WHAT THEY'RE SAYIN[...]
BARS

M000223574

"We recommend Bucket List Ba[...]
now until the day you finally qui[...]

"And I thought I'd been to a lot of bars! Bucket List Bars showed me just how many bars I still have to make it to—looks like I'm going to have to scratch the Grand Canyon off the list and, instead, head to Denver to hit El Chapultepec, Tucson for the Kon Tiki, and the dozens of other hidden gems Dr. Clint Lanier and Derek Hembree have uncovered. This book will inspire readers to get out and see the bars that built the country (not to mention the tiki movement). Finally, a guidebook for people like me — I'll never travel to an American city without it again." —Christine Sismondo, author of America Walks into a Bar: A Spirited History of Taverns and Saloons, Speakeasies and Grog Shops

"It is interesting just as reading, but also a very practical guide for the traveler who enjoys colorful bars. I have already folded over several pages for my upcoming trips." —Larry Olmsted, Forbes

"Authors Clint Lanier and Derek Hembree's new book, Bucket List Bars, lists the favorite spots of our Founding Fathers, the places where celebrities go to put a few back, and the joints that you wouldn't normally walk into—but you should." —Complex.com

"When a full day of travel leaves you thirsty for a stiff drink, you could hit up a hotel bar and enjoy a watered-down Old Fashioned or one of three beers on tap. Or you could unwind at a watering hole where Al Capone, Jack Kerouac or Clark Gable once sat. We don't know about you, but we'd go with the latter. That's why we're psyched about a new travel book called Bucket List Bars" —Hollis Templeton, Men's Journal

"Need some inspiration for your next bar crawl? Look no further than the ultimate guide to America's most historic and legendary bars, dives, saloons, and pubs, Bucket List Bars." —Marcy Franklin, The Daily Meal

"If you didn't know any better, you'd most likely pass these gems by on the street: small, graffiti-riddled, sometimes with barred windows—vestiges of their speakeasy past. Pro boozers Dr. Clint Lanier and Derek Hembree would never miss one, though: they teamed up to write Bucket List Bars, chronicling America's most historic watering holes." —Fodors.com

BUCKET LIST BARS ®

Bucket List Bars: Historic Saloons, Pubs, and Dives of America

For ordering information or special discounts for bulk purchases, please contact:
AO Media LLC
2015 Cotton Ave.
Las Cruces, NM 88001
info@bucketlistbars.com
http://www.bucketlistbars.com

Cover design by Martin Riggenbach

Printed in the United States of America
Second Edition

ISBN: 978-0-692-18274-1
Library of Congress Control Number: 2018910706

CONTENTS

GET TO KNOW A CITY AND ITS HISTORY

Hemingway once famously quipped, "don't bother with churches, government buildings or city squares. If you want to know about a culture, spend a night in its bars."

He knew what he was talking about, having spent many nights in the bars of cities like Paris, Havana, and Madrid. As a traveler, Hemingway experienced a city, a country, and, of course, a culture in this manner—over cocktails, beer, wine, laughter, and conversation. The bars of these countries taught him what the countries were really like: what was important to the people and what really mattered to them.

Bars are like that. They have this unique and strange power to unite people. They've been doing it for hundreds of years. Once upon a time, American colonists, fed up with their treatment at the hands of a king thousands of miles away, united at public houses and taverns to plot a revolution. A century later, exhausted and frustrated at the factories and foundries in which they spent most of their lives, workers united in the bars and saloons of America's industrial cities to form labor unions and demand change. In a Greenwich Village bar in 1969, gay New Yorkers united together to fight for their rights, and spawned the gay rights movement.

These places molded us every bit as much as wars or laws have. History was made in these saloons, pubs and dives. Our nation was formed in them.

At one time, every neighborhood in most every city across the country had a pub or tavern sitting squarely on the corner. They served as meeting places for the community. They sometimes acted as banks—cashing checks for the locals. They sometimes acted as soup kitchens—offering a cheap meal and drink for those who had few other options. They sheltered their neighbors and helped them find jobs, homes, or a simple, silent respite from the stress and pressure of the world outside the doors.

The bars in this book are some of the last of these bars left in the country. We're trying our best to find them, visit them, and then bring them to you, but they're closing fast. Some of the bars we covered in our first edition have since locked their doors. Some we visited for this edition closed before we could even get this printed. And some that you're reading about now might just be closed by the time you get there. You just can't tell.

And while we can't promise you'll love every single bar in our guide as much as we did, we can promise you this: you will learn much more about any city you visit by going to the bars in these chapters than you ever will by visiting those churches, government buildings, or city squares. Cheers!

Clint Lanier and Derek Hembree

SO, WHAT IS A BUCKET LIST BAR™?

We're often asked what a Bucket List Bar™ really is. Unfortunately, the explanation isn't that simple. Perhaps the most basic definition is to say that these are the places around the country and around the world you want to have a drink in before you die.

But Bucket List Bars™ are more than just watering holes. They're not places you go to just drink. They're places you go to experience. These are places that have a history. Sometimes it's good, sometimes it's bad, but it's always worthy of time and investigation.

Bucket List Bars™ have character. No two are alike and all are original. They define their own style and include décor and atmosphere often imitated but never, ever duplicated.

These aren't chain places. They might be owned by a corporation, and they might not be the only one in a portfolio of bars, but they're not places exploited, copied and then shared with the world in cut-rate versions across the continent.

Bucket List Bars™ have no defining look. Some are elegant while some, frankly, smell like last week's stale beer. Some serve cocktails that take ten minutes to make while others serve one kind of beer and nothing else.

They could have mismatched furniture or priceless artwork, gleaming brass or faded wood, crystal and porcelain, or red Solo cups.

But all of these differences—every single one—are what makes these Bucket List Bars™.

If they were people they wouldn't be Brad Pitts or Kim Kardashians, they'd be James Browns and Jack Kerouacs. They'd be people who made their own way—people who didn't try to fit in—but simply did what they did until the world took notice and then put them on their deserving pedestals.

Bucket List Bars™ are innocent in that they didn't set out to be Bucket List Bars™. They simply set out to provide the basic necessities—companionship, food, drink and entertainment—to society. At some point the world took notice and now *we're* putting them on their deserved pedestal.

WHY DO WE SELECT THE BARS WE SELECT?

Let's be honest; there are a lot of bars out there. Many are good and worth a stop-in for a drink. However, we're confident that the bars we present are the best to visit in any given area.

We can be that confident because of the research we put into finding them. We first start with the source. We tap our social media networks and then ask for recommendations. We scour the internet and look at reviews, read the history and local accounts, newspaper articles, biographies and visitor records.

But let's be even more honest; anyone can do that stuff. Many books and articles do—they rely on secondary sources for their information and recommendations.

We take it a step further and visit. Proof of this are the documentaries we make of every single one of the featured places we include.

We interview the owners, the bartenders, the customers and then give you that history in the videos. If they have a signature drink, we ask them to make it so you can see whether or not it's worth trying (they usually are).

And it's at this stage we determine if a place is a Bucket List Bar™ or not. This is the point when we figure out really quickly if this place is worthy of your visit or not. If not—if it turns out that even after our research, our visit, and interviews we determine the bar to be a loser—we don't bother telling you about it. There are a handful of bars we didn't include in this book just for that reason.

But those we do include are vetted and tried and definitely worthy of you. These places have a great history, a notorious past, and sometimes a dubious present.

WHAT ABOUT THE BUCKET LIST BARS™ IN THIS VOLUME?

This book presents the Bucket List Bars™ from 25 major cities around the United States. The focus is on the historic bars from these regions.

Historic in the truest sense has nothing to do with age—though we did track down the oldest two bars in the nation. When something is historic it is significant to the culture and society around it at the time and into the future.

There have been thousands of bars and saloons in the United States from its founding until now. Only a handful survived, but they are not all equally historic. True, they're all old and significant in terms of architecture or simply in their atmosphere, but not all saw a gunfight. Not all were used to imprison a famous British spy during the Revolutionary War. Not all have become the quintessential dive bar or Old West Saloon.

In short, not every old bar is historic.

And in fact, not all of the bars in this book are really that old. We present bars from the 1950s and 1960s. Does that make them less historic?

When you read about them, and definitely when you visit them, you'll understand.

The value of these places is in what they represent to the people who decide to have a drink in them. They reflect the history of a region, of a people, of an event, or of a way of life that's now long gone. Or, as in the case of the most recent bar—Mother's Nightclub opened in 1968—they represent the start of something. In Mother's case it's the start of whole movements in music and everything that was inspired by those movements.

And this list isn't complete. Here we present 170 of the most historic and worth-your-time watering holes from only 25 large cities around the country. There are many more we still need to discover and bring to you, and that will happen soon.

Until then, use this book to find the hidden treasures in the cities you probably already visit quite frequently. Go have a drink (or a few) in these places, and let them know you found out about them in this book.

HOW TO USE THIS BOOK

This book is divided into 25 major regions in the United States. At the end of each bar we review we also provide some nearby distractions that you really should visit if you're in the area. Many of the distractions have some kind of connection to the bar itself, so it's worth your while to see them.

Lastly we made a YouTube-hosted documentary about each of our featured bars. The documentaries help to put each bar in context, show you what they look like inside and out, and provide a much more in-depth and colorful history of the bars than a simple guide could do.

For those bars that have some type of signature drink, we've also made videos of the bartenders mixing these drinks. These are the drinks we tried and loved when we were there and are our recommendation for trying when you visit.

THE BARS OF BUCKET LIST BARS™

Not all bars are created equal, however: they are all different, not only in their personalities but also in their types. There are at least five different bar types we'll talk about over and over: Taverns/Pubs, Saloons, Speakeasies, Dives, and Tiki Bars. Here we'll try to define them in their historical context.

TAVERN/PUB

In our modern vernacular the terms, "Tavern" and "Pub" have come to mean the same things. But it wasn't always the case.

Pubs, or public houses, and taverns can trace their history all the way back to the Roman Empire. During the Empire's four-century control of Britain it created a vast and extensive network of roads throughout Britain and Europe. Along these roads were alehouses, taverns, and inns that offered travelers a place to stop for a drink, food, supplies, or a place to sleep. Alehouses of the time were usually ordinary dwellings where the householder would serve home-brewed ale or beer and, if lodging was offered, it was commonly a simple spot on the floor or a loft in a barn. A tavern on the other hand typically served only wine, and, since wine was more expensive at the time, taverns catered to the upper class. Another major difference was that taverns were limited to towns whereas alehouses could be opened in just about any dwelling where the occupant wanted to sell their home brew and possibly offer travelers a place to stay.

After the Roman Empire collapsed, and during the 18th century, the term alehouse was gradually replaced by the term public house, as alehouses were growing in size and grandeur. In 1810 we see the first purpose-built public houses erected in London, England and quickly expanding to towns across the country and eventually the world. These establishments were usually the focal point of a community and there was a time in some countries (like Holland, for example) when towns would not officially be recognized as such unless they had a pub and/or a tavern. The pub had become a place where the common public could grab a meal or a drink, talk of local, national and world news, do business and often times find some form of entertainment.

Similar to public houses, taverns began to evolve after the collapse of the Roman Empire. In 18th century England we see many of them transformed into coffee houses catering to the wealthy, while others turned into extravagant inns, and still others remained taverns. In the Colonial US taverns were an important part of the community and were often supervised by county officials. These establishments were eventually licensed to house guests, turning them into inns, and were the earliest forms of what we know today as hotels. Taverns were an essential part of life for travelers who relied on them for shelter for themselves and their horses, as well as a place to find food and entertainment. Plus, they acted as a town's post office and most importantly, a place to enjoy an alcoholic beverage.

Today for the most part a pub and a tavern are the same, though very different from a lounge, a dive bar, club, or Tiki bar. They usually have significant European influence in their décor, building, food menu and in their founding history. Their drink menu can vary vastly with beer and whiskey almost always the cornerstone of the bar. Though they were founded during the rule of the Roman Empire they still survive today as the foundation for almost any drinking establishment or hotel you find yourself in.

SALOONS

Saloons are about as American as apple pie.

When you think of a saloon the first thing that probably pops into your head is a character like Josey Wales walking into an old dusty bar with swinging doors, a piano player pelting out an old tune, gambling off to the side, ladies of the night advertising their wares and an old barman cleaning a glass behind the bar. In all truthfulness only some of what we called saloons would have been quite so extravagant.

One of the earliest saloons opened in Brown's Hole, Wyoming, in 1822 to serve fur trappers and traders. Geographically close to Wyoming's border with Utah and Colorado, this establishment was the first of thousands of similar places to be dubbed saloons during America's expansion west. Shortly after the first saloon opened its doors more started popping up just about anywhere and everywhere.

Built out of tents, wagons, sod houses, ship hulls, cut into the side of hills, built from the ground up, shady and extravagant, they were built in almost every small town, city or cross roads that dotted the western frontier. But no matter how, where or what they were constructed of, they all served the same purpose: a place for cowboys and soldiers to spend their off hours, where a lonesome traveler could find conversation or companionship, and even where a businessman could strike a deal.

Though there were many different types and differing levels of luxury in the various saloons of the country, the alcohols they served were often limited. Beer was not uncommon, but without pasteurization and refrigeration its quality would have been questionable at best. Some places served Cactus Tea or Cactus Wine, which was made from a mixture of peyote and tequila (we wonder what kind of buzz that brought on). But at the forefront of alcohol served in saloons was whiskey. Oftentimes made from raw alcohol, burnt sugar, and chewing tobacco, it was called numerous names like Tarantula Juice, Red Eye, and Coffin Varnish. Most places also served house rotgut that was often 100 proof and cut with turpentine, ammonia, gunpowder or some kind of spice, like cayenne.

Legend has it that if an unknown or foreign patron entered a saloon and ordered a strange or "fruity" cocktail, or if he was to stand around and only sip his drink, bar patrons would sometimes take it upon themselves to force the stranger to drink a fifth of rotgut for his own good.

Saloons today are for the most part a thing of the past. Most places that still call themselves saloons are either still open or reopened from the days of the old west, like the Crystal Palace in Tombstone, or are opened in the spirit of the traditional saloon, like Broken Spoke in Sturgis, South Dakota, and in Daytona, Florida. Regardless of when they were built, a saloon today is used in much the same manner as a saloon of yesterday. They exist for the common good of the public as places to find a conversation, blow off some steam, catch a game, meet some new friends, grab a bite to eat, or simply spend some time contemplating the meaning of life.

SPEAKEASY

Many believe that speakeasies came about during the notorious period known as Prohibition. And while that is when these establishments were in their heyday, they actually came into existence long before the start of Prohibition in 1920.

The term speakeasy refers to an establishment that illegally sells alcoholic beverages. There are many legends as to how the term came about but one of the most commonly told is the story of Kate Hester. Kate owned a bar in Pittsburgh, Pennsylvania which she operated as a legal establishment until 1888 when the state of Pennsylvania raised the price of bar licenses from $50 to $500 dollars. Kate refused to pay a 1000% increase and instead took her bar underground. She would tell her patrons to "speakeasy boys" when they became too loud so as not to attract the attention of law enforcement officials.

The term has become synonymous with establishments that sold alcohol during the United States' experiment with Prohibition from 1920-33. From notorious gangsters like Al Capone to the everyday working man and woman, speakeasies served as a reprieve from the oppression of the Noble Experiment. They most commonly served hard alcohol, especially gin due to its ease of distillation, and beer was an uncommon luxury. When Prohibition was repealed with the 21st Amendment, often these very same establishments turned into legal neighborhood bars or returned to being the bars they were before the onset of Prohibition.

When we refer to speakeasies in this book we are referring to places like The Green Mill in Chicago, Illinois and The Townhouse in Venice Beach, California that were actually speakeasies during Prohibition. Places like these are still in operation today and still retain that original ambiance. Walking into them will often give you the feeling of being transported to another time period. You'd almost expect Al Capone to walk in any minute and sit down with you for a drink or two.

DIVE BARS

A dive bar is one of the original American bars: a staple of Americana if you will.

The history of how the dive bar came about is steeped in mystery. Some believe the term was used to describe illegal drinking establishments similar to speakeasies, which were mainly located in basements (thus you had to "dive" under the street or building to get in). Others believe the term came about because it was in these seedy establishments that patrons would "dive" under their tables and chairs to get away from gun fights and/or bar brawls—a sometime necessary evil of being a patron of an exceptionally seedy dive bar. Further adding to the mystery is the fact that no one knows which bar was the first 'official' dive bar, and saloons or even speakeasies could also be labeled dives on their journeys through history.

One of the most notorious is the saloon/speakeasy turned dive called King Eddy's Saloon in L.A. King Eddy's is located beneath of the 120-year-old King Edward hotel and was once the hub of L.A.'s notorious bootlegging operation made possible by a gigantic network of tunnels running under the city. During Prohibition the bar was located in the basement and was a favorite among local cops.

When Prohibition ended King Eddy's moved back upstairs amongst L.A.'s rapidly declining Skid Row. Today the old-timers and youngsters mix and mingle in a diverse crowd, and the place opens at 6am which just so happens to be the same time Happy Hour blessedly starts. In the end this place was a legend among dive bars the world over until it was recently bought out by a local corporation with plans for renovations, leaving a huge question mark as to what kind of establishment will exist upon reopening.

Most places don't start off as dive bars (though some places try to) and they aren't created from a corporation's drive to take advantage of a trend. A dive bar is a reputation and an atmosphere that has to be earned and developed over the course of years. It's a badge that is worn with honor; a place that welcomes all (most of the time) and is known for the great times you typically can't remember, cheap drinks, and regulars who become like a family. If your chief mission is to forgo the craft cocktail or regional beer (most Dives specialize in cheap American beers and equally cheap shots of whiskey) and instead eliminate sobriety, then a dive is the place for you.

Today's dive bars are usually dark, run-down, with odors of questionable origin, ever-present beer signs and sports flags, and Christmas lights haphazardly hung on the walls and fixtures. Regardless of their dubious characteristics dive bars hold a special place in almost any bar patron's heart. It's in these places you feel no different than the movie star sitting on your right or the bum on the left. There's no special section, no VIP area, the prices are easy on almost any pocketbook and the food is almost always a bad idea. And while all of these characteristics may be the very reason you would avoid some bars, they're also reasons you come to a dive bar.

Regardless of how the term came about there's one thing that's certain: dive bars are one of America's greatest gifts to the world.

TIKI BARS

The 1950s and 60s found the United States in a state of change, self-discovery, and newfound world prominence on the heels of World War II. The middle class was taking the country by storm with ever-expanding lifestyles that included the suburbs, 2.4 kids, a two-car garage, and a shift in the American Dream. Concurrently consuming the nation were Tiki bars and Tiki culture, which eventually led to at least one Tiki bar in almost every US city.

It all started in 1934 when Ernest Raymond opened his Polynesian-themed bar and restaurant in Hollywood, California, called Donn the Beachcomber. Ernest, who later changed his name to Donn Beach, found inspiration for his new establishment from his time spent sailing throughout the South Pacific. He opened the bar and restaurant in the hopes of bringing a piece of Polynesian "Aloha" to the people of Southern California through a unique atmosphere, tropical drinks, and a Polynesian-themed menu. Little did he know that he had started a whole new American subculture that would both grow to epic proportions and survive the test of time.

Today Tiki bars still sweep their patrons away to an island oasis. Known for their tropical drinks with recipes guarded more tenaciously than the gold at Fort Knox, unique décor, and a one-of-a-kind atmosphere, these places are a unique gem amongst the community of bars. They have an ever loyal following that are known to literally travel the world in search of the perfect mai tai and perfect Tiki oasis. You could be in the middle of a bustling city, but when you step into the confines of one of the great American Tiki bars you will find a Polynesian oasis awaiting your arrival.

ALBUQUERQUE, NM

Albuquerque, New Mexico is probably best known for green chile and the International Balloon Fiesta (or perhaps for meth-thanks Breaking Bad), but there's also a rich drinking tradition throughout this city and surrounding area that you need to discover.

Founded in 1706, Albuquerque was a small farming village for years, consisting of both local, Native American tribes and Spanish settlers. It grew up under many national flags, belonging to Mexico and then finally the United States, and slowly developed into the largest city in New Mexico.

The history is important, because it splices together the culture, the people, and the drinking.

Just south of Albuquerque we see some of the first vineyards planted in North America. They were making wine here before they were making it just about anywhere else on the continent. That alone is pretty impressive.

During prohibition, the area was also rife with bootleggers and speakeasies. And there has long been tension between the various Native American tribes and the booze peddlers, a tension that exists even today.

Despite the long history, little remains of the rich drinking tradition of the area. The fabric of the Wild West's history is stitched together by the Albuquerque area, and the streets were lined with saloons. Filling these saloons were characters from just about every western ever made. The legendary, like Kit Carson, and the notorious, like Billy the Kid. These were the types of people that bellied up to the bars of 19th century Albuquerque.

That's not to say that there's no place worthwhile to find a drink. A short drive north or south will take you quickly back in time to an age where people wore guns to the bars and sat with their backs against the wall. In fact, there are century-old saloons spread throughout the state, but we found three close to Albuquerque that will make your stay in the Land of Enchantment truly memorable (or perhaps not, it just depends on how much fun you have there).

CAPITOL BAR, SOCORRO, NM

Address: 110 Plaza, Socorro, NM, (575) 835-1193
Website: www.socorro-nm.com/capitolbar.htm **Video tour:**
http://youtu.be/pS0wRfJKBKE
Food: Yes **Live Music:** Yes **Hours:** Monday–Saturday 12pm–2am, Sunday
12pm–12am **Type of Bar:** Saloon **What to Drink:** Cheap beer and a shot of
cheaper whiskey **Why You Should Go:** It was once owned by a judge who
held court in the saloon, was a speakeasy throughout prohibition, has a
hanging tree out back.

THE HISTORY

Sitting in Socorro, New Mexico's town plaza, the Capitol bar was originally
built in 1896 and called the Biavaschi Saloon. Built by and named after two
brothers, Giovanni and Tobashci, the saloon was meant to celebrate, serve,
and share Giovanni's locally grown and produced wine with townspeople and
travelers alike. It makes perfect sense considering Socorro is where some of the
first vineyards were planted in the US. At the time of the bar's completion,
Socorro was New Mexico's largest city and consisted of 3000 residents and 30
bars, an outrageous ratio by today's standards.

Shortly after the turn of the century, Giovanni somehow lost the bar, and it
was subsequently sold to a local district judge by the name of Amos Green.
Amos wasted no time setting up shop, literally, and started holding court
proceedings in his newly acquired bar, which was still a bar. Offenders were
held in one of the back rooms (bars can still be seen on the windows today),
and court was held in the other. It's also rumored that one of the trees outside
was referred to as the "Hanging Tree," though, today, no one knows which

tree it was. Judge Amos even presided over hundreds of marriages in his establishment, and was quoted as saying, "Those whom God and Amos Green have joined together, let no man put asunder."

Ownership eventually passed on to Fred Emilio who proceeded to paint the front of the bar green and rename it "The Green Front" in honor of Judge Green. Fred also operated the bar as a speakeasy during prohibition, complete with trap doors and tunnels, which were used to hide liquor and to escape from the coppers. The bar was known to have had some of the best liquor in the area during prohibition, thanks to Fred and his business partner having the foresight to stock up before the Volstead Act was enacted. Locally-produced moonshine of high quality didn't hurt either.

Sometime between 1937 and 1938, the bar was passed on to Emilio's sons, Willie and Frankie, who renamed it "Capitol Bar." Then, in 1969, a local alumnus of nearby New Mexico Tech, Earl DeBrine, leased and eventually bought the bar from Willie, and turned the basement into an unofficial study hall for Tech students. For the students, it was a place where knowledge and booze flowed freely and they were so enamored with it they tried to dig a tunnel from the campus to the bar's cellar for easy late night access.

TODAY

Though a lot has changed at "The Cap," a lot remains the same. Gone is the court room, though you can still see the bars on the windows in the back room, and the trap door and escape tunnel are still present from its days as a speakeasy. Sadly, most of the tunnel is filled in, but Tech students can still be found discussing higher learning over a pint of cold beer.

The crowd is extremely varied. While there, we saw bikers wearing their "colors" with pride, old and young locals, and even a few tourists. Typically, they're all friendly and simply there to enjoy a drink and some company. It's hard to see anyone feeling out of place at The Cap.

They feature live music and dancing in a large room next to the bar, and also have a small patio outside allowing drinkers to enjoy cool spring or autumn nights while slamming back a few.

When you go, ask about the local radio personality who had his ashes interred (along with his microphone) above the bar. Also look up and try to spot the bullet holes in the ceiling, evidence of The Cap's wilder days.

All of its unique characteristics make the bar a stellar example of what bars used to be out in the wild west. Add to that the fact that the current owner, someone who wishes to remain anonymous, still cherishes and celebrates the bar's history, the Capitol Bar is on track to remain a staple of southwest saloon tradition.

The Capitol Bar is truly a diamond in the rough and a welcome respite should you ever find yourself in central New Mexico on one of its hot summer days. It's well worth the beautiful, hour-long drive from Albuquerque to get here.

THE DRINKS

The Capitol Bar has a full bar, and they're used to serving college crowds, bikers, tourists and old locals, so they can whip up just about anything you could order. Don't expect a study in mixology, though, the place is a bar, not a cocktail lounge.

You can never go wrong with a beer and a shot at a saloon, and this rule holds true for The Cap. Locally-produced beers and whiskeys are gaining popularity in the area, so ask about one if you're feeling adventurous.

They also serve a really good Bloody Mary, which we tried while there and can confidently recommend.

NEARBY DISTRACTIONS

Very Large Array—www.vla.nrao.edu, 50 miles west of Socorro on US Highway 60, (575) 835-7300 (free guided tours are held the first Saturday of every month at 11am, 1pm and 3pm, and unguided tours are available from sun up to sunset daily). Do you remember the movie, Contact? How about Terminator Salvation? Remember all of the giant satellite dish-looking things? Those are part of the Very Large Array (VLA) which is about 50 miles away from Socorro, NM. The 25-meter diameter dishes are used for radio astronomy, and they, as well as the area around them, are visually stunning, especially at sunset.

Buckhorn Restaurant—www.buckhornburgers.com, 68 US 380 San Antonio, NM 87832, (575) 835-4423 (Monday–Friday 11am–7:50pm, Saturday 11am–2:45pm). Founded in 1944, the Buckhorn Restaurant is known for Green Chile Cheeseburgers. In fact, they are actually known worldwide for their burgers. So well-known, in fact, that it earned a spot in GQ's 20 best burgers in the US, and even took on Bobby Flay (and won) in a Green Chile Burger competition. A short, 11-mile drive from The Cap, it's a must-try restaurant for anyone who enjoys a good burger.

Bosque Del Apache—1001 Highway 1 San Antonio, NM 87832, (575) 835-1828 (Visitors Center open Monday–Friday 7:30am–4pm, Saturday–Sunday 8am–4:30pm, Driving Tour Loop open 1 hour before sunrise to 1 hour after sunset). A quick, 30-minute drive from the Capitol Bar will land you at the Bosque Del Apache National Wildlife Refuge. Most active in the fall and winter when thousands of birds fly in from all over the world, the refuge is home to a long list of bird species over the winter months. Time a visit for dusk when the view of thousands of birds flying in to roost for the night is a once in a lifetime experience.

THE MINE SHAFT TAVERN, MADRID, NM

Address: 2846 Hwy 14, Madrid, NM, 87010, (505) 473-0743
Website: www.themineshafttavern.com **Video tour:**
http://youtu.be/GMHvktkc4CI
Food: Yes **Live Music:** Yes **Hours:** Monday–Thursday 1130am–8pm, Friday–Sunday 11am–11pm **Type of Bar:** Saloon **What to Drink:** Horny Cadillac Margarita **Why You Should Go:** Originally built as part of a "company" town for thirsty miners, only bar with a retired antique steam locomotive sitting inside the back theatre, some of the best onion rings in the southwest.

THE HISTORY

The city of Madrid was founded in 1835 as a "company" mining town. That is to say the mine's owner—the Albuquerque and Cerrillos Coal Company—built and ran the entire town for the purpose of attracting, housing, entertaining and caring for the mine-workers and their families. From the hotel to the stores, the tavern, baseball fields, and even law enforcement, the company owned and ran everything. As a matter of fact, the town was so well built and managed, that it quickly became a model city for other "company" owned towns around the country.

The actual Mine Shaft Tavern was completed sometime around 1895 as a men's club. One of its unique features was a taller than normal bar so miners could stand up straight after hours spent hunched over in the mines. For those who are tall they might not notice that much, but for the shorter among us, it's an odd experience to drink at a bar that comes up to your chest.

Though a saloon, it was still the cornerstone of the community. There were other distractions in town to be sure, such as a theater, a minor league baseball team (with the first lit field west of the Mississippi), and even a town library, but the meeting-place for the workers was always the tavern. Through the ebb and flow of the local coal mines, the economy and the community, the beloved bar remained a place for the men of the town to come together, enjoy each other's company, and throw back a few drinks.

It was said to have been a rowdy place back in the day, and if you consider it for a moment, it only makes sense. After all, New Mexico was part of the untamed West at the time and was simply littered with outlaws, bandits, and thugs. Company town or not, there's no doubt many of them wondered through Madrid on their ramblings, so there's no doubt the Mine Shaft likely saw gunfights, fistfights, thievery, thuggery, and other nefarious deeds.

In 1944, however, tragedy struck the town as their beautiful bar burned to the ground on Christmas day. A mining town can't last long without a saloon, though, so it was rebuilt in 1947 only to be shut down again as the mines closed and the town became a ghost town.

Then in the 1970s the town owner began renting and eventually selling some of the old houses and structures, which led to the eventual revival of the town and (blessedly) the one and only Mine Shaft Tavern.

TODAY

Today, the Mine Shaft and the town of Madrid have become a mix of weekend tourists, hipsters, hippies, artists, and bikers. On any given weekend, you'll find a few hundred "hogs" in and around the town, while at the same time, find tourist and sight-seers mingling in and out of the Mine Shaft and the shops (art galleries and boutiques) lining Main Street.

The Mine Shaft itself is over 100 years old, and the current owner feels that preserving the essence of the Tavern is of upmost importance. As such, very little has changed since its rebuild in 1947 (the floors, stage and bar are original). This preservation, as well as the unique location and décor, have made the bar a favorite of location scouts, and so it's been featured in movies such as Beer for my Horses, Paul, and Wild Hogs.

While you're here, take time to walk around and look at the décor on the walls because it tells the history of this town and of the New Mexico Territory in the early 20th century. Also, stop to take in the detail of the colorful mural behind the stage. It was painted by New Mexico artist Ross Warner, who created the nearby Tinkertown attraction (numerous small, animated, carved people and things).

Also, while you're here, you owe it to yourself to take a short tour of the grounds, maybe before you start drinking.

Located behind the tavern is Madrid's Old Coal Town Museum. Renovated in 2012, the museum tells a more comprehensive story of the town of Madrid through relics, photos, and static displays, and is open (weather permitting) almost every day of the year. Included in the tour is the Engine House Theatre, which is possibly the only theatre in the world with a retired steam locomotive nosed up against the stage.

The theatre is a converted Engine Repair House that was once used to house the steam locomotive from the area's freezing nights as well as a place for maintenance and repairs. The tin roof is still stained from steam and soot from the idling trains.

The historic town, tavern, drinks and food make this a must see during a trip to Northern New Mexico.

THE FOOD

Though they have quite an extensive menu, consisting mainly of typical bar-faire, The Mine Shaft specializes in great burgers with two must-tries: the Kobe burger and the Buffalo burger.

Both burgers are made from locally raised and butchered animals. The Buffalo is free range, moist and delicious, while the Kobe burger absolutely melts in your mouth.

Add to each some green chile and cheese to make it a New Mexico-style burger, and be sure to order their legendary tempura fried and grilled onion rings to make the plate about perfect. Their fries are hand cut and almost as good as the onion rings, so you can't go wrong if you decide on the standard.

THE DRINKS

The Mine Shaft has a full bar, so they can get you whatever you might want to drink. However, that being said, you simply have to give the Horny Cadillac Margarita a try.

Perfect for a hot day, the drink uses a secret mix of crushed cucumbers and jalapenos to make it both refreshing and a little spicy. If the Cadillac is too hot for your liking, then The Shaft Margarita—more of a traditional margarita—might be more appealing. Both drinks are made with fresh-squeezed lime juice and will surely satisfy the pickiest of margarita drinkers.

NEARBY DISTRACTIONS

Santa Fe Plaza—plaza-sf.nm-unlimited.net, 80 E San Francisco St, Santa Fe, NM 87501 (open yearly, shops hold typical business hours, events go on year-round). A quick 20-minute drive from Madrid will land you in Santa Fe's historic Plaza. Established as the center of Santa Fe's commercial, political, and social scene in 1610, the plaza is surrounded by a multitude of souvenir shops, art shops and locals peddling native wares. Be sure to visit the Palace of the Governors (built between 1610-1612) and the San Miguel Mission (built in 1640).

The Lorreto Chapel—www.lorettochapel.com, 207 Old Santa Fe Trail, Santa Fe, NM 87501, (505) 982-0092 (Monday–Saturday 9am–5pm, Sunday 10:30am–5pm). Completed in 1878, the chapel originally had no access to the second story choir loft. A mysterious carpenter arrived shortly after the chapel was completed and built the staircase with two 360 degree turns using no nails and no center support. After completing the staircase, the carpenter slipped away without pay or thanks, never to be seen again. The staircase still mystifies engineers and carpenters today and is visited by thousands yearly.

SILVA'S SALOON, BERNALILLO, NM

Address: 955 S Camino Del Pueblo, Bernalillo, NM, 87004, (505) 867-9976
Video tour: http://youtu.be/qNHQptYev7I
Food: Yes (sporadically) **Live Music:** Rarely **Hours:** Monday 11am–9pm,
Closed Tuesday, Wednesday–Saturday 11am–9pm, Sunday 11pm–9pm
Type of Bar: Saloon **What to Drink:** Beer and a shot of whiskey. **Why You
Should Go:** Original owner used to bootleg for Al Capone, his mash and still
are on display in the bar today, a Danny Trejo favorite.

THE HISTORY

Silva's was opened in 1933 by Felix Silva Sr. literally the day after
prohibition ended. But this wasn't the new bar owner's first dealings with
alcohol. Felix was a long-time moonshiner and bootlegger who used to hide
his still in the family's apple orchard (the small still he used is proudly
displayed in the bar today).

He would transport his moonshine in the back of his pickup truck all the
way to the Blacksmith Hotel in Oklahoma City. Many believe his moonshine
was being used to supply none other than Al Capone's gang, but no one
knows for sure as Felix Sr. refused to ever talk about his dealings with the
notorious crime boss. In fact, he mysteriously told his granddaughter when
asked why he didn't want to talk about his dealings, "when you give a man
your word, you hold true to it."

Even after opening his bar Felix still didn't see fit to follow all of the local
laws. Senior ran 'round-the-clock poker games in the back room. His son,
Felix Jr., remembered letting people into the hidden rooms to gamble. And

though it was illegal to sell alcohol on Sundays, Felix Sr. was happy to pour for regulars and friends alike on the Sabbath (he was also happy to serve Native Americans, which was also illegal).

But despite his lawless streak, Felix had a heart of gold and never turned away a weary traveler looking for a hot meal and a place to sleep, and he was always quick to give away candy and ice cream to the customers' children.

Silva's was a bar that welcomed everyone. It was common to find locals, travelers, farmers and ranchers bellied up to the horseshoe-shaped bar throughout the day. As time passed, so too did the bar's regulars. Many of their families brought in articles from the deceased to leave a part of a loved one in a place they loved. Hats, boots, glasses, pictures, and even a few driver and hunting licenses were used to decorate the walls of the bar, a tradition that continues today.

Felix Sr. is no longer with us. His son found him early one morning in 1995, slumped over the bar, having passed in the place he poured his heart and soul into. Felix Jr. insists that his dad's spirit is still here, keeping watch over his legacy and ensuring that it lasts many years into the future.

TODAY

Silva's remains a local's bar, but it's welcoming to all. When you walk up to the place you may initially be intimidated by the outside décor, or by some of the rough looking patrons. Don't be! This is one of the most welcoming and enjoyable bars we've ever been to. In fact, according to Denise, Felix Sr.'s granddaughter, no nonsense is tolerated in the bar. Ever.

Felix Jr., along with his daughter, Denise, own and run the place today. And while Felix isn't behind the bar as much as he used to be, he's always happy to meet new customers. While we were visiting, a local in his late 60s mentioned to us that he'd never been inside. We told him he really needed to, that the place wasn't a biker hangout, but simply a neighborhood pub. By the time we left, Felix and he were talking as if they'd known each other for years.

On Friday, it's customary for one of the regulars to bring in a huge meal to share with any and all in the bar. Sunday mornings find the bar full of local men who take turns buying breakfast for everyone and talking about the weather, sports, news or just about anything else over a cup of coffee or an ice-cold beer.

The décor has changed little since the bar's founding, except it could be getting a little more crowded. Patrons continue to bring in favorite articles of loved ones who've passed on. Additionally, recently married men have been known to bring in some of the more provocative items adorning the walls today, at least that's what we were told (you will no doubt notice the high number of nudes hanging on the walls, ask about them for some entertaining stories).

You'll also notice a payphone on one of the walls. It's striking that you really don't see payphones in bars anymore, so why does Silva's have one?

Apparently, in the 1990s, a CIA agent was running an anti-spy program in the area trying to find out who was selling secret information from nearby Los

Alamos and Sandia National Laboratories. The agent regularly used the phone at Silva's Saloon to call his headquarters and make his reports. Once finished with his call, he'd get off the phone and buy a beer.

When the operation was declassified, Felix Jr. thought the phone should remain (though he gripes about the monthly fee for having it).

Silva's is a dying breed. Few, if any, bars today have that welcoming feeling or that ambiance that makes anyone feel welcome and a part of a family. Replacing places like Silva's are the Tilted Kilts, Applebees and TGI Fridays: cookie cutter establishments that have little or no true essence, or feeling, or community. Go to Silva's while you can, you never know when it could go away.

THE FOOD

Silva's doesn't really serve food. However, stop in on just about any occasion and you may find a spread provided compliments of one of the regulars. While we were visiting on a Friday evening, pots of beans and other regional favorites were brought in and set down for anyone to pick at.

The next morning of our visit, Felix Jr. (who in his 80s still opens on Saturday mornings) and two men were gabbing it up when a third entered with a bag of breakfast burritos to share among them. If you really want to make friends here, bring some food!

THE DRINKS

When we asked the owner's daughter, Denise, about specialty drinks, she just kind of looked at us like we were a little crazy. She said they can make just about anything in her bartender's guide (she is still learning the trade) and doesn't mind giving any drink a try. We say order just about anything you desire and cross your fingers.

While at the bar, look towards the top and see a row of dusty old bottles, still full of whatever liquor they carried when they were made. Many are from the 30s and 40s and so contain some very rare spirits. Felix Jr. sealed each bottle with wax years ago and, on occasion, he opens one up to share amongst friends. If you're lucky you'll be there when he does!

NEARBY DISTRACTIONS

New Mexico Wine Festival—Bernalillo, NM 87004, (Labor Day weekend, 12pm–6pm). Every year over Labor Day Weekend, vineyards from across the world descend on Bernalillo to present their wines in one of the largest Wine Festivals in the US. If you find yourself in or around the area over Labor Day Weekend, this is a must.

Coronado State Monument—Address: 485 Kuaua Rd, Bernalillo, NM 87004, (505) 867-5351 (Wednesday–Monday 8:30am–5pm, closed Tuesday). When Coronado entered the area in search of the fabled Seven Cities of Gold, he came across a multitude of villages inhabited by prosperous natives. Unearthed in 1930, this is the Kuau, one of the villages he visited. Visit the site to get a look into Coronado's expedition, the historic earthen pueblo, and the way of life at the time. It's also worthwhile for the beautiful scenery (the monument is right up against the lazy Rio Grande river, and there are some spectacular view of the territory).

Albuquerque Balloon Fiesta & Museum—Address: 4401 Alameda Blvd NE, Albuquerque, NM 87113, (505) 821-1000 (morning session 5:45am–8am or 10am depending on the events for the day, evening session 4pm–8pm check schedules and dates). Every October, Balloonist from all over the world crowd Albuquerque for the 10-day balloon fiesta, the largest of its kind in the world, and make it a must-see if you are anywhere close to the area. If you can't make the fiesta, check out the museum which gives visitors an inside look into the fiesta, its history, and ballooning.

ALBUQUERQUE'S HISTORIC BARS

El Matador Lounge—Address: 707 California Ave. Socorro, NM 87801, (575) 835-1180 (Monday–Friday 10am–8pm, Saturday 12pm–7pm, closed Sunday). If you find Socorro charming and would like to find another place to drink at after you get thrown out of The Cap, make your way to El Matador Lounge, connected to the retro-looking El Camino Restaurant. Retro is actually a fitting word for the place. The booths are red vinyl, the walls are lined with dark, wooden paneling, and you'll quickly find yourself looking for the velvet paintings on the wall (oh, there they are!). It's kitsch—complete kitsch. But, what you must understand about this bar, is that it simply hasn't changed. The Brady Bunch was airing weekly when this place started up, and it honestly looks like it hasn't been touched since then.

Owl Café—Address: 77 US 380, San Antonio, NM 87832, (575) 835-9946 (Monday–Saturday 8am–8:30pm, closed Sunday). Established in 1949, the Owl Café has been serving beer and green chile cheeseburgers for over 60 years. Though it features locations in San Antonio, New Mexico (just about five miles south of Socorro) and the east side of Albuquerque, we prefer the original in San Antonio. They serve really tasty burgers, and really cold beer, a great combination any day of the week.

El Farol—Address: 808 Canyon Road, Santa Fe, NM, (505) 983-9912 (Monday–Saturday 11am–12am, Sunday 11am–11pm). This the oldest bar and restaurant in Santa Fe. They have reportedly been serving here since 1905, and the place is really popular with locals. So popular, in fact, that the bar quickly gets crowded, and there's typically a long wait. The key is to get here early. But when you do, you'll be immersed in old-time Santa Fe. Both the old-world artwork and the old hippies will show you what the state's small capital used to be like when it was filled with so much weird that Austin was jealous.

Lately, when people think of Atlantic City, two images come to mind. The first is the shady home of fictional 1920s gangster, Nucky Thompson in the HBO series, Boardwalk Empire. The other is of a bunch of fake-tan-sporting, muscle-bound guys and bubble-headed women getting drunk and cavorting on the beach and in the bed on MTV's old show, Jersey Shore.

Neither one is really that honest or flattering for the small city by the sea, but both is correct on some level.

Atlantic City's history does have a touch of what both shows present. It was, and still is, a summer destination for residents up and down the East Coast. It does swell in the summer months with droves of young beachgoers and (sadly), you can find many people not too different from those presented in Jersey Shore (yes, they do exist).

Atlantic City (or AC as locals call it) has, in fact, been a summer destination since the early 1900s, when the first elegant hotel was built on the beach in 1903. The summer crowd was much different, however, typically catering to the very rich: the upper-crust from New York, Pennsylvania and New Jersey.

And it was in this era that the other show's reality is unveiled. The character in Boardwalk Empire is based on the real-life crime boss, Nucky Johnson, who ruled the criminal underground as mob boss from 1910 until he was finally locked up in 1941.

During Nucky's rule, the small town saw racketeering, prostitution, illegal gambling and, of course, bootlegging during prohibition. In fact, prohibition was so loosely enforced in AC that most any restaurant one walked into would gladly serve wine, beer or liquor as soon as the customer sat down.

AC, henceforth, became known as "The World's Playground," and the roaring 20s truly roared here. Nucky Johnson was making about $500,000 annually off of his crime-rings, and the city was swelling with tourists, eager for a good time.

As is typically the case, Atlantic City declined after World War 2. The automobile allowed people to come and go as they please, so instead of staying for a couple of weeks, they stayed for a couple of days. There was no major airport, so tourists flocked to other areas of the nation as air transport became cheaper. AC became a forgotten model of crime and poverty.

In 1976, though, gambling was legalized and the city has been on a steady run to reinvent itself. There were setbacks in the 90s when Vegas became the popular gaming destination (plus two casinos opened in Connecticut), then the recessions in 2000 and 2008 slowed progress, as did Hurricane Sandy.

But the small city is strong, and is always making strides as new, elegant hotels, reminiscent of the old elegance, are being built. Though many of the bars from the golden years of Atlantic City have been leveled, we did manage to find two that we consider worthy of a bucket list.

KNIFE AND FORK INN, ATLANTIC CITY, NJ

Address: 3600 Atlantic Ave., Atlantic City, NJ 08401, (609) 344-1133
Website: www.knifeandforkinn.com **Video tour:**
http://youtu.be/dUbfJZoVHws
Food: Yes **Live Music:** No **Hours:** Bar open daily from 4pm–11pm, Dinner
served daily at 5pm, Friday lunch 11:30am–4pm **Type of Bar:** Tavern **What
to Drink:** An Aviator or a Jezebel **Why You Should Go:** Direct link to
notorious gang-boss, Nucky Thompson—he ate and drank here. In fact,
many of those in high society frequented the Knife and Fork. This is where
the richest of the gangsters would have assembled.

THE HISTORY

So, you might have heard of Nucky Thompson, and he's certainly someone
worth the notoriety, but Atlantic City was filled with many more colorful
characters, all neck-deep in prostitution, kick-backs and other nefarious
crimes. One of those characters is named William Riddle.

William Riddle was part of the Republican political machine that ran
Atlantic City for decades. He was a wealthy, well-educated man who believed
that AC should be turned into the next Monte Carlo. In fact, as mayor, he
publicly stated more than once that gambling and prostitution should both be
legalized in his city. In the early 1900s, though, they weren't, and neither
were Sunday liquor sales.

Making these activities illegal, however, did little to stop them. Atlantic City
had a segregated portion of town, called the Tenderloin, where gambling and
prostitution went on with everyone's knowledge (in a five year span the area
was raided only once). The problem, though, was that this area was a rough
part of town. The joints in which one could gamble, drink on Sundays and

enjoy the companionship of women (other than the wife), were pretty decrepit places.

So, in 1912, William Riddle founded the Knife and Fork Inn, a "gentleman's club" where the well-heeled of the city could spend their time in pursuit of sin amongst others of the genteel class.

The names of the men who helped to initially establish the Inn are inscribed on a brass plaque on the Inn's fireplace, and the list reads like a who's who of mob-bosses and political cronies. Among them is Louis Kuenhle, called the Commodore, who was also a political boss of the city. He didn't have long to enjoy it, though: a year after the founding of the Knife and Fork the Commodore was sentenced to a year in jail for corruption and kickbacks.

On the second floor of the Knife and Fork Inn, Riddle ran an exclusive club that had curtained (meaning private) dining alcoves and a full bar. There was a room outside of this main dining room that featured a separate entrance where women would gather and wait to be summoned by the gentlemen inside.

The third story rooms were used for gambling and prostitution. In short it was a veritable fantasyland for the rich, where all their tasteless needs were met.

The place remained as such, seeing just about every political and mob boss, right through prohibition. As you can imagine, nobody really took the 18th Amendment seriously in Atlantic City, and so most places, including the Knife and Fork, served openly right through the early years. In 1927, though, the Feds finally got tired of America's playground flaunting its disrespect for the law, thus they clamped down.

Riddle saw the writing on the wall and knew his speakeasy-days were coming to an end. He eventually sold the restaurant to the Latz family, who converted the building into a public restaurant, which it has remained ever since.

TODAY

The Knife and Fork Inn remained in the Latz family through two generations until it was sold in 2005 to a local restaurateur, Frank Dougherty, whose family has owned another local restaurant (Dock's Oyster House) since 1897.

Dougherty immediately set about renovating the old building to bring it back to its prohibition luster. He installed a long, mahogany bar on the ground floor, and turned that section into a fine-dining area.

Upstairs, where the hidden and private alcoves used to hide married gentlemen and their night's entertainment, another bar was installed, and the area restored to another dining room.

The third floor room, where gambling used to take place, is now their wine room, with a floor-to-ceiling wine cellar that shows off their collection of hundreds of bottles.

The (ahem) *other* room now serves as office space.

What's nice about the renovations that Dougherty undertook is that they kept the spirit of what William Riddle had intended for the Knife and Fork Inn. While no longer an exclusive gentlemen's club, it's very easy to see yourself dining and drinking in the days when Nucky ruled the city.

In fact, underneath the booths that surround the 2nd floor dining area are the original lockers used to stash booze on the rare occasions the place was raided. The Knife and Fork truly celebrates this heritage.

It could be argued that this is more restaurant than bar now, and the argument certainly has merit. But the sheer history of the place, the notoriety of its patrons, the atmosphere of old-world Atlantic City, all combine to make this a great place to sit and enjoy a few cocktails, away from the circus that the city has become.

THE FOOD

The food at Knife and Fork is legendarily simply because it's classical. They serve steaks grilled to perfection, as well as seafood, and classic poultry dishes. The one thing that sets them apart from anywhere else is their Lobster Thermidor.

Lobster Thermidor is a classic French dish in which the lobster is completely de-shelled, the meat is mixed with leeks, onions, tomatoes and sherry, cooked, and then stuffed back into the shell.

The dish is certainly a nod to the decade of Knife and Fork's establishment—it's a dish ripe with history and something that the well-to-do "gentlemen" of early Atlantic City would have enjoyed. You're here to splurge, after all, so splurge on something you won't find anywhere else.

THE DRINKS

Their cocktails remain fixed in history as well. As the manager told us, they don't try to reinvent the wheel, but instead stick to the most classical of drinks that would have been served to Nucky and his cronies.

One of their most unique and most popular cocktails is the Aviation cocktail. This cocktail, mixing gin, maraschino liqueur, crème de violette, and lemon juice, has been around since 1916, and is rarely served at bars anymore. However, the Knife and Fork's attention to detail and its dedication to its own roots make this a must-try drink when you stop in.

Another cocktail to try—though not a period one— is called the Jezebel, which they make with their fresh Jalapeno Sorbet shaken with vodka.

Of course, they have a full bar, an expansive wine list, and talented bartenders so they can get you drunk with just about anything you request.

NEARBY DISTRACTIONS

Lucy the Elephant—Website: www.lucytheelephant.org **Address:** 9200 Atlantic Avenue Margate, NJ 08402-2449, (609) 823-6473 (Seasonal hours, check online for current times and day). The iconic, Lucy the Elephant, is a six-story hotel originally built in 1881 as a tourist attraction to get people to what was called "South Atlantic City" (about 15 minutes south of AC). The scheme worked, and it became an instant sensation. Now, the world's largest pachyderm is a visitor's center and they offer tours every half hour.

Exotic Driving Experience—Website: www.exoticdriving.com **Address:** New Jersey Motorsports Park 8000 Dividing Creek Rd., Millville, NJ 08332, (855) 822-0149 (Call ahead for booking and reservations). Drive the car of your dreams around a state of the art track and learn how to race like the pros. Exotic Driving Experience offers numerous dream cars for track driving rental, including Ferraris, Lamborghinis, and Aston Martins.

THE IRISH PUB, ATLANTIC CITY, NJ

Address: 164 St. James Place, Atlantic City, NJ 08401, (609) 344-9064 **Website:** www.theirishpub.com **Video tour:** https://youtu.be/n-7abXpkATw **Food:** Yes **Live Music:** No **Hours:** 24 Hours Sunday–Saturday **Type of Bar:** Pub **What to Drink:** A Guinness or a Jameson **Why You Should Go:** The oldest existing bar in Atlantic City, plus the adjoining hotel above it. Great boxing history and is a stone's throw from the boardwalk.

THE HISTORY

Situated at St. James Place and Boardwalk (refer to the Monopoly board to locate it), the Irish Pub started off in life as the bar inside the Elwood Hotel in 1903. This is actually pretty amazing because just about everything old on the island has been razed to make way for newer places, and that's especially true for the hotels. The fact that this bar, with adjoining inn above it, actually exists, speaks to how beloved it is.

While not large like the boardwalk hotels (it's only 6 stories tall), the Elwood Hotel became a popular destination. Visitors from around the world have checked in here and drank at the bar on the ground floor. This was especially true during prohibition.

Like the Knife and Fork Inn, the bar at the Elwood Hotel refused to stop selling booze just because of the 18th Amendment. And (again), like the Knife and Fork, the proprietors of the Elwood served alcohol openly, especially in the early years. In fact, the guest registration desk upstairs served as an impromptu bar during the roaring 20s, and the bell clerk was quick to pour guests a drink when they checked in.

According to a New York Times article, the Elwood Hotel was amongst a number of locations in Atlantic City that was raided by prohibition agents on September 7, 1920. In total, the agents seized $100,000.00 worth of liquor during the raid, which amounts to about $1.1 million today.

The Elwood allegedly remained a speakeasy, however, and continued to delight its guests with its full bar. After prohibition, the place remained popular and saw a number of famous guests and drinkers, most notably Joe DiMaggio who frequently stayed, ate and drank here. It was also heavily patronized by Hall of Fame boxing writer Bert Sugar, who reported on the many fights hosted by the city.

Another interesting piece of trivia is that the red hotels used in Monopoly were alleged to be modeled on the Irish Pub. Take a look and you'll quickly notice the resemblance.

As Atlantic City decayed in the 1960s and '70s, the Elwood was spared the fate of many other old buildings. In 1972 she was bought by Atlantic City locals, Richard and Cathy Burke. They changed the name from the Elwood Hotel to the Irish Pub & Inn and then left everything else alone. In fact, we were told that the newest thing in the place is the elevator, which was installed in 1930.

TODAY

This place is vintage pub. Once you enter you are embraced by warm, gleaming wood from the floor to the bar and even on the walls. The wood has been there for over 100 years and looks pristine, polished by the hands of thousands of visitors.

The memorabilia on the walls tells the story of Atlantic City's history. There are original newspapers from the 1920s, framed photos from the 1930s, and just about every other type of bric-a-brac imaginable collected over a century.

The large bar you see upon entering is welcoming and so authentically vintage you'll swear you recognize it from someplace else. You probably do: the copycat chain places that claim to be what this place actually is.

There are numerous tables if you choose not to sit at the bar (which seems a crime), or if you have a large party. There's also a small patio behind and outside the bar that's perhaps the most peaceful spot in the city. In fact, a local told us that it's the one spot you can go to and not feel like you're even in AC.

The time to visit is St. Patrick's Day. Sure, it gets wild and crowded simply because of its name and atmosphere—but it feels like it should at a Irish Pub on Saint Patrick's Day. But, they also have an odd tradition here that has been around for years. Here, St. Patrick's Day is also known as "Bag Day," and hundreds of people show up wearing bags on their heads. Yes, strange. But it sounds like fun, and it would be fun to at least watch the drunken shenanigans unfold.

The place is open 24 hours a day, which is pretty remarkable. In fact, they are the only place this close to the boardwalk that serves food and drink at all hours.

It's also a welcoming place. It almost sounds cliché to say that once you enter you immediately feel comfortable, but it's the truth. It seemed that there wasn't any certain crowd here, instead what we saw was a diverse mix of old and young, hipsters and normal people.

It's doubtful many of the patrons know or understand the rich history of the bar they're drinking in, but in the end, it probably doesn't even matter as long as they're here.

THE FOOD

Comfort-bar-food is the best way to describe the plates at the Irish Pub. They serve a number of sandwiches, burgers, fish and chip offerings, salads, and hearty meals like meatloaf and crab cakes.

Impressive is their late-night menu. From midnight to 6am, the Irish Pub serves a number of appetizers, burgers and meals meant to soak up all the booze you've been consuming on the boardwalk. This is actually a rare find, and one you'll be grateful of when the munchies kick in at about three in the morning.

Further, they have some of the cheapest meal specials around. Four dollars gets you a homemade soup and sandwich for lunch and $8 gets you a dinner special.

THE DRINKS

They have a full bar that can mix up just about anything you can think of. The classic cocktails are certainly their specialty, so a martini or Old Fashioned would be great choices. They also have decent selection of beer on tap, including a wide selection of local and craft brews.

But, because of its connection with the Emerald Isle, you would be committing a crime not to drink the traditional pint of Guinness finished with a shot of Jameson's Irish Whiskey. Yes, it's cliché, but it seems to just make sense here.

NEARBY DISTRACTIONS

Steel Pier—Website: www.steelpier.com **Address**: 1000 Boardwalk Atlantic City, NJ 08401, (609) 345-4893 (Monday–Friday 3pm–7pm, Saturday–Sunday 12pm–6pm). The original Steel Pier opened in 1889 and featured amusements for everyone, including rides, concerts, theaters and various spectacles. After years of neglect it burned down in 1982, but when the Taj

Mahal was built in 1996, it was resurrected. Now, like in the days of old, it is an amusement park by the sea and features rides and games for everyone.

Atlantic City Boardwalk—(Opened year round, though many attractions and shops close for the winter). The Atlantic City Boardwalk was installed in 1870 and was the first boardwalk in the nation. It was immortalized in the Monopoly board game and is pretty much what people picture when they hear the word "boardwalk." It stretches four miles from end to end and is lined with hotels, bars, restaurants, gift shops and amusements.

Central Pier Arcade & Speedway—**Address:** 1400 Boardwalk, Atlantic City, NJ 08401, (609) 345-5219 (Monday–Friday 11am–12:30am, Saturday 10am–2am, Sunday 10am–1am). This is the quintessential boardwalk arcade, with a variety of midway-style games. But, they also have other, more exciting distractions, like paintball and a huge over-under go-kart track with NASCAR style karts.

ATLANTIC CITY'S HISTORIC BARS

Ducktown Tavern—**Address:** 2400 Atlantic Ave., Atlantic City, NJ, 08401, (609) 449-1212 (Open 24 hours, Monday–Sunday). There's not a big selection of bars in Atlantic City, but if you need another, darkly lit space to drink at, Ducktown Tavern fits the bill. In fact, it's probably one of the more popular dives in the area. When we were there it was filled with locals and college-age kids. They also have an attached liquor store so you can take the party back to the hotel with you.

Dock's Oyster House—**Address:** 2405 Atlantic Ave., Atlantic City, NJ, 08401, (609) 345-0092 (Monday–Sunday 5pm–10pm). Dock's is the oldest continually-operated family-owned restaurant in the United States. It was opened in 1897 by Harry Dougherty and has been shucking oysters steady since then. Though mainly a restaurant, they do have a small bar and mix classic (but pricey) cocktails. It's a great place for a nice meal and some local history.

AUSTIN, TX

Austin, Texas, is one of the most dynamic cities in the United States. The mix of politics, western history and of course the state's largest university creates a lively and sometimes eccentric environment.

Austin is known as an entertainment destination. From concerts to sporting events, the city seems to have something to offer everyone. That includes those looking to quench their thirst. Most famous is the downtown area where 4th and 6th Streets overflow with bars and nightclubs. Most of these are trendy music venues for the Austin "weird" crowd: hipsters, college students and young professionals.

We don't want to have anything to do with this area. The bars change often, the scene is more in tune with what sells at the moment and less about authenticity. Instead, we want to get off these streets and look at other places where we can hoist a cold one.

The legacy of Austin's drinking history is intertwined with the huge influx of German settlers coming into the region. In the 1830s, a German immigrant wrote a letter to a friend back in Germany that described the beauty and wealth of Texas. The letter was subsequently published in the town's paper and ended up being quite influential in drawing more immigrants to the area.

The German influence can easily be seen in the local architecture (more a Bavarian influence than Mexican or Spanish), in the history of brewing (lagers over other types of beer), and even in the last names of many of the oldest families.

The influence was also substantial on the bar history of the town, and at least two of our picks for Austin Bucket List Bars™ reflect that legacy.

SCHOLZ GARTEN, AUSTIN, TX

Address: 1607 San Jacinto Boulevard, Austin, TX, 78701, (512) 474-1958
Website: www.scholzgarten.net **Video tour:** http://youtu.be/GvR0vzMUNoI
Food: Yes **Live Music:** Yes **Hours:** Monday–Thursday 11am–10pm, Friday–
Saturday 11am–11pm, Sunday 11am–10pm. **Type of Bar:** Beer Garden
What to Drink: Beer. Any kind. **Why You Should Go:** One of the oldest bars
in the United States, great tradition and history, German immigrants,
experience the thrill of UT football game night.

THE HISTORY

Scholz Garten was founded in 1866 by August Scholz, a German immigrant
and confederate veteran. Originally purchased in 1862 from Sam Norville for
the sum of $2400, the property contained a boarding house above which
August eventually built his bar and café. Scholz Garten quickly became a
popular meeting and hangout location for Austin's German population.
Eventually August converted the downstairs to a bar as well and installed a
traditional Bavarian beer garden—an outdoor sitting area where bands play
and beer flows like water.

After August's death in 1891, his stepson, Theodor Reisner, took over the
operation of the Garten until selling the establishment to the Lemp Brewery,
makers of Falstaff Beer, in 1893. That year just so happened to be the same
year the University of Texas football team went undefeated, and thanks to the
Garten's geographic location, only two blocks from the stadium, it quickly
became THE place to celebrate the school's wins (a tradition that continues to
this day).

The bar was again sold in 1908 to the German singing club "The Austin Saengerrunde," who still own the property today though the bar and restaurant are leased.

And as it did for so many establishments across the nation, the 18th Amendment had a dramatic effect on Scholz Garten. To survive, they created a non-alcoholic brew called Bone Dry Beer and increased the focus on their food, featuring both German and Texas favorites, a tradition that continues today.

TODAY

Today Scholz Garten is well known for being exactly the same as its always been, and in a time of constant changes, updates, and renovations, that's a unique characteristic. Little is different about the place after over 100 years of operation. As a matter of fact, in 1962 when then operator Bob Bales decided to add air conditioning, he claimed he was almost run out of town by unhappy patrons. Needless to say, the regulars like the Garten and want it left just the way it is.

Scholz Garten has become a rite of passage for University of Texas students and fans, an iconic location to celebrate UT victories and to mourn their losses. It's also a staple in Austin's bar scene and continues to be a local favorite.

Also, because of its geographic location and historic importance, Scholz Garten has had more than its fair share of politicians stop in for a cold beer, bite to eat, and a friendly debate or two. Notable visitors include almost all of Texas's governors (the Democrats, anyway), Bill Clinton, Al Gore, and more than a handful of Texas state representatives. The outdoor Garten attracts the more liberal politicians, while the indoor area tends to attract the conservatives (makes one wonder where the independents go).

During you visit you might hear a mysterious sound while standing around the outdoor beer garden. It's an occasional rumble and boom, kind of like rolling thunder, but heard on both stormy and clear days. Its source is known by only a few: it's the Scholz' bowling alley (now you know too).

The bowling alley is located on opposite side of the north wall lining the beer garden. It was built by the Lemp Brewing Company sometime around 1893 and is still in operation today. If you ask around, find the right person and beg for admission (it is a private club) you too could enjoy a few rounds of bowling with a nice cold pitcher, just feet away from the historic beer garden.

THE FOOD

The most obvious choice is going to be the more traditional stuff. Brats and beer go together like, well, brats and beer. This is especially true at a beer garden. Order a bratwurst, sauerkraut, hard roll and mustard, and you can't go wrong.

They're also really well known for their barbecue, especially the Texas specialty: the brisket. They let us watch them preparing it, and we were drooling in no time. Get a plate of it and sit outside to listen to some traditional music. Give their four meat BBQ plate a try for a little of everything, and wash it down with an Austin Beerworks Pearl Snap Pilsner. Either way you go, you really can't go wrong.

THE DRINKS

While they used to only serve beer, they now feature a full bar and can make just about anything you might want. Though it's tempting to order Jaegermeister or maybe schnapps, you need to go with beer; after all, it is a beer garden.

They serve an immense amount of beer here, especially during a UT football game. And while we're typically not fans of the common American lagers and pilsners, it would actually be fitting to order it here. So take your pick, a Bud, Coors or Miller product outside in the garden would make for a great day (or night).

NEARBY DISTRACTIONS

Texas State History Museum—Website: www.thestoryoftexas.com **Address:** 1800 N. Congress Ave. Austin, TX, 78701, (512) 936-4639 (Monday– Saturday 9am–6pm, Sunday 12pm–6pm). Located less than a half mile from Scholz is the Texas State History Museum. Featuring three floors of interactive exhibits, a special effects show and Austin's only IMAX theatre, it is truly a Texas-sized museum (about one of the largest and most colorful states in the nation). Be sure to check out their website, as they often have special exhibits and events.

Bobalu Cigar Co.—Website: www.bobalu.com **Address:** 509 E. 6th Street Austin, TX, 78701, (888) 332-4427 (operating hours vary, check website or call ahead). Only a mile from Scholz is Bobalu Cigar Company. Makers of their own line of cigars, they pride themselves on being the microbrewery of the cigar business, with the freshest, best tasting cigars and fairest prices you'll find. They even have experienced Cuban Cigar Rollers on site that you can watch via cameras as they roll some of the finest cigars in the country. So whether you're a cigar connoisseur, a beginner or somewhere in between, Bobalu is worth checking out.

Joe Jamail Field Texas Memorial Stadium—Website: www.texassports.com **Address:** San Jacinto Boulevard Austin, TX, 78712, (512) 471-7437 (games, events, and tour times vary. Trophy room is open to the public Monday– Friday 8am–5pm). Few college sports programs or stadiums are as storied as that of the Texas Longhorns football program. Less than a mile from Scholz (you can see it from the front door), the stadium is a beacon in Austin. If you can swing going to a game it will be an unforgettable experience, and if not, then go on their self-guided tour, which ends in the trophy room containing their multiple national titles and Heisman trophies.

HISTORIC SCOOT, INN AUSTIN, TX

Address: 1308 East 4th Street, Austin, TX, 78702, (512) 524-1932
Website: www.scootinnaustin.com **Video tour:**
http://youtu.be/aPzCazDjAmo
Food: Food trucks **Live Music:** Yes **Hours:** Wednesday–Saturday 4pm–2am
Type of Bar: Dive, Beer **What to Drink:** Local craft beer, shot of Jack Daniels
Why You Should Go: History of Austin, beer garden, live music.

THE HISTORY

The Historic Scoot Inn was originally built as a railroad saloon in 1871 and played host to a long list of thirsty train passengers, railroad workers, bankers, outlaws, ranch hands, pioneers, travelers, and of course ladies of the night. From its opening in 1871 until around 1940 the place went through a long succession of owners, made a few changes, but refused to stop serving. Legend has it that the saloon has never closed its doors, even operating through Prohibition, faithfully serving locals and travelers alike.

In 1940 Scoot Ivy and his buddy Red bought the bar and named it Red's Scoot Inn. They served many of the same customers as those served 70 years before: warehouse workers, railroad workers, travelers, and locals (not to mention themselves; rumor has it Red and Scoot were themselves big drinkers and sometime finished multiple cases in a day). The place got quite the reputation during their tenure when most considered it the bar to be avoided in Austin through the 1970s. They owned, operated, and drank at the bar until 1980 when they both passed away.

The bar continued to operate, but it was a bit of a rough spell for a while until Vera Sandoval took ownership in 1997. Vera and her mother immediately set about cleaning up the place's image and attracting a new and more refined crowd. They ran the place until 2006, when the owners of the now closed Longbranch Inn just up the street purchased the Scoot Inn. From then until now, the saloon has changed hands another three times, but as long as the doors stay open, a 140+ year old tradition continues in Austin.

TODAY

The Scoot Inn is now a lively destination for many in Austin, and for many that travel to Austin. It features regular live music and is has become one of the go to musical venues in the city (it is owned by a live music production company). They have extensively remodeled it from the dive it used to be into a rather nice, nostalgic throwback lounge with large beer garden on the outside.

Once here, you'll find a long, shiny bartop and modern décor. The lounge area features overstuffed chairs, taxidermy longhorns, and cow skin rugs. In most any other place, it would look a bit laughable, but considering the history of this bar it actually works.

This is a place to listen to music and sip some fine cocktails with friends. It is a bit dark and gets pretty crowded, but it's the last and oldest of the Austin saloons, so you can forgive the many other patrons for also wanting to check the place out.

THE FOOD

They don't have a kitchen, so don't cook or serve their own cuisine, however they have a nightly rotation of food trucks with some great, local gourmet food to try.

THE DRINKS

The Historic Scoot Inn features a mixology program with signature drinks. They also serve top shelf whiskies. We would suggest asking them for a signature, bourbon-based drink. If you're in the mood for beer, then definitely try something local.

NEARBY DISTRACTIONS

Juan In A Million—**Website:** www.juaninamillion.com **Address:** 2300 Cesar Chavez Street Austin TX, 78702, (512) 472-3872 (Monday–Sunday 7am–3pm). If the beer and live music at the Scoot Inn leaves your stomach rumbling, then drive or walk the one mile from the Scoot Inn to Juan in a Million, and take on the breakfast taco challenge. To win, all you have to do is eat more Don Juan breakfast tacos than the current record, which as of now stands at eight, and you'll get your picture on the Juan Wall of Fame. Good luck.

Live Oak Brewing—**Website:** www.liveoakbrewing.com **Address:** 1615 Crozier Lane, Del Valle, TX, 78617, (512) 385-2299 (tours occur twice per month, check website or call for information and reservations). You can never go wrong with free beer, especially when it is good free beer. At Live Oak

Brewing Company the beer is good and on tours it is free, at least a small amount anyway. Only two miles away, it is yet another opportunity to taste some of Austin's outstanding craft beer offerings.

THE TAVERN, AUSTIN, TX

Address: 922 West 12th St., Austin, TX 78703, (512) 320-8377
Website: www.tavernaustin.com **Video tour:** http://youtu.be/4OcauzoWuSQ
Food: Yes **Live Music:** Yes **Hours:** Daily 11am–12pm **Type of Bar:** Sports Bar **What to Drink:** A Fireman's 4 Blonde (local beer) **Why You Need to Go:** Oldest sports bar in Texas, speakeasy and brothel through Prohibition, tons of local history.

THE HISTORY

A phrase you'll hear often around Austin is "You're never too far from 12th and Lamar." It's a reference to the Tavern, the oldest sports bar in Texas, located on the corner of 12th Street and Lamar Boulevard. It is one of Texas' oldest bars and has a colorful history that makes any trip worthwhile.

The building was originally built in 1916 by owner R. Niles Graham, who had planned to build a bar at the location since day one; he hired Hugo Kuehne, a first generation German immigrant, to design and build the building. Hugo decided to model the building after a traditional German public house, but plans had to be "modified" after the 18th Amendment was passed. In true can-do, can-win and can-make-the-best-of-the-situation attitude, Graham decided to build a grocery store in the bar's place (or at least that is what he wanted everyone to believe).

Rumor has it that the establishment was a grocery by day and a speakeasy by night. After closing, the downstairs was turned into a popular speakeasy complete with booze and gambling, and the upstairs contained a prominent brothel—some of the employees of which are said to still be with the place!

Like so many old establishments across the country, the Tavern is rumored to be haunted. Most believe the ghost of a prostitute named Emily, and possibly her daughter, still reside in the building today. It is thought that they were killed during an altercation between two men sometime in the early 1940s, though there is no hard evidence to prove this story. People have witnessed TV channels changing for no reason, glasses and plates falling unexpectedly, footsteps in the halls when no one is around, tray tables falling and unexplained phone calls.

One particularly creepy incident occurred late one night when the manager was upstairs on the third floor for closing. With nobody in the building, the manager received a call from the gas station attendant across the street, who wanted to know if the place was still open. The manager replied no, and the attendant asked why there was someone standing in the window on the second floor. The manager went to investigate and found no one and nothing out of the ordinary, so he called the gas station attendant back, but the attendant still insisted that the lady was in the window looking right at him.

Haunted or not, we didn't see anything, but if you do happen to see Emily or her daughter, tell her we said hello and would love an interview.

The grocery store was moved in 1929 and an upscale restaurant took its place. Finally, when Prohibition ended in 1933, Graham got his wish and was able to start serving alcoholic beverages (legally, of course).

TODAY

Today the saying "You're never too far from 12th and Lamar" continues to be an Austenite favorite as does the Tavern. The bar is a common hangout for people from all walks of life and, due to the huge number of high-definition flat screens, it's also a favorite on game day.

When entering, try a seat at the bar, carved up from artistic vandals over the years (if you have a pen knife you're welcome to carve your name as well). Or if you're brave enough and the place is kind of empty, take your drink and dish up to the top floors and hang out with one of the ghosts that haunt the joint.

Earlier, when we said that the crowd was varied, we weren't kidding. Today you'll find doctors, students, politician, businessmen, tourists, and professors, the Tavern seems to have something for everyone.

THE FOOD

The Tavern serves up a large array of sports bar-type fare, including burgers, salads, soups and the like. One of the more interesting dishes (for sports bar grub) is the plate of White Wings.

The White Wings are traditional chicken wings wrapped in bacon and jalapenos and tossed in their special wing sauce. They're actually pretty spicy but really tasty—the combination of wing sauce and bacon is just right.

THE DRINKS

The Tavern features a full bar, so they can mix up just about anything you want. However, they pride themselves on their local and craft beers, many of which aren't available outside of Austin.

We recommend the Fireman's 4 Blonde, a local beer that goes really well with the White Wings (if you decide to have them). They will also be happy to serve the beer in one of their oversized souvenir steins. Word of advice, though: if you do go for the oversized stein, be sure to get a cab ride home. Those things are no joke!

NEARBY DISTRACTIONS

K1 Speed—Website: www.k1speed.com **Address:** 2500 McHale Court Austin, TX, 78758, (512) 271-5475 (Monday–Thursday 12pm–10pm, Friday 11am–11pm, Saturday 10am–11pm, Sunday 10am–7pm). If you're in the mood for some head-to-head racing with your friends, then head out to K1 speed, about 10 miles from The Tavern, for some fun indoor go-kart racing. For the ultimate experience, call ahead and plan an adult-only event.

Texas State Capitol—Website: www.tspb.state.tx.us **Address:** 1100 Congress Avenue Austin, TX, 78701, (512) 463-0063 (operating hours vary by building and event). An extraordinary example of 19th-century architecture, the Texas Capitol is approximately 22 acres of grounds and monuments. Less than a mile from the Tavern, admission is free and self-guided tours are available.

AUSTIN'S HISTORIC BARS

Deep Eddy Cabaret—Website: www.deepeddycabaret.com **Address:** 2315 Lake Austin Boulevard Austin, TX, 78703, (512) 472-0961 (Monday–Sunday 12pm–2am). This staple of Austin is a quiet place, geared towards relaxing with a drink in your hand and talking to friends. The place actually started life as a grocery store and bait shop in the 1920s, but in 1951 they converted to a beer joint. If you want to escape the loud music and crowds at other places, this might be your bar of choice.

Threadgill's Old #1—Website: www.threadgills.com **Address:** 6416 N Lamar Blvd, Austin, TX, 78752, (512) 451-5440 (Monday–Saturday, 11am–10pm, Sunday, 10am–9:30pm). This place is the quintessential Austin music bar, featuring a wide variety of musical genres and range throughout the week. This didn't just happen recently, it's actually been going on since about day one. Opened in 1933 as a filling station, it became the first bar in the county after prohibition was repealed that same year. Soon, musical acts began performing here. In the 1960s, Threadgill's became a regular venue for none other than Janis Joplin. The tradition continues at Threadgill's every day, and this place should be a stop for anyone visiting Austin.

Carousel Lounge—Website: www.carousellounge.net **Address:** 1110 E 52nd St, Austin, TX, 78723, (512) 452-6790 (Tuesday–Sunday, 3:30pm–1am).

Have we mentioned Austin is weird? Well it is. And they celebrate it. In fact celebrating "weirdness" is itself celebrated, and that's why Carousel Lounge is such a popular, long-lasting dive. You'd think the circus theme of this place would wear thin after a while, but since 1963 this place has been going strong. It's known not only for its eclectic décor and history, but also for its great live music, cheap drinks and great feel.

BALTIMORE, MD

A stone's throw from Washington DC, Baltimore is dripping in history, and, luckily, we can still find some of it at her bars. Despite its proximity to the Nation's Capital, traffic can make it a tough place to get around, yet when you find any of the places here, you're rewarded with an amazing trip through time. Baltimore is a fun place, and a great area to spend a Friday afternoon having a few beers and catching a baseball game.

Though founded in 1729, well after some of the older cities and colonies on the East Coast, Baltimore has done a remarkably great job at preserving its past. So good, in fact, that over a third of the buildings found in the city are on the National Register of Historic Places. They know how to respect the past here, and it shows. Aside from historic buildings, you'll also find more monuments and statues per capita than in any other city in the US. Many of these were erected in honor of some of the remarkable and famous past residents, like Edgar Allen Poe, Frederick Douglass, Babe Ruth, and Billie Holiday.

In terms of drinking, the city's history is unrivaled. One of the most popular beers in the region is National Bohemian, locally called, Natty Boh (be sure to order it by this name, not National Bohemian). This beer has been quenching Baltimore's thirst since 1885, and is still about the most popular beer in the region—about 90% of all that's produced is consumed in Baltimore, and much of it in Fells Point, the historic district that at one time was one of the busiest ports in the nation. In all, Baltimore is a great place to visit, and a great place to find some of America's most historic haunts.

THE HORSE YOU CAME IN ON, BALTIMORE, MD

Address: 1626 Thames St, Baltimore, MD, 21231, (410) 327-8111
Website: www.thehorsebaltimore.com **Video Tour:**
https://youtu.be/lvhc3S2dJzE
Food: Yes **Live Music:** Yes **Hours:** Monday–Sunday 11am–1:30am **Type of Bar:** Dive **What to Drink:** Jack Daniels **Why You Should Go:** The oldest bar in Maryland and rumored to be the drinking spot for none other than hometown favorite, Edgar Allen Poe.

THE HISTORY

This part of Baltimore, Fells Point, was a fun place when The Horse You Came In On opened in 1775. Back then, this was one of the busiest ports in the new nation, and they saw goods and trade from all over the world arrive here. There was also a significant shipbuilding industry, so all told you must try to imagine this place crawling with sailors, shipbuilder, immigrants, and other rough and tumble-type crowds.

And following along with these groups was, of course, the ladies that loved them (by the hour, that is). Brothels were practically stacked on top of each other and at one time, it was reported, that in this little space in the city alone, there were over 300 bars and over 100 brothels. Needless to say, this is where we'd be hanging out in the late 18th century!

Sadly, none of that exists, but The Horse You Came In On (affectionately, and simply called, The Horse, by locals), gives you a brief moment of time travel. This small, stone tavern once saw these sailors and other ne'er-do-wells night after rum-soaked night, and it's somehow lasted all these years.

When the saloon was originally built, the buildings just to the south of The Horse weren't yet constructed, and so any patrons visiting had a perfect view of Fort McHenry on the night of September 13, 1814 when the British attacked. The Star-Spangled Banner was written the next morning, giving a first-hand account of the battle that would also have been seen by those at The Horse.

Perhaps one of the most notorious stories of The Horse has to do with a particular regular. It's rumored that Edgar Allen Poe, Baltimore resident during many stages of his life, was often seen here. It would make sense, as this was reportedly the last saloon between the port and his house on Amity Street, so he would surely stop in here for a nip or two. What's even more interesting, though, is the final night of Poe's life. On October 3, 1849, Poe was found delirious and rushed to a hospital. Some say he smelled of alcohol and attributed his death to drinking heavily and being left outside in the cold night. Others argue he was poisoned. In either case, his death is a mystery.

Adding to this mystery is the account from some that he was seen at a local saloon getting soused. The saloon he was reportedly in was none other than The Horse You Came In On. If that's true, then it was here where Poe took his last drink, and it may also have been that visit that eventually killed him. While this account is rejected by many Poe fans, it makes for an interesting night of conversation while drinking at the same bar as one of America's most famous writers!

TODAY

The saloon was named in the 1970s by an irreverent owner to The Horse You Came In On, and it's kept its tongue-in-cheek moniker ever since. The theme he chose for his place was a western-type saloon, not too common in a port-city like Baltimore. The theme is toned down a bit today, but can still be seen in the name, the logo, and the saddles for barstools you get to sit on when having a cold one at the bar.

The northernmost part of the saloon is the oldest and most original, seen in the architecture and building materials used. There are a total of four bars here, with three more to the south of the original. This area (including the back rooms they used for the kitchen), were originally stables that were since purchased and folded into the bar. The architecture here is still quite old, but has been remodeled and added to extensively. However, each of the bars is a bit different, and includes a tequila bar with a huge selection of tequilas.

They sell a lot of Jack Daniels here. A lot! They even have a bottle program that lets patrons purchase a bottle and then leave it there for consumption when they stagger in with friends. The Horse was also, reportedly, one of the first bars to infuse their own Jack Daniels. In fact, according to the owner, Jack Daniels got the idea for its cinnamon and honey whiskies from infusion program The Horse already had.

They have live music that ranges in genre, but is typically upbeat. When we visited, there was a small crowd dancing to a single, acoustic musician. It was fun, or at least it looked like fun (we were busy eating). They have a full kitchen so you can settle in for a meal with your drink, which we would highly suggest, because the drinks do flow.

The crowd is pretty diverse, but includes tourists and locals. There was a pretty big college-type crowd here, and we saw a bachelorette party or two as well. They were rowdy people, but well-mannered and generally quite friendly.

Know that there are some mysterious goings-on late at night here. While the rumors of Edgar Allen Poe are disputed, one thing that many are sure of is that the place seems to be haunted. The owner and manager call the spirit "Edgar" and think it might be Poe that's haunting the place considering he may have had his last night in this saloon. The manager we talked to said he wasn't necessarily a believer in the supernatural, but became one when, closing late at night, a beer mug sitting on the bar exploded for no reason. Have a few Jack Daniels and you might see Edgar yourself!

All in all, this place definitely needs to be on your short list of bars to visit in Baltimore.

THE FOOD

They do have a full kitchen here that pumps out some great pub grub. We tried the Jumbo Crab Pretzel, made with a from-scratch jumbo pretzel smothered with crab dip and melted cheese, and the Mahi Mahi Tacos with the battered mahi fillet. Combined with some dark, locally-made craft beer, we almost literally had to roll ourselves out of the place. Everything we ate was delicious and highly recommended. But they also have burgers and sandwiches, salads and wings, so you're sure to find something worth eating.

THE DRINKS

You'll find a great selection of local brews and the more commonly found stuff. You'll also find Natty Boh, the locally made hipster beer that's been a staple in this city since 1885. Jack Daniels is a good option considering the aforementioned bottle and infusion programs. They also mixed us up a great Old Fashioned, so try one of those if you're looking for a cocktail.

NEARBY DISTRACTIONS

Edgar Allen Poe's House—Website: www.poeinbaltimore.org/poe-house **Address:** 203 N Amity St, Baltimore, MD, 21223, (410) 462-1763 (Thursday–Sunday 11am–4pm). From 1832 to 1835, Poe lived in this small house with his aunt, his grandmother, and his two cousins (one of which he would marry). Restored and open to the public, visitors get to see what life was like for a 23-year-old, budding writer, including the poems and stories he penned while in Baltimore. You can also take a look at his chair, lap desk, and telescope. This would be a great place to visit before hitting The Horse later on.

Edgar Allen Poe's Grave—Website: www.eapoe.org/BALT/poegrave.htm **Address:** 515 W Fayette St, Baltimore, MD, 21201, (410) 706-2072 (Monday–Sunday 8am–6pm). Yes, another Poe-related distraction, but considering the history of the saloon we're featuring, it makes complete sense. Poe was originally buried in an unmarked grave, and in 1865 a movement began in the city to give him the memorial he deserved. After a community drive to raise the money, this memorial was completed and installed in 1875. When you go, you'll notice the knick-knacks and souvenirs left on the gravestone, including the occasional bottle of cognac from an unnamed person every year on the poet's birthday. Definitely worth seeing either before or after you drink!

Fort McHenry—Website: www.nps.gov/fomc/index.htm **Address:** 2400 E Fort Ave, Baltimore, MD, 21230, (410) 962-4290 (Monday–Sunday 9am–5pm). It takes a little more work to get here, but it is well-worth the time and trouble to see the fort made famous by Francis Scott Key. Made a historical landmark in 1939, and then subsequently fully restored by the US Government, this is a must-see distraction when in Baltimore. Here visitors learn about the War of 1812, about the part that Baltimore played in that war, and about the famous battle on the night of September 13, 1814.

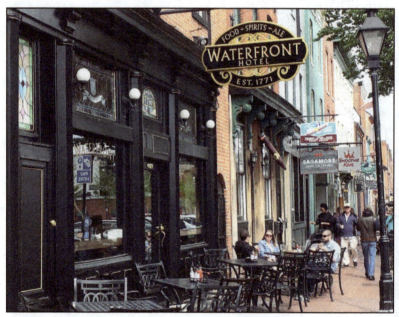

WATERFRONT HOTEL, BALTIMORE, MD

Address: 1710 Thames St, Baltimore, MD, 21231, (410) 537-5055 **Website:** www.waterfronthotel.us **Video Tour:** https://youtu.be/lvhc3S2dJzE **Food:** Yes **Live Music:** Yes **Hours:** Monday–Sunday 11am–2am **Type of Bar:** Dive **What to Drink:** Natty Boh **Why You Should Go:** Originally a private residence that was built in 1771, it was later converted into a hotel and tavern in 1861 and played a huge part in housing (and quenching the thirst of) troops during the Civil War.

THE HISTORY

Thomas Long constructed the building at 1710 Thames St. (about two blocks east of The Horse You Came In On) in 1771 as private residence. If you ask the bartenders, they'll point out the loose bricks in the wall that Long hid cigars from his disapproving wife. Ten years later it was Irish immigrant Cumberland Dugan who transformed it into a hotel (with included tavern). Dugan was a fun fellow who was formerly a flour merchant before he got into commercial real estate. He started a tradition of leaving an open clam on the pillow of each guest to welcome them. Yes, we find that odd too, but for some reason it was considered endearing.

The hotel was popular, and with two stories of guest rooms above the ground-floor tavern, it was also (most likely) quite lively with the sailors, shipbuilders and merchants. We can't confirm that there was a brothel here, but because they were so common in Fells Point at the time, we certainly can't rule it out. Dugan, however, was a prominent area businessman, so it's doubtful he'd want to get caught up in the more unsavory aspects of running a hotel.

Like The Horse, one of the Waterfront's more notable visitors was Edgar Allen Poe, who enjoyed tipping a glass here as he worked his way up the saloons of Thames St. In fact, while he may have had his last drink at The Horse, he may have had his first of the night here. Who knows? The Waterfront Hotel was also charged with housing troops during the Civil War, and there are tales of them causing a bit of a ruckus here while they stayed.

Another notable drinker to hang out here was Dashiell Hammett, who enjoyed visiting in the 1920s while working for the Pinkerton Detective Agency. Hammett went on to write some pretty notable books, like The Maltese Falcon and The Thin Man. Then, in 1955, after over a century and a half of hosting some of Baltimore's finest visitors, The Waterfront Hotel stopped being a hotel, and converted to a tavern and restaurant (while keeping the existing name just to confuse everyone).

TODAY

The Waterfront is still a really active and lively place, despite the missing sailors and shipbuilders. The bar is popular with visitors and locals alike, all of them partying in Fells Points on the weekends. If you come by, and it looks a bit familiar, it might be because it was used as one of the more noticeable backdrops for the TV show, "Homicide: Life on the Street."

When you visit, take some time to just explore the downstairs tavern. Unlike The Horse You Rode In On just up the street, this place has changed little, and it certainly hasn't had any other buildings added to it or folded into it. This is legitimately over two centuries of unchanged structure. And though the interior has been remodeled, and then remodeled again over the years, it will still be very similar to the space that Poe drank in.

Like many old buildings are, this place is reportedly haunted. Visitors have reported hearing voices and footsteps coming from the upper floors, even though they're vacant. Though they haven't named any their ghosts like other places have, it's still enough to give you the creeps on a late night.

For a great view of the harbor, try to sit upstairs on the second floor. This space is more of a lounge-like area where you can relax with a drink and enjoy some scenery. Also, they do have live music every night, with different genres and local bands. Check their website for the full music schedule. All in all, The Waterfront Hotel is a great place for a drink, and a wonderfully preserved part of Baltimore's past.

THE FOOD

The crab dip is amazing and we could eat it by the gallon. But, of course, they have other offerings. In fact, they have a full kitchen and make a wide variety of burgers and sandwiches. If you want something other than pub grub, though, they also have a great selection of full meals, including steaks and southern classics. By the way, did you know this was the South?

THE DRINKS

They have a full bar, and a really good cocktail program. They can make just about anything you'd like to order. They also have a variety of locally made craft brews on tap, so you're sure to find something you like. For us, though, we went with the Natty Boh—National Bohemian, the beer of Baltimore. They have it on tap, it's fresh, light and pairs well with most anything you order from the kitchen.

NEARBY DISTRACTIONS

Baltimore Ghost Tours—Website: www.baltimoreghosttours.com **Address:** Sidewalk Outside Max's Sidebar, 731 South Broadway, Baltimore, MD, 21231, (877) 293-1571 (Friday–Saturday 7pm–9pm). Fells Point has some of the oldest real estate in the nation, so you know there's going to be some great ghost stories that go along with it. Take a tour of haunted Baltimore, or more precisely, haunted Fells Point, for some creepy stories. They also have a haunted pub crawl, which is right up our alley.

Urban Pirates—Website: www.urbanpirates.com **Address:** 911 S Ann St, Baltimore, MD, 21231, (410) 327-8378 (Seasonal, April 7–June 10, check website for options and times, June 12–September 3, check website for options and times). Okay, you can get a tour of the harbor and see Baltimore by ship from just about every tour company in the area, but how about doing it while drinking rum and firing water cannons? Urban Pirates lets you explore your inner Black Beard on an adults-only cruise, complete with pirate costume and fake tattoos (but you supply your own booze).

Baltimore Electric Boat Rental—Website: www.baltimoreboatrental.com **Address:** 40 International Drive, Baltimore, MD, 21202, (443) 949-2855 (Monday–Friday 10am–8pm, Saturday–Sunday 9am–8pm). Why not just rent your own boat for a few hours and tool around the harbor? It's a bit pricey, but for a group of up to 10 people, it could be a bargain. They have party boats too (just add your own "supplies" for the party), so you can rent yourself a floating fiesta. And remember, there's no better partying than partying on the water.

BALTIMORE'S HISTORIC BARS

The Owl Bar—Website: www.theowlbar.com **Address:** 1 E Chase St, Baltimore, MD, 21202, (410) 347-0888 (Monday 4pm–12am, Tuesday–Thursday 11:30am–2am, Saturday 11am–2am, Sunday 11am–12am). Housed inside the basement of the opulent Belvedere Hotel, this elegant bar started serving drinks in 1903. The hotel was the first luxury hotel in the city, and soon was playing host to every class of visitor, including US Presidents and even royalty, so it's safe to say the bar has served both the famous and the influential through the years. The liquor didn't stop flowing during prohibition, either, as the place kept the hotel's guests quenched with illegal hooch. The room-length, oak bar is all class, and there's just enough taxidermy on the wall to keep it securely in the category of "hunter's lodge" and not dive bar. They have a full bar (of course) and are great at classic cocktails, so try a Gin Rickey or some other prohibition-era drink. They also have a full-service kitchen with upscale pub-grub. The food isn't cheap, but it's made from locally sourced ingredients and is a far cry better than the hot wings you'll find at other bars in the area.

Leon's of Baltimore—Website: leonsbaltimore.tripod.com **Address:** 227 W Chase St, Baltimore, MD, 21201, (410) 539-4850 (Monday–Sunday 4pm–2am). "Are you a friend of Dorothy?" If you uttered that phrase at 227 W. Chase in Baltimore during the 1950s and 60s, the door would open and you'd be able to have a drink in what's now the oldest gay bar in Baltimore. Though a bar of some kind since 1890s, the place started catering to the artistic and beatnik crowd in the 1940s. The crowd often included gay men and women, who found an accepting getaway at Leon's (named for Leon Lampe, the bar's owner in the 1930s). In 1957, the bar finally became a gay bar exclusively. This is pretty special if you think about the fact that being gay was illegal in many parts of the country (and the world) during that era. In any case, Leon's stayed low-key and quietly played host to the city's gay crowd until it didn't really have to stay in the shadows any longer. In the 1970s, Leon's was an open secret in Charm City, and it was visited by an array of distinguished guests of the day, like Liberace and Joan Rivers. This is a special place and deserves credit for its longstanding service to the community. Definitely check it out when you visit Baltimore.

Muir's Tavern—Address: 36 E Fort Ave, Baltimore, MD, 21230, (410) 385-0344 (Monday–Saturday 10am–1am). Muir's was founded in 1944 by Roland Muir, who spent his life as a tugboat captain before he started spending it behind the bar. Since then it's been nothing but family that's manned the helm at this small tavern. When it opened, family-run bars were a common sight in Baltimore, but as the years have gone by, all the others have closed, leaving just a handful serving the locals. And of those left, Muir's is the oldest. Here the beer is cheap and the atmosphere is purely old-school Baltimore. Here you'll find a portrait of Johnny Unitas and vintage Natty Boh signs. The crowd is warm and friendly, and the bartenders are quick to strike up a conversation with you. This is, simply speaking, the type of bar that used to dot every neighborhood in the country, but which has slowly been edged out. Also, they do sell package bottles and beer, so if you need something to take back to your hotel room, look no further.

Irv's Basement Bar—Address: 2054 Knollview Ave, Pasadena, MD, 21122, (Monday–Sunday 11am–1:30am). In 1963, Irv Koch and his brother Harry (both plumbers, because of course they were), bought a small house in the small Baltimore suburb of Pasadena and opened a bar…in the basement. Today that house with the ultimate man cave in the basement still exists, and Irv, at 94, is still pouring the drinks. According to Irv there were, at one time, basement bars throughout the region, but now Irv's is the last of them. This is the ultimate find for the bar lover, and there's little doubt it won't be around much longer. If you can make it, and if the bar is closed, simply knock on the door and ask Irv to open up. When you get inside you'll find some scattered tables, a pool table, and even a disco ball. You'll also see underwear and bras hanging from the ceiling (always a great sign), and knick-knacks from the decades of patrons who've passed through the place. Irv serves up classic and easy-to-make cocktails, as well as inexpensive bottled beer. The prices overall are really low and make this place a bargain to boot. This is one you need to go out of your way to visit, but when you do, it will be oh so worth it!

BOSTON, MA

There are few cities in America with the history boasted by Boston. Founded by Puritans in 1630, it's come to represent much of what we think of when we think of the early years of the United States. Not only was it one of the first colonies, but it was also one of the most important, and was a leading center for rebellion and uprising during the Revolutionary War.

As can be imagined, this early history has itself played a role in shaping how the city has progressed. As a result, Boston identifies itself as much for its history as for its modern contributions to the country. And though it strives to be taken seriously for its current drive to be a focus of the high-tech industry throughout New England, it's also constantly reminding visitors of its past and place in history at every opportunity.

For the traveler looking for a new place to drink, a welcoming pub, or a slice of early American bar life, Boston is a great place to get lost in.

Those who remember the 80s might recollect Cheers as being here. It was. It was a genuine imitation of a not-very-old bar you can still go to today.

And as far as the old, historic bars, there are still a few worthy of your money.

What you have to remember about this city, though, is that so many historic characters traipsed through here during the most important moments of our history. And that pretty much means that everyone claims the presence of historic figures. That's why if you go anywhere in the city short of a Walmart you'll probably see a plaque claiming that John Adams, Sam Adams, or even Paul Revere had been there/drank there/evacuated himself there.

We don't want to cast any doubts on the authenticity of any of these places but do take these claims with a grain of salt (unless we tell you otherwise – we've done the research). Enjoy!

WARREN TAVERN, CHARLESTOWN, MA

Address: 2 Pleasant Street, Charlestown, MA, 02129, (617) 241-8142
Website: www.warrentavern.com **Video tour:**
http://youtu.be/UO0qJmM6rfE
Food: Yes **Live Music:** No **Hours:** Monday–Friday 11:00am–1am, Saturday–
Sunday 10:00am–1am **Type of Bar:** Tavern **What to Drink:** Samuel Adams
Why **You Should Go:** Founded in 1780 it's one of the oldest original taverns
in the country (not moved from some other location or rebuilt later with the
same name), and the most authentic in Boston.

THE HISTORY

Just feet from the historic Freedom Trail, tracing the history of our
country's founding through Boston, sits the Warren Tavern. Erected in 1780
in Charlestown, Massachusetts, today it is over 225 years old and is the oldest
and most celebrated bar in the area.

Rumored to have been one of the first buildings built after the British
burned down Charlestown following the legendary Battle of Bunker Hill
(1775), this place simply oozes American history and is what we feel truly
embodies what a tavern should be.

Captain Eliphelet Newell, himself a participant in the Boston Tea Party,
built and named the tavern after the legendary Patriot leader Doctor Joseph
Warren, who was killed at Bunker Hill.

After construction was completed the tavern quickly became Paul Revere's
favorite watering hole. George Washington is also known to have stopped by
on more than one occasion and even over-indulged in a drink or two.

As it was intended when it was originally built and throughout its history the tavern has been a local watering hole, where one could stop in for a drink, a meal and be updated on local and national news.

TODAY

Today the Warren Tavern is a cornerstone of the city of Charlestown and its residents. It continues its tradition of being a true tavern where locals and tourists alike mingle in the historic structure sharing ideas, arguing differing views, conversing about local, national and international events and simply having a good time. The tavern is exactly what Captain Newell had intended when he originally built it, and we honestly believe that if either Newell or Warren himself were to walk into the bar today, he would not only approve but would also feel right at home.

Upon entering, a tall person might feel a bit claustrophobic. The low-hung ceilings were typical for the time period and built that way to keep heat in during the winters. The place is inviting, and the bar is scattered with a handful of regulars. This is a great place to watch a game or just spend an afternoon or evening relaxing and enjoying the great atmosphere.

THE FOOD

The Warren Tavern is famous for its Tavern Burger, (featuring their house made garlic-herb cream cheese), and their garlic-mustard (a perfect addition to the burger). The mustard, which is something of legend, can be bought by the jar, and you should plan to buy a few jars to take home.

Beyond the burger and mustard there is the clam chowder and there was little doubt in our minds we were in for a treat when the Warren Tavern's manager, John, told us he would put their clam chowder against any in the nation without hesitation. And we have no hesitation when we tell you that the clam chowder at the Warren Tavern is the best we've ever had. Don't get a cup—it won't be enough; Get a bowl and love every bite. You can thank us later.

THE DRINKS

The Warren includes a full bar that serves just about every cocktail you can imagine. Their beer selection is also regional and seasonal, so there's little doubt that you'll find something you like.

For us though, it had to be a Sam Adams. Boston Beer Company is just across the bridge, and Sam Adams Lager and Ale permeate this area of the country. What better beer to drink than one that was named after one of our Founding Fathers, all while sitting in such a historic setting—a setting that also entertained the very men we've read about in history books.

NEARBY DISTRACTIONS

Bunker Hill Monument—Address: Monument Square, Charlestown, MA, 02129, (617) 242-5641 (Monday–Sunday 9am–5pm). Only four blocks northeast of Warren Tavern is the site of the famous Battle of Bunker Hill, ironically enough not on Bunker Hill but on Breed's Hill. The granite obelisk and visitor's center mark the sites of one of the most famous and earliest battles of the Revolutionary War (occurring in 1775). It was here that Dr. Joseph Warren lost his life and the Patriots infused the colonies with their spirit and bravado.

USS Constitution—Address: Building 22, Charlestown Navy Yard Boston, MA, 02129, (617) 426-1812 (November 1–March 1, Thursday–Sunday 10am–6pm, April 1–September 30 Tuesday–Sunday 10am–6pm, October 1–October 31 Tuesday–Sunday 10am–4pm). Located about 10 long blocks east of the Warren Tavern sits Old Ironsides herself: the USS Constitution. Launched in 1797, she's still an active US Navy warship and crewed by sailor and Marine tour-guides in period costume. It's actually really stunning to view this ship and see how the sailors used to live and fight.

Samuel Adams (Boston Beer Company) Brewery Tour—Address: 30 Germania Street, Boston, MA, 02130 (617) 368-5080 (Monday–Thursday 10am–3pm, Fridays 10am–5:30pm, Saturdays 10am–3pm). You'll need transportation to get here, but it'll be worth it. You'll see how the biggest independent brewer in America operates and get a couple of beer samples to boot. The beer is found all over the area anyway, so you might as well make the trip to its origin while you're here.

BOSTON'S HISTORIC BARS

The Green Dragon—Website: www.greendragonboston.com **Address:** 11 Marshall Street Boston, MA, 02108, (617) 367-0055 (Monday–Sunday 11am–2am). This is an imitation of the real and important landmark tavern that was frequented by so many of the Patriots leading up to the Revolutionary War—in fact the real one was where the Boston Tea Party was planned (probably after too many shots of rum). This one, on the other hand, is really nothing like it. Never mind the fact it was built in the '90s (1990s that is), but this one is more of an Irish-type pub and probably little like the real one at all. However, it's fun to say you were here, plus the locale is boozer central, so if the scene is lousy you can walk across the alley to the another historic bar.

The Bell in Hand Tavern—Website: www.bellinhand.com **Address:** 45 Union Street Boston, MA, 02108, (617) 227-2098 (Monday–Sunday 11:30am–2am). Emblazoned across the top of the first floor are the worn, gilded wood letters proclaiming "America's Oldest Tavern." It's not. Its claim lies in the fine print of *continuously operating*, meaning it's been going since 1795, though even this claim is dubious since it moved from the original 1795 home blocks away to its current residence sometime in the late 1800s, and surely they had to close for a period then. But, in any case they do have pieces of the original place in here, like a section of the original bar and the original sign. It's worth it to be close to many other Irish pubs and close to the water. Not truly authentic but still a fun time.

Union Oyster House—Website: www.unionoysterhouse.com **Address:** 41 Union St, Boston, MA, 02108, (617) 227-2750 (Sunday–Thursday 11am–9:30pm, Friday–Saturday 11am–10pm). This is a must see restaurant and bar when visiting. Serving continuously since 1826, the Union Oyster House serves fine seafood meals with fresh, local ingredients. At the same time, it's been serving libations since its founding and can arguably be called a tavern just as much as any of the other old places. Imagine the history of this place, and what life was like when it was founded.

Doyle's Café—Website: www.doylescafeboston.com **Address:** 3484 Washington St, Jamaica Plain, MA, 02130, (617) 524-2345 (Monday–Thursday 11am–12:30am, Friday–Sunday 9am–12:30am). This classic Irish pub was opened in 1882 and has been a fixture of the city ever since. This is also the closest pub to the Samuel Adams Brewery, and so features many of their experimental beers that aren't served anywhere else. In fact, this was the first place that had Sam Adams on tap. Doyle's was also a known hangout for many of the local elite and political classes, including the Kennedy's (in fact, Ted Kennedy himself dedicated a room there to his grandfather, John Fitzgerald).

Sligo Pub—Address: 237 Elm St, Somerville, MA, 02144, (617) 625-4477 (Monday–Thursday 11am–1am, Friday–Saturday 11:15am–1:45am, Sunday 11am–12am). This Irish bar has been serving local residents since 1932 and is considered the oldest post-prohibition pub in the city. Inside you find a bar with messages and names scrawled in every square inch by past patrons. You also find cheap beer and tall pours. Here you want to order a Jameson or Dewar's neat. If you come by at night or during the weekends, you'll find it filled by a twenty something crowd, but during the week you'll find grizzled regulars who started coming with their grandads back in the day.

Sullivan's Tap—Address: 168 Canal St, Boston, MA, 02114, (617) 742-6968 (Monday–Sunday 9am–1am). Just around the corner from the "Garden," this narrow, long bar, named the best "Bruins Bar" in the city, has been quenching the thirst of Bostonians since 1933. This is a dive bar to be sure, but a special one. Here, regulars and locals have been watching the Celtics, Bruins and Sox play, probably since it was founded. They serve cheap drinks and only take cash, so come prepared. There's no food served, but they do have a great game room, with basketball hoops, pool tables and arcade games.

Chicago's long bar history—not to mention its stellar brewing and distilling history—was cut short by the great fire of 1871. The fire, which ravaged the city and destroyed over 3.3 square miles in the heart of Chicago, left over 100,000 people homeless and (more to our point), leveled most every old saloon there was.

People rebuilt, of course, but a result of the fire was that the city forbade wooden structures, and so many of the glorious old city bars were never to be rebuilt.

That aside, though, Chicago's historic boozing was unharmed. This city, after all, was home to Brunswick, famous for its bowling legacy, but in the 1800s (and even early 1900s) was the primary supplier of ornate, hardwood bars shipped across the country.

Brunswick bars ended up in the most obscure of places, including Tombstone, Arizona, and Goodsprings, Nevada. Ultimately, if you see the Duke belly up to a big beautiful bar in an old Hollywood Western, it was modeled after the furniture coming out of Chicago.

Perhaps what comes to mind for many when they think of Chicago is Prohibition. After all, this was home to some of the more notorious bootlegging mobs in the country at the time. Not only that, the place was absolutely rotten with speakeasies and blind tigers. In fact, it's estimated that there were about a thousand of these illegal bars in the city at any given time during Prohibition.

And this is what makes the bars in this city great. We're not going here to find the founding of our country, as we would in Philly or New England, or even to soak up the atmosphere of the grogshops and alehouses of the 19th century like we would in New York City. Here we're looking at bars that had some kind of tie to America's dumbest of laws—the 18th Amendment.

THE GREEN MILL, CHICAGO, IL

Address: 4802 N. Broadway Ave., Chicago, IL, 60640, (773) 878-5552
Website: www.greenmilljazz.com **Video tour:** http://youtu.be/0oHCAYX8-Iw
Food: No **Live Music:** Yes **Hours:** Monday–Friday 12pm–4am, Saturday 12pm–5am, Sunday 11am–4am **Type of Bar:** Speakeasy **What to Drink:** Gin martini **Why You Should Go:** Capone's personal speakeasy that remains perfectly preserved and ready for him to visit.

THE HISTORY

The Green Mill was opened in 1907 (as Pop Morse's Roadhouse) originally as a stopping place for funeral goers in transit to or from St. Boniface's Cemetery not far away. The area was in a state of transformation during the early 1900s and considered part of the up-and-coming entertainment district of Chicago.

New owners purchased the roadhouse in 1910 with the hopes of recreating Paris' famous Moulin Rouge, notorious at the time for its excess—free-flowing champagne, constantly changing décor and dancing girls in provocative outfits.

When the Green Mill opened in 1910, it was considerably larger than what you will find standing today, taking up almost an entire city block and containing a huge ballroom, stage for dancing girls, multiple lounges, live music, and a restaurant. The original entrance is still found next door: look for the windmill carved into granite right above the entrance to (at the time of writing) a Mexican food restaurant.

After the Volstead Act was passed in 1919, the place—in its original size—was no longer sustainable. However, the Green Mill was promptly downsized and transformed into a speakeasy.

Sometime during the 1920s one of Al Capone's henchmen, "Machine-gun" Jack McGurn gained a 25% stake in the club. McGurn as a person was pretty rotten; he ordered a gruesome hit on one of the Green Mill's performers and—according to many—masterminded the St. Valentine's Day Massacre.

Once Prohibition ended the place remained a destination for jazz acts and fine cocktails, which still holds true today.

TODAY

Today the bar is over 100 years old and is what many consider both the best jazz club in the US and the crown jewel of Chicago's Uptown. When you walk in you feel like you've just been deposited into a 1920s speakeasy: all of the elements are present—dim lighting, paneled paintings on the walls, green velvet booths and some of the best jazz bands in the area.

While we were there, we both commented that we wouldn't be surprised to see Al Capone himself come strolling in the door and take a seat at his favorite booth. It is a place one can go to enjoy either a top-dollar martini or a cold draft of Schlitz while listening to some outstanding live acts.

Speaking of live acts, the Green Mill has a long and rich history of great music and entertainment, and its stage has legends perform almost nightly. Their list of acts includes Joe E. Lewis, Frank Sinatra, the Mighty Blue Kings, David Liebman, Kurt Elling, Sheila Jordan and Mark Murphy, to name just a few. It also has the longest running poetry slam in all of Chicago (every Sunday night, when a $6 cover will get you in to see amateur poets perform). If you come for the live music, arrive early (it was getting crowded at 8:00 pm) to get a table, booth or seat at the bar. However, be prepared to wait, because the first act may not go on until 11:00 pm or later.

When you get here you've got to ask for Capone's booth. Legend has it that when Capone arrived the band would stop playing whatever song they were in the middle of and start up Capone's favorite song, "Rhapsody Blues." He would then take a seat at his favorite booth located at the end of the bar and opposite the side door leading to Lawrence Street (this gave him good views of both entrances and allowed him to see who was coming or going). Arrive early if you want the booth since, unsurprisingly, it is the most popular table in the bar.

THE DRINKS

The Green Mill sells more of a drink specific to Chicago than anywhere else in the world: Malort. Malort is a liqueur made with grapefruit and wormwood—the ingredient also found in Absinthe. It's certainly an acquired taste and not for everyone (think grapefruit plus bile).

They're also very traditional when it comes to their cocktail menu (in fact, they don't have one). The Green Mill is of the opinion that if you don't know what it is you want, you probably shouldn't be drinking it. We suggest a classic drink, the gin martini. We like gin because that's what they would have put in the drink in the '20s. A classic drink for a classic bar.

NEARBY DISTRACTIONS

The Aragon Entertainment Center—Address: 1106 West Lawrence Avenue, Chicago, IL 60640, (773) 561-9500 (operating times vary by show; check their website or call). Since you're in Chicago's historic uptown theater district, why not try and catch a show at the Aragon. Built in 1926 for a healthy sum of two million dollars, it was modeled to resemble a Spanish palace courtyard complete with crystal chandeliers, mosaic tiles, terra-cotta ceilings, balconies and grand arches. Acts vary, but stopping by the Green Mill before and/or after a show will make for a fun-filled night.

Riviera Theater—Website: www.rivieratheatre.com **Address:** 4746 North Racine Avenue, Chicago, IL, 60640, (773) 275-6800 (operating times and shows vary throughout the year; check their website or call). Originally built in 1917 as a movie theater, it was transformed into a private nightclub in 1986. Featuring a long list of up-and-coming as well as legendary performers and entertainers, the Riviera is another gem in Chicago's uptown theater district.

Spacca Napoli—Website: www.spaccanapolipizzeria.com **Address:** 1769 West Sunnyside Avenue, Chicago, IL, 60640, (773) 878-2420 (Tuesday 5pm–9pm, Wednesday–Thursday 11:30am–3pm, 5pm–9pm, Friday 11:30am–3pm, 5pm–10pm, Saturday 11:30am–10pm, Sunday 12pm–9pm). Just a short one mile jaunt from the Green Mill is Spacca Napoli Pizzeria. Step out of Chicago's deep dish norm and try some authentic Italian wood-fired pizza before heading to a show or to the Green Mill for a few drinks.

SIMON'S TAVERN, CHICAGO, IL

Address: 5210 N. Clark St., Chicago, IL, 60640, (575) 878-0894
Website: www.simonstavern.com **Video tour:** http://youtu.be/fwRj3uPChQ8
Food: Yes **Live Music:** Yes **Hours:** Monday–Friday 11am–2am, Saturday
11am–3am **Type of Bar:** Pub **What to Drink:** Glogg or a shot of Aquavit
Why You Should Go: Original speakeasy, Swedish culture, Chicago history,
Nickel Tour.

THE HISTORY

Simon's Tavern is named after its founder, Swedish immigrant Simon
Lumberg. The history of the bar is really the history of Simon, his
immigration to the United States, and the neighborhood bar he had always
dreamed of owning.

Simon emigrated from Sweden in the early 1900s and joined the US
military during World War I to gain US citizenship. After the war, Simon
moved to Colorado, worked for the railroad and saved his money so he could
eventually start his own business. In 1922 he moved to a small suburb of
Chicago known as Andersonville, using the money he had saved to open a
small café.

One day two gentlemen reportedly came in and ordered coffee. One then
added whiskey to it, slid it over to Simon, and told him to try it. Simon did
and exclaimed that it was "some very good whiskey!"

The bootleggers (rumored to be members of Al Capone's gang) told Simon
they could get him a regular supply and put the word out that he was to be
left alone. He accepted, and as word got out that whiskey was available in

Simon's cafe his business grew rapidly. By 1926 he needed to expand the size of his "bar," and he purchased the building where the bar remains today.

Initially he merely sold the laced coffee, but he quickly realized it would be more profitable to sell the whiskey alone. So in the mid-1920s he opened a speakeasy below the café, calling it the N. N. Club (reportedly standing for the No Name Club) and painting the door green.

1933 marked the end of Prohibition and the closing of illicit speakeasies. It also enabled Simon to go public (so to speak) with his bar. He moved from the basement to the café above, modeling it after the cruise ship Normandy (at the time the most expensive ever built), with a 60-foot-long mahogany bar, images of the ship etched into the glass above the registers and portholes in the bar-back.

Simon also started a community bank of sorts, cashing the paychecks of his patrons every Friday (over $14,000 worth in 1934 dollars). The "bank" is under the stairs to the top stories of the building and still retains all of Simon's security features, like bullet-proof glass and a heavy steel door.

TODAY

Today Simon's Tavern continues to operate at the same location and with much of the same décor. Current owner and operator Scott Martin bought the bar from Simon's son, Roy, and has continued to keep the bar's rich traditions in place. As one example, every year Scott makes over 2,000 gallons of traditional Swedish glogg—a hot, spiced wine—serving it from Thanksgiving through the end of winter.

Another of the artifacts left from Lumberg's tenure is a huge hand-painted canvas mural on the wall opposite the bar. The mural, painted by Lumberg's friend and fellow Swede, Sig Olson, depicts what was known as the Deer Hunter's Ball, a celebration held in a distant cabin on the last weekend of deer hunting season every year. The mural took Olson six years to paint and was presented to Lumberg in 1956. Look for five hidden animals in the painting, and if you find them all, drinks are on the house all night (and you get to wear the Viking helmet). Also, ask the bartender about the ghost that haunts Simon's and the revenge she exacted on the painting.

THE FOOD

The food menu is limited to small, frozen, oven-baked pizza. It's bar food at its worst, but honestly, who cares about the food with all of the other rich history in this place?

THE DRINKS

Almost every Swedish family has their own, closely guarded secret recipe for glogg, and Simon's is no different (Scott wouldn't reveal his recipe to us no matter how hard we tried).

Because glogg is a hot holiday drink, Scott doesn't serve it all year. Instead he has come up with a frozen glogg recipe that is available via a frozen margarita machine for the warmer months. Because we visited in July that's what we had to try, and try it we did. Essentially it is a spiced-wine slushy and actually very good. If you visit after Thanksgiving but before the end of winter, definitely try the real glogg.

Another drink to try is Aquavit, a popular Scandinavian spirit that takes its name from the Latin words "aqua vitae," meaning water of life. It is a potato-based spirit like vodka, but flavored slightly with caraway, cardamom, cumin, anise, and fennel (but caraway is by far the dominant flavor). The particular brand of Aquavit they serve is Linie, made in Norway. Definitely try a shot, yelling "skol!" before you drink.

NEARBY DISTRACTIONS

Swedish American Museum—Address: 5211 N. Clark St. Chicago, IL, 60640, (773) 728-8111 (Monday–Friday 10am–4pm, Saturday–Sunday 11am–4pm). Located directly across the street from Simon's Tavern is this nonprofit museum and cultural center. Featuring both permanent and special exhibits, it celebrates Swedish American culture of Chicago and is a worthwhile visit to better understand the history of Swedish immigrants and therefore the history of Simon's Tavern and its founder.

Graceland Cemetery—Address: 4001 North Clark St. Chicago, IL, 60613, (773) 525-1105. A walkable 1.3 miles from Simon's Tavern, Graceland Cemetery has drawn admirers to its highly regarded architecture, art, and horticulture since opening in 1860. With world-famous monuments reminiscent of ancient Egyptian grandeur, this is a Chicago must-stop for any architectural admirer.

ORIGINAL MOTHER'S, CHICAGO, IL

Address: 26 West Division St., Chicago, IL, 60610, (312) 642-7251
Website: www.originalmothers.com **Video tour:**
http://youtu.be/s96r5JIuz_M
Food: No **Live Music:** Sometimes, typically a DJ **Hours:** Wednesday–Friday
8pm–4am, Saturday 8pm–5am **Type of Bar:** Nightclub **What to Drink:**
Schlitz, Adios Motherfucker (AMF) **Why You Should Go:** One of the first
venues for Cream, the Velvet Underground and other milestone bands.

THE HISTORY

Mother's opened in 1968 and has been a Chicago favorite ever since.
Starting in the 1970s it was and still to this day is THE singles club in the
Rush and Division district (and arguably in the city of Chicago). However it
wasn't the only club of its kind to open in that area. Not too far away was the
famed Whiskey a Go Go, which opened in 1958 and then spread throughout
the country.

At its roots, Mother's origin was about live music, and it hosted many of the
bands we think of today as icons. At the time the bands were small or
underground acts, which makes it even more significant, as Mother's gave
them a fairly sizable venue in which to play.

Some of the more notable bands it hosted included Andy Warhol's Velvet
Underground, Eric Clapton and Cream, The Mekons, and, of course,
Chicago. What's amazing about this list is all of these bands are cited as some
of the most influential bands and musicians ever, influencing many more to
come after them.

In the late 1970s and early 1980s, after a brief but depressing disco period, Mother's became the source for the genre known as "house music," an electronic synthesized style invented by resident DJs. As before, the influence of what started at Mother's went on to create further styles of dance and hip-hop music, and formed the talent of contemporary artists like Madonna, Janet Jackson and Bjork.

Throughout its history, Mother's became known for both its architectural style—a kind of industrial war zone effect—and its consistent focus on music and changing trends. Though only 34 years young, Mother's has a significant place in the history of bars in the US.

TODAY

Today Mother's tradition of outstanding house music, live bands, and a karaoke setup that would satisfy any karaoke fiend, is still firmly grounded and keeps the place crowded virtually every night. In addition to its continued prolific music scene, it plays host to some of the best and most popular events around Chicago, including Elvis Fest, the Indie Incubator Film Fest, and the always popular Mardi Gras party.

When you enter the front door and head downstairs, you are welcomed into what can only be described as a cavernous venue. The place has three bars and two VIP lounges that regularly host an ensemble of local and national celebrities as well as locals and visitors. Make time to walk the dance floor and stage if you can, remembering that this is where Clapton came into his own in 1969 and 1970.

The décor can only be described as inspired; it is truly unique and has been left alone for the last 40 years (though we're told they moved the statuary around somewhat). It probably never goes out of style because it is pretty much its own style.

One of Mother's biggest claims to fame is the 1980s "Brat Pack" movie "About Last Night" – which was partially filmed here. In this romantic comedy, viewers follow Rob Lowe and Demi Moore, who are veterans of the Chicago singles scene, on their journey to becoming comfortable with commitment and with each other. It is a mildly funny movie that gives viewers some insight into 1980s Chicago.

Significant to Mother's is that the original play the movie was based on featured the bar as a character itself. In fact, it was set at Mother's—that's how well-known this place was in the area. Before you go, give the movie a try, just to catch the décor and bars that you'll see when you arrive.

THE DRINKS

Mother's loves its drink specials. In fact, when we arrived they were featuring "Recession Buster Monday," with inexpensive beer and well drinks. And by inexpensive we mean about half the cost of anywhere else in the Rush and Division area: $3 domestic bottles, $3 house shots, $4 import bottles, and $7 Long Islands and other well drinks.

To make this a true experience, try a mixed drink typically found at nightclubs, the Adios Motherfucker. Sip it, and then hand it off to the 21-year-old hipster next to you. Then order a Schlitz and imagine Clapton tearing it up onstage.

NEARBY DISTRACTIONS

Rush and Division—The area Mother's resides in is known as Rush and Division, an area known for its assortment of dining, drinking, nightlife and entertainment. Featuring historic bars like The Lodge Tavern, She-nannigans and Mother's Too, to name just a few, a trip to Mother's isn't complete without visiting at least one of the legendary surrounding bars.

Gibson's—Website: www.gibsonssteakhouse.com **Address:** 1028 North Rush Street, Chicago, IL, 60611, (866) 442-7664 (Daily, lunch 11am–3pm, dinner 3pm–12am). In the mood for steak? Then Gibson's is the place for you. Considered one of the top two places for steak in all of Chicago, it is less than a quarter mile from Mother's. Stop here for an outstanding steak dinner before you head out to Rush and Division for a night of drinking. If you're a fan of the television show, The League, you'll immediately recognize the outside sign.

Newberry Library & Washington Square Park (aka Bughouse Square)— **Address:** 60 West Walton St. Chicago, IL, 60610, (312) 943-9090 (operating hours vary, check website or call). Less than a half mile from Mother's, this world-renowned independent research library has free exhibitions, speaking events, and a rare and vast collection of non-circulated works. Directly across the street is Washington Square Park, which was donated to the city in 1842 and designated as a place of assembly and discussion.

THE BILLY GOAT TAVERN, CHICAGO, IL

Address: 430 N. Michigan Ave. at Lower Level, Chicago, IL, 60611, (312) 222-1525
Website: www.billygoattavern.com **Video tour:** http://youtu.be/BIW47KJLi-Q
Food: Yes **Live Music:** No **Hours:** Monday—Thursday 6am-1am, Friday 6am-2am, Saturday 6am-3am, Sunday 9am-2am **Type of Bar:** Pub **What to Drink:** Schlitz **Why You Should Go:** History of Chicago, Saturday Night Live, Curse of the Billy Goat.

THE HISTORY

The original Billy Goat Tavern was located across the street from the Chicago stadium, now the United Center, and was founded in 1934 by Greek immigrant William "Billy Goat" Sianis. When he originally purchased the place it was called the Lincoln Tavern, and Sianis paid the sale price in full with a $205 check that bounced (he later paid for it in full with the profits from his first weekend's sales).

The name of the tavern was changed when a goat fell off a passing truck and wandered inside. William decided to adopt the goat, naming it Murphy, and then grew a goatee and took the nickname "Billy Goat." Finally, he decided to change the name of the bar from the Lincoln Tavern to the Billy Goat Tavern.

Billy Goat Sianis was a true master of PR and used his skill to keep the bar packed and constantly in the public eye. In 1944 the Republican Convention was being held in Chicago, and with it came numerous media trucks. The trucks blocked the front of his bar and restaurant, so Billy posted signs stating

"No Republicans Allowed," which of course packed the place with hundreds of Republicans and got Sianis tons of great press.

Another (perhaps the most notorious) publicity stunt occurred during the 1945 World Series. The Cubs were playing game four and were cruising to victory. Billy tried to bring his goat in to watch the game, but was denied because patrons said the goat stunk. He left dejected, and when the Cubs ended up losing the last two games, Sianis sent a telegram saying, "Who stinks now?"

This made the paper, and when a reporter asked if he cursed them, he said he did, and The Curse of the Billy Goat began.

In 1964 Billy Goat moved his tavern to its present subterranean location at 430 N. Michigan Avenue and slowly expanded to nine locations, with more on the way. His move to Michigan Ave. put the Billy Goat right in the center of the many Chicago-based newspapers and turned it into a regular spot for reporters.

On October 22, 1970, William Sianis passed away at the St. Clair Hotel where he had made his home. He passed the bar on to his nephew, Sam Sianis, who currently owns and operates it with his wife and six children.

TODAY

Today the Tavern is considered a Chicago tourist landmark and is visited by hundreds of locals, world travelers, politicians and actors on a daily basis. Some of the more notable guests include President George W. Bush, President Bill Clinton, Jay Leno, Bill Murray, John Belushi, and Frank Sinatra. Almost all of them have their picture on the wall posing with either William or Sam.

The place has a long bar that takes up most of one side of the restaurant, red-and-white checkered tablecloths, and walls filled with pictures of the many celebrities that have stopped in. There are also newspaper articles written by the many regular columnists and reporters, a whole wall dedicated to the "Billy Goat" himself, and TVs that are constantly showing Chicago sports teams.

In the center of the room is a U-shaped counter, and behind that is a long, flat grill, on which meat - topped with cheese - is heard sizzling just below the sound of shouting from the people working the grill.

The place feels busy and even a little cramped, but it also feels like a good old-fashioned family restaurant, not the icon it is. Here you won't find the sterile feeling of the chain restaurants on Michigan Ave. above you. This is a place to enjoy the food and the characters working the grill and bar.

And if you're a Saturday Night Live fan, the grill may seem a bit familiar to you, but there's a good reason why. In the 1970s when the place was busy, Sam (who has an oatmeal-thick Greek accent) rushed from customer to customer taking and calling out orders. It sounded something like this:

"Who's next!?! WHO'S NEXT!?!"

"Don't look at menu, look at ME! I order for you–DOUBLECHEEZ!"

"No! DOUBLECHEEZ!!!!"

"It's Friday, doublecheez for everybody! It's payday! Triplecheez for the big guy!"

"No fries–CHEEPS!"

"No Pepsi–COKE!"

This was all immortalized in 1978 when Saturday Night Live aired a skit called Olympia Café, starring John Belushi, Bill Murray, Dan Aykroyd, and Loraine Newman. John Belushi and Bill Murray knew of the Billy Goat from their days at Second City, a nearby comedy sketch theater. Look up the video on YouTube BEFORE you get here.

THE FOOD

Speaking of Cheezeborgers, the food at the Billy Goat is simple, quick, and consists mainly of those world-famous burgers, which by themselves are worth coming in for.

The beef used in the patties is ground and prepared fresh by the family. You can get single, double, or triple cheese, with all the fixings you could possibly want. Holding true to their roots, the location on Lower Michigan Avenue still does not serve Pepsi or fries (although we were told that some of the other locations have started to serve fries due to popular demand). Either way, the burgers are great, the atmosphere is fantastic, and the trip to grab a bite to eat, watch some Chicago sports, and listen to the interaction of the cooks is well worth the journey.

THE DRINKS

Billy Goat doesn't carry many of the popular brands on tap—they never have. Coors Light and Budweiser fans will have to go elsewhere. But they've had a Schlitz account forever and still pour it fresh from the tap all day long. Luckily, Schlitz is no longer rotgut; they've gone back to their original recipe that made them so famous years ago. It's a good beer, especially with a burger and good conversation.

NEARBY DISTRACTIONS

Chicago Tribune Building—Address: 435 N Michigan Ave #1, Chicago, IL, 60611, (312) 222-3994 (operating hours vary; call ahead). Located directly across the street from the stairs that take you down to The Billy Goat is Tribune Tower. Home of the Chicago Tribune Newspaper, this neo-Gothic-themed building was completed in 1925 after a worldwide architecture competition in 1922. The lobby has a relief map of the United States made from shredded US currency, and it still houses offices for Chicago Tribune writers, whose predecessors were the original regulars at the legendary Billy Goat. Take a minute on your way down to or up from the Billy Goat to appreciate an outstanding example of Chicago's unique skyline.

Giordano's—Website: www.giordanos.com **Address:** 130 E Randolph Drive, Chicago, IL, 60601, (312) 616-1200 (Daily 11am–11pm). No trip to Chicago is complete without some deep dish pizza, and few places do it better than Giordano's. Originally opened in 1974 by Italy born Efren and Joesph

Boglio, and only a half mile from the Billy Goat, the pizza is worth the walk and the wait. Usually a busy place, so expect a wait during prime dining times. Order your pizza before you are seated to get your pie a little quicker.

Navy Pier—Website: www.navypier.com **Address:** 600 E Grand Ave., Chicago, IL, 60611, (Hours vary with season and events). Less than a mile from The Billy Goat is Chicago's Navy Pier. Featuring an amusement park, Landshark Beer Garden, regularly scheduled fireworks, seasonal events and a multitude of stage shows, the Navy Pier has something for just about everyone. Check their schedule of events before you go.

GREEN DOOR TAVERN, CHICAGO, IL

Address: 678 N. Orleans St., Chicago, IL, 60654, (312) 664-5496
Website: www.greendoorchicago.com **Video tour:**
http://youtu.be/NqK4ywT1s08
Food: Yes **Live Music:** Yes **Hours:** Monday–Friday 11:30am–2am, Saturday 10am–3am, Sunday 10am–12am **Type of Bar:** Pub **What to Drink:** French 75 **Why You Should Go:** Original Chicago speakeasy, last wooden structure built in downtown Chicago.

THE HISTORY

Immediately following the Great Chicago fire of 1871, James McCole, an area engineer, built a two-story wooden building and a detached cottage on a piece of property located close to downtown Chicago. He initially rented the property to a grocer, Lawrence P. Ek, as a combination grocery store and apartment.

Shortly afterwards Chicago passed a law prohibiting any commercial wooden structures in the Central Business District. McCole's building, however, was grandfathered in, making the building not only one of the few wooden-framed structures built in the district after the fire, but also the last freestanding wooden structure in downtown Chicago.

In 1921 an Italian restaurant called The Heron Orleans replaced the grocery store. Soon after opening the owner passed away, and so his kids did like any entrepreneurs of the time would do: they opened a speakeasy downstairs.

During Prohibition, a green door on the street meant there was a speakeasy located on the other side. Opening to the street below the Heron Orleans was the green door leading downstairs (the fixture for which the Green Door Tavern gets its name).

Their alcohol was supplied by the North Side Gang and more specifically by Irish-American mobster and bootlegger Dean O'Banion. This would have made the Green Door and its suppliers an enemy of the more notorious Al Capone (who had O'Banion killed in 1924).

TODAY

Today the Green Door Tavern continues to be the last freestanding wooden structure in downtown Chicago, and is described by manager and co-owner Jeff Lynch as "a neighborhood watering hole that serves great food and outstanding drinks." A statement we wholeheartedly agree with.

The exterior has changed very little since its building and it still maintains that very classic 1920s persona. Upon entering through the heavy green, crooked door, visitors are greeted by a bar interior decorated in the manner most chain restaurants try to copy. The bar is comfortable, dripping with varnished wood and personality. It's a place you feel at home in, with great food, powerful and well-crafted drinks, and one of the coolest original speakeasies in the entire country found just downstairs (rented for private parties and events).

Another unique aspect of the Green Door Tavern is the leaning or "racking" of the building. If you don't notice the lean from the outside, you definitely will when you come through the front door, which not only swings in but swings up as well. It can also be seen when compared to the building next door, or in the entrance to the office below the bar.

The racking is a common occurrence of wooden buildings after settling over the years. However, as disconcerting as it might seem, the building is as solid as can be, and there's no danger of impending collapse.

THE FOOD

The food at this place is simply outstanding. They're known for their chili and burgers, but when we visited we tried the corned beef sandwich, which we promptly fell in love with. The corned beef is slowly baked (not boiled) for hours, making it moist and melt-in-your-mouth tender. Combined with some seasoned, fresh-cut French fries and a dill pickle spear, and you've one of the best meals available downtown.

THE DRINKS

There really isn't a wrong drink to order here—as long as it's a classic cocktail, which they excel at making.

One to try is the French 75, a Prohibition-era cocktail invented in 1915 and named for the French 75 MM howitzer (what it's supposed to kick like). It's made with gin, simple syrup, sweet and sour, and then topped with champagne. It is much sourer than it might sound, and it's really refreshing on a hot, humid Chicago day.

NEARBY DISTRACTIONS

Chicago Brew Bus— (773) 340-2739 (Fri-Sun, times vary; check their website or call, private tours available). If you're into craft beers and pub food and want to try a few of Chicago's best in a short period, then the Chicago Brew Bus tour may be just the thing for you. Starting at the Goose Island Brewery (less than two miles from the Green Door) the tour takes you to at least three local breweries with approximately one hour at each. It includes free samples at every stop, and they'll even store and chill any growler you decide to purchase. A great way to spend an afternoon after having lunch at the Green Door.

Willis Tower (Formerly Sears Tower)—**Website:** www.theskydeck.com **Address:** 233 South Wacker Drive Chicago, IL, 60606, (312) 875-9696 (operating hours vary by season; visit the website or call for more information). Formerly known as the Sears Tower, a name most refuse to relinquish, it's the most iconic and recognizable skyscraper in the Chicago skyline. Just over a mile from the Green Door, no visit to Chicago is complete without at least getting close enough to stare up at this impressive example of American ingenuity. For the complete experience, head up to the Skydeck to get an experience of a lifetime while standing in a clear box extended out from the tower.

HALA KAHIKI, CHICAGO, IL

Address: 2834 North River Road, River Grove, IL, 60171, (708) 456-3222
Website: www.hala-kahiki.com **Video tour:** http://youtu.be/xpcY_vQk2X4
Food: No **Live Music:** No **Hours:** Monday–Tuesday 6pm–2am, Wednesday–
Friday 4pm–2am, Saturday 4pm–3am, Sunday 4pm–2am **Type of Bar:** Tiki
bar **What to Drink:** Scorpion Bowl, Lava Bowl, Puffer Fish **Why You Should
Go:** Original Tiki bar from early '60s, huge collection of period furniture and
art, all booze no food.

THE HISTORY

Originally opened in 1963 by Rose and Stanley Sacharski, Hala Kahiki
started life as the Lucky Start. Stanley was a mortician in his family's
mortuary business, but after a falling out with his family, he decided to do
something different with his life, and thus opened the bar.

The original bar didn't have a tropical theme. In fact that didn't happen
until Stanley was making some renovations and wanted to hide the poor
condition of the walls. So he hung some bamboo siding purchased from Sears
and Roebuck, mainly because it was cheap. But customers saw the change and
asked if the bar was turning into a Tiki bar (which were popular at the time),
and the idea snowballed from there.

The bar quickly grew in popularity, and so they moved it to a larger venue
in River Grove, Illinois. The location was previously a trucker bar called the
Glasshouse (originally an old Greenhouse). It still resides there today, only a
short cab ride from Chicago's O'Hare airport.

The name was changed to Hala Kahiki after Stanley's son, Sonny, was
reading a Dennis the Menace comic titled "Dennis the Menace Goes to

Hawaii." Hala Kahiki was mentioned in the comic and, after a bit of investigation, it was discovered that Hala Kahiki is a pineapple plantation in Hawaii (it actually means, "House of Pineapple"). So, the Sacharski's decided it was the perfect name for their new Tiki bar.

TODAY

Upon entering you find yourself in a tropical paradise located in the middle of the busy Chicago Metro area. The décor is all original and features the largest collection of original Witco artwork of any Tiki bar in the US. Witco was one of the most popular designers of South Sea décor during the 1960s and 1970s. Witco was so popular, in fact, that Elvis commissioned them to design and decorate the Jungle Room in Graceland.

Much of the rest of the décor is standard Tiki—outrigger canoes on the ceiling, bamboo furniture and fixtures, and tapa cloth and netting on the walls.

There are Tikis strewn about as well, especially on the outside patio, a lush oasis complete with tropical plants, fountain and pond. This place is the perfect escape at night when the torches are lit and Hawaiian music is piped in through the speakers.

THE DRINKS

The bar features over 125 drinks, and while we asked to try them all (we were told no), we were lucky enough to try a handful of them and came up with some favorites.

The first is the Chi Chi, a different spin on the piña colada and made with vodka instead of rum. Because of the more neutral taste of the vodka, the coconut and cream become the main focus of the drink and not the rum.

We were also pretty impressed with their Scorpion Bowl, which they wouldn't give us the recipe to. While expecting something somewhat sweet like the drink at other Tiki bars, we were really surprised at the sharp kick of the spirits.

Our final recommendation is the Puffer Fish, a martini made with pineapple vodka, pineapple juice, and some secret ingredients.

NEARBY DISTRACTIONS

Ernest Hemingway Foundation Oak Park—Address: 200 North Park Avenue, Oak Park, IL, 60302, (708) 445-3071 (Sunday–Friday 1pm–5pm, Saturday 10am–5pm). About five miles from the Hala Kahiki is Ernest Hemingway's birthplace. Born on the second story of this Queen Anne-style house on July 21st, 1899, Ernest spent the first six years of his life here. A short walk away is the Ernest Hemingway Museum, which is housed in the Oak Park Arts Center. Offering guided tours throughout the day a visit here is well worth the trip to get a glimpse into the life and works of arguably the most influential author of the 20th century.

Maywood Park Racetrack—Address: 8600 West North Avenue, Melrose Park, IL, 60160, (708) 343-4800 (Open year-round with varying live racing days). Featuring live harness racing since 1932, this is considered the US's fastest harness race track. Stop in to watch a live race, place a small wager to make things a little more interesting, and enjoy a reprieve from Chicago's hustle and bustle.

CHICAGO'S HISTORIC BARS

The Berghoff—Website: www.theberghoff.com **Address:** 17 West Adams Street Chicago, IL, 60603, (312) 408-0200 (Monday–Friday 11am–9pm, Saturday 11:30am–9pm). This Chicago institution was founded in 1898 by German immigrant Herman Joseph Berghoff, who wanted to bring a piece of home to the many other German immigrants flooding Chicago at the time. They serve authentic German cuisine and, of course, beer—lots of it. Berghoff made his own lager, and apparently his brewery was pretty popular. His beer was so popular, in fact, that during Prohibition when he actually did go dry and made near beer, he still sold gallons of it to locals.

Southport Lanes—Website: www.southportlanes.com **Address:** 3325 North Southport Avenue Chicago, IL, 60657, (773) 472-6600 (Monday–Friday 12pm–2am, Saturday 12pm–3am, Sunday 12pm–1am). Yep, we're talking about a bowling alley. But one with history and notoriety. This place was originally built by Schlitz in 1922—which doesn't really make sense if you think about it. In any case, all it could serve was Schlitz, but it apparently did well. However, that wasn't always the case. Once Schlitz sold the bar the new owners had a tough time making ends meet. So, they put prostitutes on the menu and ran a brothel out of the top floors. Being discreet folks, they advertised by the murals on the walls depicting naked nymphs and other erotica.

DENVER, CO

Denver, Colorado started as a stop on the route to supply nearby mining towns during the Pike's Peak gold rush of the 1850s and 1860s. As such it was a really wild place in its heyday. Like surrounding towns, Denver featured dozens of bars, alehouses and grocers where booze was had for cheap.

Granted, the booze may not have been that good, but it could be had at any rate. So, of course, could prostitutes and gambling.

During this time the town was becoming home to a number of immigrant groups, including the Irish, the Spanish and the Italian. What resulted was a melting pot not unlike many of the cities on the East Coast, with whole neighborhoods and sections of town that identified with one of these new populations.

There were also a number of famous characters that walked the streets of Denver in the 19th century. Men like Buffalo Bill Cody and Doc Holliday spent their time in the city's many gambling joints and brothels, as did the thousands of miners, travelers and cowboys bringing herds of cattle up from Texas.

While not as wild in the 20th century, Denver still saw its share of celebrities and sometimes dangerous episodes, with people like Jack Kerouac and Frank Sinatra making their way through (and stopping over at some of the bars we'll tell you about).

Denver grew into a major metropolis, now with over 600,000 people, major sports teams, music and concert arenas and, of course, some great places to drink.

MY BROTHER'S BAR, DENVER, CO

Address: 2376 15th Street, Denver, CO, 80202, (303) 455-9991
Video tour: http://youtu.be/KgFoHR12kO4
Food: Yes **Live Music:** No **Hours:** Monday–Saturday 11am–2am **Type of Bar:** Pub **What to Order:** A craft beer or classic cocktail **Why You Should Go:** This classic bar is a mainstay for Denver natives and is a throwback to another time—when bars were quiet places you went to talk to friends and strangers.

THE HISTORY

My Brother's Bar, though known by another name at the time, was established in 1873 and is the oldest continuously operating bar in Denver, Colorado. Since that year booze has always been peddled out of this location. Both Jimmy the bartender and the previous owner, Jim Karagas, confirmed that the bar even operated through Prohibition (they both cited the lack of interest in enforcing Prohibition west of the Mississippi River).

The place has had its ups and downs. When first opened the neighborhood was mostly Italian Immigrants, and legend has it the very first Columbus Day celebration took place here, complete with parade. It lost a lot of its luster in the 1950s and 1960s though, becoming a dive bar and drawing a unique crowd, including Neal Cassady—Jack Kerouac's buddy and cohort.

Jim Karagas, the previous owner, and his brother Orlando moved to Denver in 1968 and bought the bar shortly after their arrival, stating on more than one occasion that the bar was a dump when they first set eyes on it. In fact they bought it at night and never saw what it looked like during the day until it was too late.

The brothers spent the next few years cleaning up the bar and returning it to its original appearance (minus an original upstairs floor, which had been removed long before they purchased the bar). A running joke about both the name of the place and the lack of a sign outside is that after they purchased it they couldn't think of what to call the place. When bill collectors, delivery men or patrons with questions would come in looking for the owner, James and his brother would tell them, "It's my brothers bar, go talk to him." This continued until the name finally stuck and the bar was referred to as My Brother's Bar permanently.

TODAY

The bar today will immediately remind you of a classic, Irish-style pub found on the East Coast, which is ironic considering the brothers were Greek. Nevertheless, you'll find gleaming mahogany and oak, classical music piped in through the stereo and a friendly atmosphere with a lot of locals and regulars.

There is also a patio out back if you'd like to soak in a nice Denver day, otherwise there's ample room to find a seat in either the bar area or a large room just next door.

The crowd is a mix of professionals from nearby office buildings, state and city government employees, college students and Denver locals. We're told they're a regular spot for local sports celebrities, too, so bone up on your Rockies, Nuggets, Avalanche and Broncos players before arriving.

Something you may notice missing from the bar is the dull glow of any television. According to previous owner Jim and Jimmy the bartender, they have no televisions because they ruin the whole point of a bar. You can watch TV at home, but when you're at a bar you should be enjoying a good conversation with friends, family or even one of the many bartenders. After all, don't you go to a bar to enjoy the company of others?

THE FOOD

My Brothers Bar serves a lot of your typical bar food but with a few custom twists. The kitchen originally started with a very simple menu and only expanded slowly over the years and mainly through the use of their own employees' recipes. The most popular, and frequently imitated but never duplicated, is the JCB which stands for Jalapeno Cream Cheese Burger. It was created when Jim came in one morning to find Lana Harris, sister of NFL player Franco Harris, making some kind of cream cheese concoction. Turns out she was in the process of making Jalapeno Cream Cheese, which she then threw on a burger and gave it to Jim to try. It was on the menu the very next day.

Jimmy stated that on more than one occasion, they have had patrons come in, sit really close to the kitchen (it is connected to the end of the bar), order a JCB and watch with hawk-like intensity as it is prepared. They usually become quite flustered and even embarrassed when Jimmy asks them when *their* grand opening is and if they've figured out how to replicate the burger.

THE DRINKS

My Brothers Bar doesn't really have any signature drinks; rather the signature drink is actually the lack of certain drinks, or more specifically, certain brands. When Jim first bought the bar, he tried to buy from both Coors and Budweiser. But as Mr. Karagas came to find out, his lack of large volume sales made Coors and Budweiser very unmotivated to make deliveries on time or sometimes at all.

After getting fed up with both brands, Jim decided to go with alternate brands, namely smaller and more local breweries, and to this day will not serve or buy Budweiser or Coors products.

Today Budweiser and Coors both constantly bug them, asking them to carry their beer, but they stick to their guns and refuse to carry any of their products. They still have some of the finest beers and spirits you could hope for; we recommend Golden City Red or Fuller's London Pride.

NEARBY DISTRACTIONS

REI—Website: www.rei.com **Address:** 1416 Platte St. Denver, CO, 80202, (303) 756-3100 (Monday–Saturday 9am–9pm, Sunday 10am–7pm). Located directly behind My Brother's Bar in the restored 1901 Denver Tramway building is one of REI's flagship stores. This place is huge, featuring a 47-foot monolith climbing wall offering a variety of climbing terrain, almost 95,000 square feet of outdoor adventurer shopping and a Starbucks. It's worth checking out just to see (or maybe try) the climbing wall and enjoy the view of the river from their deck.

Commons/Confluence Park—Website: www.denvergov.org **Address:** 2101 15th St. Denver, CO, 80202, (720) 913-1311 (Hours vary by season). Located directly across the river from My Brother's Bar is Common's Park. The park is nestled on the edge of downtown Denver and offers extensive paths and areas for picnics and sporting activities. But the true gem of the location is access to the Platte River. On a hot summer day there are few better activities than grabbing a tube to float down this small section of the river.

Denver Aquarium—Website: www.aquariumrestaurants.com **Address:** 700 Water Street Denver, CO, 80211, (303) 561-4450 (Sunday–Thursday 10am–9pm, Friday–Saturday 10am–9:30pm). Taking the Colorado Front Range Trail, along the Platte River, the Denver Aquarium is a short half-mile walk from My Brother's Bar. Featuring extensive fresh and salt water aquariums, sharks, exotic and local fish and even a tiger exhibit, it leaves little to be desired (if you desire fish, that is). But for those who want to get a little closer to the life aquatic you can also dive with the sharks! In the middle of downtown Denver, certified or not, you can get up close and personal with sharks, barracudas, giant sea turtles and more. Just make sure you do this before visiting My Brother's Bar.

EL CHAPULTEPEC, DENVER, CO

Address: 1962 Market Street, Denver, CO, 80202, (303) 295-9126
Website: www.thepeclodo.com **Video tour:** http://youtu.be/dx9mGXtD_hk
Food: Yes **Live Music:** Yes **Hours:** Monday 11am–1am, Tuesday–Sunday
11am–2am **Type of Bar:** Dive **What to Drink:** Coors Banquet Beer **Why
You Should Go:** Best jazz bar west of the Mississippi, great history, wonderful
Denver lore.

THE HISTORY

The bar was founded by Tony Romano in what was at the time one of the
grittier parts of Denver. Obtaining liquor license #2, The Pec originally
opened as a mariachi joint serving Mexican food and catering to the local
population of migrant workers. It obtained its tongue-twisting name after
many of the workers asked Romano to cash their checks so they could send
the money to their families, back in El Chapultepec, Mexico.

In 1958 the bar changed fairly dramatically when Romano's son-in-law,
Jerry Krantz, took the place over. Jerry had developed a deep love of jazz
music over the years and began featuring live jazz almost immediately. One of
the first artists Jerry was able to book was Buddy DeFranco, whose
performance put The Pec on the map.

Over the next 40 years, the tiny, pink neon-lit bar played host to some of
the biggest names in the history of jazz. Artists that played there included
William (Count) Basie, the three Marsalis brothers, former president Bill
Clinton and even Frank Sinatra himself. They and hundreds of local, national
and international musicians played on the tiny stage making The Pec the
unofficial capital of jazz west of the Mississippi.

Aside from the stories of Ella Fitzgerald listening to music in her limo parked in the alley, or of Jack Kerouac sitting quietly stoned in the booth immediately right of the front door, El Chapultepec really became famous because of Jerry Krantz himself. He was a hard-nosed bartender/owner/bouncer who took no shit from no one. He had a baseball bat behind the bar and was happy to tap some ne'er-do-well upside the head because, as he told us, "you gotta get their attention before you can talk to them."

Jerry passed in May, 2012, but his spirit doggedly lives on at this little-known treasure in Denver's former red light district.

TODAY

Jerry's daughter, Angela, has continued her father's legacy with only a few minor tweaks. She assured us that they no longer handle rowdy customers (or "assholes" as Jerry would refer to them) with a baseball bat. And while the bar still features the best live jazz bands they also mix in blues and funk (all live of course) for a change of pace. Other than that she's left things alone.

Visitors are greeted with a long, waist-high, Formica covered bar and glowing pink neon. Along the wall on the right are the booths so famous for hosting Kerouac and his band of miscreants in the early '50s. And at the end of the room is the famous stage, so tiny you wonder how the hell bands could fit up there. Be sure to take a look at all the famous headshots lining the wall. The tough guy standing next to the celebrities is Jerry.

The biggest change to The Pec is actually in the surrounding area. In 1995 the Colorado Rockies built Coors Field almost directly across the street from The Pec. The move was all part of the revitalization of Denver's downtown which included attracting new bars and restaurants to the surrounding areas. It's such a sharp contrast to see the building housing The Pec, squat and stucco, next to the taller, polished brick of the "revitalized" downtown.

THE FOOD

There is a small dining room with pool table just on the other side of the bar. The kitchen, featuring fairly traditional Mexican food—rice, beans, tacos and so forth—is located there and is a popular place to grab a bite while having a beer.

We didn't get to try them, but we hear the tamales are pretty outstanding. It's all relative, of course, when you combine the atmosphere, music and history of this place, everything tastes good.

THE DRINKS

The Pec holds Liquor License # 2, yet for some reason they never brag about it. In any case, think of this as your beer-and-shot bar, not the kind of place to make fancy shots or mixed drinks.

They also have the oldest Coors contract in Denver. In fact, the Coors family often let Jerry and his kids use their Sky Box at the next door stadium whenever they'd like. So aside from a shot of whiskey, get a Coors Banquet Beer for tradition's sake.

NEARBY DISTRACTIONS

Coors Field—Website: www.colorado.rockies.mlb.com **Address:** 2001 Blake Street Denver, CO, 80205, (303) ROCKIES, (operating hours vary by game times and events). Just steps from the front door of "The Pec" is Coors Field, home of the Colorado Rockies baseball team. Also contained in the stadium is The Blue Moon Brewing Company @ the Sandlot, which is where Blue Moon was invented and where the four employees spend most of their time making one-off beers for their patrons to enjoy. Keep in mind, with the exception of special events the stadium is only open during the baseball season, as is the brewery and tours are only available during this time unless a group or private tour is arranged. It's a perfect stop on the way to or from "The Pec."

16th Street Mall—Website: www.16thsteetmalldenver.com, **Address:** 1001 16th St. Denver, CO, 80265, (720) 282-9610 (shop, gallery and restaurant hours vary). Less than a mile from El Chapultepec and itself over a mile long, sits the 16th Street Mall. Featuring a long list of galleries, shops, restaurants, bars, clubs, street vendors and street performers, it has become Denver's version of Venice Beach, though not quite as hipster and a little more mainstream. It's worth a visit if for nothing else than its extensive bar and food choices as well as some outstanding street performers.

Coors Brewery—Website: www.millercoors.com **Address:** 13th Street Golden, CO, 80401, (303) 277-2337 (Thursday–Monday 10am–4pm, Sunday 12pm–4pm, hours differ slightly during the summer). A short, 20-minute drive from "The Pec" will deliver you into Golden, Colorado, and more importantly the Coors brewery. With daily self-paced tours of the world's largest single-site brewery that concludes with free samples of Coors products, this is about as good as tours get. And considering the relationship between The Pec and Coors, it's pretty fitting as well.

BUCKHORN EXCHANGE, DENVER, CO

Address: 1000 Osage Street, Denver, CO, 80204, (303) 534-9505
Website: www.buckhorn.com **Video tour:** http://youtu.be/lniCr3CBZiY
Food: Yes Live Music: Yes **Hours:** Monday–Thursday 11am–9pm, Friday
11am–10pm, Saturday 5pm–10pm, Sunday 5pm–9pm **Type of Bar:** Saloon
What to Drink: Buffalo Bill Cody Cocktail **Why You Should Go:** Western
saloon with colorful history including Teddy Roosevelt (always fun), and
great Western lore.

THE HISTORY

The Buckhorn Exchange was founded by Henry H. Zeitz in 1893. Zeitz's
life reads more like a novel than that of a real person and so, to truly
understand the Buckhorn Exchange you must take look at Zeitz's life.

In semi-chronological order, the story goes like this: he hitch-hiked out
West at the ripe old age of 10, met the great Indian chief Sitting Bull (look up
the story of General Custer if you don't know who that is), became a scout for
and close personal friend of Buffalo Bill Cody (who gave him the nick name
Shorty Scout), was a bodyguard for Horace Tabor in the silver mining town
of Leadville, Colorado (Tabor was also known as the Silver King during that
time), founded the Buckhorn Exchange, guided President Teddy Roosevelt
on hunts in Colorado and then later hunted with Teddy in Africa.

Henry got his start in the bar business when the US switched from the Gold
to Silver standard late in the 19th century. With the switch, Zeitz decided to
head back down to Denver from Leadville because his father had started a
saloon in the downtown area. A common complaint Zeitz heard from railroad
workers was that there was nowhere near work or home to drink. Henry,

recognizing an opportunity, purchased the Niff's breweries office and warehouse located across from the rail yard. He then moved the family saloon into the building and, seeing yet another opportunity, offered to cash the rail workers checks on payday. The one catch to cashing the check at the Exchange was that the workers only received part of their checks. A percentage was saved for the wives to pick up later that day for use in the Exchange to purchase food and supplies.

TODAY

Though the focal point used to be the saloon, today the Buckhorn Exchange has become more of a restaurant than a bar. With featured foods like rattlesnake, alligator tail, 64-ounce steaks and Rocky Mountain oysters, the Exchange has become a legend in the Denver culinary scene. But the Buckhorn was founded as, and still is, a bar at its core. If you head upstairs, you will find a white oak bar that has played host to Buffalo Bill Cody and President Theodore Roosevelt, even the bar itself has story almost as interesting as Henry Zietz himself.

It was hand carved for the Zeitz family for their original saloon in Germany in 1856. When they immigrated to the US they brought the bar by boat to New York, moved it from New York to the Great Lakes via the Eerie Canal, the Great Lakes to Prairie Deshane by rail and then made the final leg of its journey to Denver in 1871 by oxcart.

The décor of the Buffalo Exchange is, to put it mildly, a study in taxidermy. Zeitz's life was full of excitement and adventure, and the walls certainly reflect it, with mountain lions and mounted deer peering over cases, watching as you munch on a buffalo steak. You'll also see Zeitz's extensive gun collection, an array of Native American artwork he often accepted as payment and even a forlorn looking elk dork (which he'd use to tame rowdy customers).

Be sure to look behind the bar for Colorado liquor license #1, the very first issued after Prohibition had ended.

THE FOOD

As already mentioned, the Buckhorn Exchange specializes in fine cuisine, especially dishes featuring game such as alligator or even rattlesnake. They are most well-known though, as the place in Denver to get a great platter of Rocky Mountain oysters.

Now, if you're not familiar with them, Rocky Mountain oysters are bull testicles, sliced thin, battered and deep-fried. They have a…unique taste. And for certain they're probably the most unique of bar foods that you'll find anywhere. Try them with cocktail sauce and you probably should have a drink handy.

THE DRINKS

Speaking of drink, the Buckhorn Exchange specializes in a multitude of drinks in their full-service bar but the one we recommend as a must-try is none other than Buffalo Bill's drink of choice, and later named in his honor, the Buffalo Bill Cocktail.

According to oral history—provided by the manager—Cody was told by his doctor to limit his alcohol to one drink per night. So, when down from Golden, he'd stop in at Zeitz's saloon and sip a tall glass of rye whiskey and apple cider on the rocks. This drink is still served here, though they've substituted bourbon for the rye and apple juice for the cider. It's a refreshing drink, not sweet, with a heavy taste of the whiskey. It's easy to see what Buffalo Bill liked about it.

NEARBY DISTRACTIONS

Mile High Stadium—Website: www.sportsauthorityfieldatmilehigh.com **Address:** 1701 Bryant St. Denver, CO, 80204, (720) 258-3333 (operating hours vary by game times and event, call or check their website). Home of the Denver Broncos and a mere two miles from the Buckhorn Exchange sits Sports Authority Field at Mile High or simply Mile High as it is called by most locals. Containing the Colorado Sports Hall of Fame and available for tours, both occur year-round with varying hours, this is a must-see for any Denver Broncos fan.

Fort Collins—Located approximately one hour north of Denver sits the sleepy town of Ft. Collins, Colorado. Home of Colorado State University, HP and what is probably the heaviest concentration of world-class breweries in the US. If you have the time (and a designated driver wouldn't be a bad idea either) head up and check out the free tours at Anheuser-Busch, Odell, New Belgium, Ft. Collins and Equinox to name just a few. Most tours end with free samples or low-priced samples, and touring them all can easily take up an afternoon ending with anyone over 21 feeling pretty good or not good at all, depending on your tolerance.

US Mint—Website: www.usmint.gov **Address:** 320 West Colfax Avenue Denver, CO, 80204, (303) 405-4761 (tours run 8am–11am and 1pm–4pm). Less than two miles from the Buckhorn is one of the United States Mints. Producing over 50 million coins per day, the mint offers free daily tours, which must be scheduled in advance via their website and can be scheduled as much as three months in advance. The tour gives you a glimpse into how dull, blank scrap metal slugs (gone are the days of actual metal worth something) are turned into shiny pocket change used to tip the bartenders in the lousy saloons not in this book.

DENVER'S HISTORIC BARS

Buffalo Rose—Address: 1119 Washington Street, Golden, CO, 80401, (303) 278-6800 (Monday–Sunday 11am–2am). One of the oldest bars in the area and, according to them, the oldest in all of Colorado (established in 1858). This is a saloon-turned-dive that caters to live music acts, primarily loud rock. The food is cheap and so are the drinks. We've heard good things about the burgers, but this is only hearsay. At the very least this will give you an excuse to get out of Denver and check out Golden.

Ship Tavern-Brown Palace Hotel—Address: 321 17th Street, downtown Denver, CO, 80202, (303) 297-3111 (Monday–Sunday 11am–12am). This bar was opened in 1934 after the repeal of Prohibition. It was designed to resemble a waterfront tavern you might find in New England in the 19th century, with gleaming brass, polished wood and antique nautical décor. It's the polar opposite of the Buffalo Rose, with nary a dive bar qualifier (like Christmas tree lights or stale beer smell) to be had. But that being said, the Brown Palace itself is a great place to have a drink in anyway. It was opened in 1892 and at one time had a pretty wild saloon, catering to many of the ne'er-do-wells as one of the less reputable joints in the area.

DETROIT, MI

Known as the Motor City, Motown, The D, Hockeytown, Hitsville USA, The Paris of the Midwest, the 313, (the list goes on and on), Detroit has more nicknames than just about any major city in the US. It's also had more ups and downs than any other city in the US. The city's motto is: Speramus Meliora; Resurget Cineribus, which means "We hope for better days; it shall rise from the ashes." A fitting one for a city that would climb the ladder to become one of the greatest cities in the world, and, just a few short decades later, be the first major US city to claim bankruptcy.

Ironically enough, one of the city's highs came during prohibition, a time when many cities struggled. When prohibition started, Detroit had 1,500 bars, saloons, and taverns, but by 1929, it's estimated it had 15,000 speakeasies. That same year, the illegal production and distribution of alcohol was the 2nd largest industry in the city—second only to auto making—to the tune of 300 million dollars annually (4 billion in today's dollars). It's easy to see why when you consider that it's estimated that over 70% of the illegal booze in the US during prohibition came from or through Detroit (much of it due to our Canadian neighbors to the north, thanks, eh!).

Through it all, Detroit and its residents have remained loyal to the city's motto, and today it isn't all doom and gloom as it was just a short time ago. The future looks bright thanks to new investors, such as Quicken Loans founder and Cleveland Cavaliers owner, Dan Gilbert. People like him are breathing new life into the city. And, with new investors and new life, comes new residents, new businesses, and—more importantly—new life for many of the historic bars and taverns that have been serving Detroit residents through the city's tumultuous past.

NANCY WHISKEY, DETROIT, MI

Address: 2644 Harrison St., Detroit, MI, 48216, (313) 962-4247
Website: www.nancywhiskeydetroit.com **Video Tour:**
https://youtu.be/XOHN-dSfaQs
Food: Yes **Live Music:** Yes **Hours:** Monday–Saturday 11am–4am, Sunday
12pm–4am **Type of Bar:** Dive **What to Drink:** Tullamore Dew **Why You
Should Go:** One of the last Irish Bar's in Detroit, Jimmy Hoffa Hangout,
maintains Detroit's oldest liquor licenses, Tullamore Dew shots.

THE HISTORY

When Irish immigrants began showing up in Detroit, Michigan in the
middle of the 19th century, fleeing the Great Irish Potato Famine, many
settled just west of downtown Detroit. Most of these Irish immigrants were
from Cork County, Ireland, and thus, the area quickly became known simply
as Corktown. It was here, in 1898, that Digby's general store opened (the
name is still featured on the doorstep today). In 1902—realizing there was
more money to be made in booze—Digby's converted into a full-fledged bar,
known simply as Digby's Saloon. But, in a fashion similar to the city of
Detroit, Digby's was quickly faced with some historic challenges.

Less than 20 years after the saloon opened its doors, the nation, and
Digby's, were faced with what many refer to as the modern-day dark ages, aka
prohibition. But, in true Irish (or perhaps Detroit) spirit, it refused to let
something as trivial as the 18th Amendment stand in its way. The good times
continued to roll as Digby's turned into one of the thousands of speakeasies
dotting the city. Following prohibition, Digby's reverted to a neighborhood

bar and maintained its service to the neighborhood regulars, including one Jimmy Hoffa.

Located just steps away from Nancy Whiskey's front door you find the offices of Truck Drivers Local Union 299 and Teamsters Local Union No. 337. These are where Jimmy Hoffa's offices were once located. According to legend, Jimmy's office phone was tapped, an annoyance of which he knew. So, to get around this he would stroll down to the local bar (now known as Nancy's), and place calls in the phone booth. It's also rumored he held more than one informal meeting with some of the more colorful residents of the city, including union representatives, community leaders and mobsters. If only these walls could talk, maybe they'd tell us where Jimmy is.

Nancy McNiven-Glen, the bar's namesake, took over the bar in 1987 and the good times, regardless of rollercoaster-ride that is Detroit, continued to roll. Shortly after taking the bar over, Nancy frequently traveled back Ireland to visit friends and family. She was known to oftentimes bring back cases of Tullamore Dew to serve up to her thirsty patrons (it wasn't imported in those days). Later, as Tullamore Dew began officially exporting to the US, Nancy arranged for the bar to receive some of the first cases, and Tullamore Dew became an integral part of the historic bar from that point on.

But it hasn't always been smooth sailing for Nancy and the bar. In 2009, it was almost completely burned down due to an electrical fire. The community, realizing the importance of the bar, rallied together to save it. A local shop teacher, who was also a Nancy's regular, rebuilt the bar, while another repainted the ceiling. Everyone did their part and the bar was rebuilt to the glorious divey-ness you find today.

TODAY

Nancy Whiskey describes itself today as "Detroit's oldest party," and, with a liquor license that spans over 110 years, that claim is probably pretty close to the truth. They are also one of the nation's last true classic neighborhood bars, located in the middle of a neighborhood with houses surrounding all sides.

As you walk in you see head-gear strewn across the bar back, each representing members of law enforcement, firefighters, emergency responders and military members (we were told some of these items saw action in their various fields). Pictures of the bar's history also fill the walls visually detailing some of the bars biggest events over the course of its history. You'll also find a less conspicuous historical item in the bar, located just off to the side of the front door, a phone booth.

As mentioned earlier, Nancy's is just a stone throw away from Jimmy Hoffa's old office where his phones were tapped. It's allegedly this phone booth to your left that Jimmy Hoffa utilized to circumnavigate the snooping feds. And while it's no longer working, it's worth a look and maybe even a photo or two—one can just imagine the conversations that took place in there.

While Nancy no longer owns the bar, many things remain the same from the days she did own it. You'll still find firefighters, cops, military veterans, locals, regulars and newbies bellied up to the bar holding their own form of church almost any day of the week. Additionally, Corktown, and therefore Nancy Whiskey, is lucky enough to find itself in one of the up and coming areas of Detroit, as is reflected not only by the clientele, but also by the ongoing renovations to the neighborhood.

In the end, Nancy Whiskey is more than your average Detroit dive bar. It remains one of the last, true neighborhood bars in the nation. It hosts some outstanding Blue's acts, is one of Detroit's few remaining Irish tavern's, and has navigated some of our nation's toughest and darkest days (prohibition, the world wars, the great depression, the great recession, etc.). Nancy Whiskey is a bar to be celebrated with a shot of Tullamore Dew, Stroh's back, and a toast to her history.

THE FOOD

Nancy Whiskey serves up your typical pub grub, like burgers, chicken fingers, and sandwiches. But, if you're really looking for a treat, head over on a Friday to enjoy one of their fish fries.

THE DRINKS

You won't find high-priced craft cocktails at Nancy's, but that isn't to say you won't find good cocktails. This place typically sticks to the classics, and, in true dive bar tradition, serves up an excellent heavy-handed shot and beer back. We recommend a shot of Tullamore Dew (the locals say it's like having an angel piss on your tongue) with a Stroh's back to get a true taste for the bar and the city she resides in.

NEARBY DISTRACTIONS

Teamsters Local Union 299/337—Address: 2801 Trumbull Ave, Detroit, MI, 48216. Jimmy Hoffa's old hangout, which is located just a few blocks away makes for a fun photo opp. They don't really have a visitor's center or anything, and, due to the notoriety of Hoffa, would probably get a bit upset if you wandered in asking questions about him, so it's probably best just to glance at it from the street.

Motor City Casino—Website: www.motorcitycasino.com **Address:** 2901 Grand River Ave, Detroit, MI, 48201, (866) 782-9622 (Open 24 hours, 7 days a week). Like it or not, casinos have arrived in Detroit and it looks like they are here to stay. Located a brief half mile walk from Nancy's, Motor City Casino and Hotel not only offers additional drinking and eating choices but also a nice hotel option if you happen to overindulge. Maybe try this place out after Nancy's that way you have enough money to drink with before you gamble it all away.

TOMMY'S DETROIT BAR & GRILL, DETROIT, MI

Address: 624 3rd Ave., Detroit, MI, 48226, (313) 965-2269
Website: www.tommysdetroit.com **Video tour:**
https://youtu.be/qYe6a270nrw
Food: Yes **Live Music:** Yes **Hours:** Monday–Sunday 11am–2am **Type of Bar:** Dive **What to Drink:** Local beer. **Why You Should Go:** Haunted, known speakeasy, Al Capone hangout, free shuttle to local professional games.

THE HISTORY

The building that contains Tommy's has more of a story to tell than the bar itself. The original building here was a wooden structure, built sometime in the mid-1800s, and was utilized as part of the Underground Railroad (in addition to the church next-door). Later, sometime around 1880, the structure was demolished, and a brick structure was erected in its place. That structure still stands today, though it has had multiple owners, businesses, rooms and even floors added and removed over the years. But, throughout it all, it's always served alcohol (both legally and illegally) in one form or another.

In 1893, the original Union Depot train station was opened just across the street from the bar, and travelers were able to swing by Tommy's for a cocktail, cigar, shoe shine, and a shave. Later, during World War I, the train station served as a major departure point for soldiers heading to the war. Many would stay at the next-door Ford Presbyterian church, where they had their own private entrance that just so happened to face the bar. It's easy to imagine these soldiers spending time praying for a safe return, and then downing a few cocktails here prior to heading out.

Records show that in 1920, an Italian restaurant occupied the main level of the structure, and, later, when prohibition was the law, the basement was turned into a speakeasy. It was known as Little Harry's, and historians have found business cards with the name, address and phone number of the speakeasy—making us wonder the extent to which prohibition laws were actually enforced in Detroit. Little Harry's was rumored to have been supplied and frequented by the notorious Purple Gang.

Also known as the Sugar House Gang, the Purple Gang was a predominantly Jewish gang that operated in Detroit in the 1920s and 30s. And, since it's believed that at least 70% of all illegal liquor coming into the US during prohibition came across the Detroit river (thank you Canada), they were in the right spot at the right time to operate and control a sizeable percentage of the illegal hooch arriving in the US. As a matter of fact, there is rumored to be a photo of Al Capone outside of Little Harry's during prohibition, and it's said he was at the mercy of the Purple Gang and their supply of booze, not the other way around.

The building remained a speakeasy and restaurant throughout prohibition, and was a favorite stop for travelers with a layover at the Union Depot, until the Depot closed in 1973. Over time, the bar took on different owner's and names, such as Thomas's Bar, Tom's Tavern and Tommy's Bar, but has always been a bar and important part of the community.

TODAY

When you walk into Tommy's, the first thing you'll probably notice is how modern it feels, but don't let this fool you, the place celebrates its historic past. Tommy, the owner, renovated the establishment shortly after purchasing it, but he's exceptionally proud of the history, as you'll see when you move into the back-lounge area and are greeted with walls full of the place's history. This history includes pictures of a recent dig by Wayne State Archeologists, who found many clues to the bars past, proving and disproving some of the legends.

To truly get a feel for the history of this place we recommend you schedule a tour in advance with the owner. During the 25-minute tour, you'll get a chance to hear and see some of the historical aspects of the bar, including the basement, the tunnel entrance that was used to smuggle liquor up from the river (and freed slaves to the river), false walls, hidden rooms, and ghost stories that will give you goose bumps. It's well worth it.

If you happen to show up on a game day (whether it's the Wings, Lions, or Pistons), Tommy's is a great place to watch the game. Better yet, if you have tickets, stop by Tommy's for a bite to eat, a few cold beverages, and then take advantage of the free shuttle to the arena.

Tommy's is truly a great historic bar, which, while it has been modernized, still clings to its historic past. If you find yourself with an opportunity to swing by, or better yet grab a meal and take the tour, you won't be disappointed.

THE FOOD

Tommy's has a full-service kitchen and the food is tasty! We have a fondness for their Andouille Pretzel Burger, a burger topped with andouille sausage, cheese, and peppercorn horseradish sauce served on a pretzel burger bun. Start with an order of the wings or pretzel bites if you're gearing up for a heavy night of drinking. If you're on a tight budget or just want to snack on something, they do feature free popcorn, which is always a nice touch.

THE DRINKS

Tommy's has a full-service bar and you can get just about anything your heart desires. We recommend trying one of the many local craft beers they have on tap.

NEARBY DISTRACTIONS

American and Lafayette Coney Island—Address: 114 and 118 W Lafayette Blvd, Detroit, MI, 48226 (Monday–Sunday, open 24 hours). "Lafayette or American" or "American or Lafayette?" The same question posed in two different forms, but each asking the same thing: which of these two legendary Detroit hot dog restaurants do you prefer? Located a mere half mile from Tommy's, you'll find these legendary Detroit eateries literally right next door to each other (they share a wall). And, it's here that you can answer the previously posed question, "Lafayette's or American?" We can't recommend this experience enough! The food is tasty and a perfect late night stop after making the rounds at the local bars. Start at either place, order a Coney Dog (or Coney Island Hot Dog, a crisp dog topped with chili, mustard and onions), and maybe a Coney Loose Burger, (add the smothered fries if you are really hungry), scarf it all down, and then head next door and repeat. Then answer the question, "Lafayette or American?"

The Renaissance Center (GM Building)—Address: 100 Renaissance Center, Detroit, MI, 48243 (Hours vary by business, but you can walk by and get a great view 24 hours a day). You have probably all seen the GM building portrayed in movies (such as Grosse Pointe Blank and Bird on a Wire) and in news clips about Detroit or the auto industry. Erected in 1977 it remains Michigan's tallest building, and hosts multiple businesses, including a Marriott hotel, multiple restaurants, and both GM and state offices. It's worth a visit to see the iconic building and its surroundings.

Joe Louis Monument—Address: 5 Woodward Ave, Detroit, MI, 48226 (Open 24 Hours). Located just over a half mile from Tommy's, you will find the Joe Louis Monument. This 24 x 24 x 11.5 foot 8,000 lbs cast bronze monument honors boxer, Joe Louis, a former Detroit resident and heavyweight champion of the world from 1937 to 1950 and widely considered to be the first African American national hero. The famous boxer died in 1981 and the monument was dedicated in 1986. The meaning behind the sculpture is meant to be open, as intended by the originally artist, so many have concluded it to represent anything from Joe's iron fist to Detroit's willingness to fight through anything (which it needed through the great recession). Regardless, the monument, along with its surroundings is worth a visit during your stint in Detroit.

2 WAY INN, DETROIT, MI

Address: 17897 Mount Elliott Street, Detroit, MI, 48212, (313) 891-4925
Website: http://2wayinn.com **Video Tour:** https://youtu.be/5kT7sqEq5Qw
Food: Yes **Live Music:** Yes **Hours:** Tuesday 12pm–5pm, Wednesday 12pm–12am, Thursday–Saturday 12pm–2am **Type of Bar:** Dive **What to Drink:** Beer and a shot. **Why You Should Go:** The 2 Way Inn is Detroit's oldest bar, serving drinks non-stop for over 140 years.

THE HISTORY

The 2 Way Inn was established by Colonel Philetus Norris in 1873 in the small town of Norris, Michigan. The building was originally utilized as the town's jail, general store, and the Colonel's residence until it was turned into a saloon in 1876. Norris was annexed by the city of Detroit in 1924 landing the bar in its current location of eastern Detroit (also called the Nortown neighborhood).

Over the years, the 2 Way Inn continued to morph and change. In addition to being a jail, general store, residence, dentist office, and saloon, the 2 Way Inn was also utilized as an inn, a stagecoach stop, railroad depot, dance hall, and a brothel. Through it all, it's always served its patrons booze (legally and illegally), a run that has lasted for over 140 years.

During prohibition, it was turned into a combination Dentist office and speakeasy, which sounds weird at first until you consider the laws of the time—since the Volstead Act allowed doctors to prescribe alcohol to patients, having a dentist office in the building was exceptionally beneficial. Locals could swing by the Dentist office, complain about a toothache, get a prescription for whiskey, and then pick up their "prescription" downstairs. No prescription? No problem, step into the speakeasy (one of approx. 15,000 located in Detroit during prohibition) and get your needed fix.

As time ticked by and Detroit's economy ebbed and flowed, so did the 2 Way Inn. Hit just as hard as Detroit during the "great recession" the Two Way Inn survived thanks to its loyal patrons and neighbors, a fierce loyalty that remains today.

TODAY

Today the bar is best described as a homey neighborhood bar, or, as it's owners, bartenders and patrons like to describe it, a "fine dive," meaning dive bar pricing without the smells. As you get ready to head into the bar, be warned, you can't just walk in, you need to be buzzed in. Find and press the button next to the door and give your least threatening smile (you're on TV). If you pass the visual inspection, you'll hear a buzz as the door is unlocked, open the door and head in. The process kind of reminded us of sneaking into a speakeasy back in the day, and in our opinion adds to the charm of the place.

As you walk in, you're greeted by a dimly lit pool room complete with tables and chairs, wall art, and taxidermy. Move past this and head down the ramp to find the original Stroh's bar. You'll quickly notice there are no taps, but the bottled beer and spirit selection is vast. We recommend sticking to a classic cocktail or the dive bar specialty—a beer, a whiskey, or a whiskey shot with beer back, depending on your mission and time.

The 2 Way Inn has a saying, "you are a stranger here but once, so stop being a stranger," and we recommend you let the bartender know it is your first time. You'll be encouraged to participate in the quarter toss in which you lean up against the bar, stand on the foot rail, make a wish, and toss a quarter up to the top of the bar back. If you make it, your wish will come true, miss and you just lost a quarter for nothing, except a great experience.

Another tradition you should be aware of has to do with the big cow bell hanging enticingly above the bar. Read the sign carefully before you touch it. Ringing the bell signifies your wish to buy a round for the bar. It does happen from time to time, but unless you're willing to buy the round, we recommend you leave the bell alone.

The bar is dark and has an almost underground feel to it, which isn't to say it is unwelcoming. We found the bartenders to be friendly, the patrons fun-loving, and the atmosphere almost addictive. It's easy to imagine an afternoon and night slipping away as you enjoy the company and reasonably priced drinks. Tradition and history simply permeate the atmosphere of this historic neighborhood "fine dive," and we highly recommend a visit.

THE FOOD

The 2 Way Inn does not have a formal menu, but Mary (owner and part-time bartender) does host the occasional "popup" meal featuring tasty homemade food (like shepherd's pie, lasagna, etc.). If you're lucky enough to be there for one of these, the food is hearty, tasty, and worth the paltry price. Additionally, during the first Sunday of cold-season months (aka December, January, February etc), they host a brunch that features cheaply priced and flavorful food as well as house made vegetable infused alcohol for those Sunday brunch cocktails, a must if you happen to be in the area at the time.

THE DRINKS

The 2 Way Inn is definitely a shot and beer type of place. We recommend a Stroh's (the bar is after all an original Stroh's bar, and you're in Detroit, the home of Stroh's in the first place), and a shot of your choice (though whiskey is always a safe bet in our opinion).

NEARBY DISTRACTIONS

Comerica Park, Ford Field, and Little Caesars Arena—Unlike many of the other major sports cities across the nation, Detroit not only has a professional hockey, basketball, baseball, and football team, their venues are all located within walking distance of one another. If you're any kind of a sports fan, then a stroll through the area is worth your time. Better yet, time your visit for one of the games.

Monroe Avenue—New Orleans has Bourbon St., Memphis has Beale, and Detroit has Monroe. Located in Greektown, and considered one of the liveliest places in the downtown area, Monroe Ave. features multiple places to eat, drink and even gamble (the Greektown Casino). The area is especially lively during the warmer months and anytime there's a home game for one of Detroit's major sports franchises. Stroll down to Monroe if you're looking for a concentration of bars, restaurants, and shops, you're sure to find something going on.

Elwood Bar & Grill—**Website:** www.elwoodgrill.com **Address:** 300 E Adams Ave, Detroit, MI, 48226, (313) 962-2337 (Hours vary by local events, check website or call). If you head down to check out Comerica Park or Ford Field, the Elwood Bar and Grill is a must. Founded in 1936, located across the street from Comerica Park and Ford Field and within walking distance of Little Caesars Arena (home of the Piston's and Red Wings), the Elwood is the perfect place to stop in for a drink and bite to eat on the way to or from an event.

DETROIT'S HISTORIC BARS

Abick's Bar—**Address:** 3500 Gilbert St., Detroit, MI, 48210, (313) 894-9329 (Monday–Saturday 9am–2am, Sunday 12pm–2 am). Believed to be one of Detroit's Oldest Continuously Operating Family-owned bars, Abick's is steeped in history. The bar was built in 1907 and became Abick's in 1919 when George Abick purchased it. Later, during prohibition, it's believed to have been a speakeasy (of course). During World War 2, it was run by Marie Abick, who was known to collect and pool the neighborhood ration stamps and cook up feasts for the locals, which was especially helpful as rations ran lean. Today the bar remains in the Abick family and it proudly retains its history with as little changed as possible. The old mahogany bar still remains with the antique bronze cash register still perched at its station. Memorabilia dots the walls and ceilings, telling the story of the bar's past. If you get the chance to head back to the secretive Scotch and cigar lounge, we highly recommend a visit to get a unique insight into the bar, the family who owns it, and the community it has so loyally served.

Tom's Tavern—Website: 10093 W Seven Mile Rd., Detroit, M, 48221, (313) 862-9768 (Wednesday–Saturday 7pm–2 am). Tom's, not to be confused with Tommy's, isn't pretty to view from the outside, and, to be honest, it isn't much to view from the inside. What it is, is a true Detroit dive bar. Opened in 1928, Tom's is one of the younger bars in Detroit, but what it lacks in age it makes up for in stories. Believed to have been supplied and frequented by the Purple Gang, it's easy to imagine 1920s mobsters hanging out here. The place isn't a craft beer or fancy cocktail kind of place, but it does have some great live music, so try and time your visit on a night when a band is playing. Ask if Ron is working, and if you're lucky (and he's in the mood), you'll get a tour of the place followed up by some of his legendary Gumbo.

Painted Lady Lounge—Website: 2930 Jacob St, Hamtramck, MI, 48212, (313) 874-2991 (Monday–Friday 4pm–2am, Saturday–Sunday 12pm–2am). An unpretentious dive bar located inside a Victorian era house is probably the best way to describe the Painted Lady Lounge. One of the many bars claiming to be Detroit's oldest, the bar features an interesting coral pink and turquois color combination that is peeling off the walls…quickly. Inside you will find PBR on tap, cheap well drinks, unpretentious attitude, and rumors and stories of ghosts, speakeasies, and illegal card rooms in the basement. Stop by the Painted Lady Lounge to get a taste of the classic, humble Detroit attitude, a decent whiskey selection, vintage beer signs, bathroom graffiti, and a good time.

EL PASO, TX

There are few Wild West towns in the United States that are as overlooked as El Paso, Texas. While places like Tombstone and Dodge City garner the imagination of Hollywood screenwriters, El Paso, with its much more interesting and amazing history, seems to go completely unnoticed.

But in fact, this area was awash in the factual accounts of what we normally think of as movie fiction.

Brothels abounded in the city, and there are dozens of true tales of madams who killed their lovers, themselves or someone else. Shoot-outs on the street were a regular occurrence, with many putting legendary shootouts you've heard of (like the gunfight at the OK Corral) to pitiful shame.

The most deadly gun in the West, outlaw gunfighter John Wesley Hardin, walked El Paso's streets and—ironically enough—practiced law. He also met his end here in the form of a bullet through his head from another gunfighter.

Throughout the region are found stories like this, all of them true, and most of them you've probably never heard of.

Another point to consider about the region is that just on the other side of the river from El Paso is a city that has rivaled the most dangerous cities in the world, Juarez, Mexico. Juarez has been locked in a bloody drug war since the mid-2000s. In 2010 they reached a high of 3,111 murders, which fell to a still-staggering 1,955 in 2011. And these are only the ones that have been reported.

The area covered here is large, and it will take some driving to get to all of the bars on the list. But they are well worth it.

ROSA'S CANTINA, EL PASO, TX

Address: 3454 Doniphan Drive, El Paso, TX, 79922, (915) 833-0402
Video tour: http://youtu.be/ms9I4OWY6zU
Food: Yes **Live Music:** Yes **Hours:** Tuesday–Thursday 11am–12am, Friday–Saturday 11am–2am, Sunday 11am–12am **Type of Bar:** Saloon **What to Drink:** A bottle of Lone Star and a shot of Cuervo **Why You Should Go:** The song by Marty Robbins, El Paso, was written based on this place. What more do you need?

THE HISTORY

Rosa's wasn't always Rosa's. It was actually founded in the early 1940s (by the name of Los Tigres) outside of El Paso in what was called Smelter-town (so named because of the many factories and smelters in the area). It was a quiet neighborhood bar like any other until 1957 when it was bought by Beto and Anita Zubia. That started a chain of events that would put the place on the map for years to come.

One of the first things Zubia did was change the name, liking the sound of "Rosa's Cantina" after one of his waitresses, and the name stuck. Then, a by-chance stop when the place was closed one day created a legend and the reason why people flock to it today.

The story goes that Marty Robbins was driving from Nashville to Phoenix when he and his crew happened upon Rosa's Cantina. At the time the main road taking travelers from west Texas to southern New Mexico passed right in front of the bar. According to legend Marty stopped, got out of the car and looked around and then, inspired, got back in the car and headed to Phoenix.

By the time he hit Phoenix the song, "El Paso", was complete.

The song tells the story of a cowboy who falls in love with a Mexican dancing girl. In a jealous rage he shoots a potential suitor and then flees the bar to the badlands of New Mexico. Drawn back by his love he crosses back into Texas on his way to Rosa's but is chased and shot by a posse. His love, Felina, witnesses the cowboy's valiant effort to make it back to her and runs to comfort him as he lies dying.

One thing you must do if you find yourself heading to Rosa's is actually listen to the song. Marty talks about the badlands of New Mexico, easily viewable right across the street from Rosa's. He also talks about looking down on the town of El Paso from the badlands, easily imaginable looking at the hills in the distance.

TODAY

Historically Rosa's wasn't always the most inviting place for outsiders. Take for example the time Beto Zubia locked all of the doors because a couple of buses loaded with college athletes and tourists pulled up expecting to visit the world-renowned establishment. He and the regulars sat quietly as the out-of-towners knocked on the doors. When asked why he did it, Zubia said it was because they would have drunk all the beer.

Today Rosa's is a more welcoming saloon, with a mix of locals, celebrities, and tourist from all over the world. Some of the more recognizable names to frequent Rosa's are Chip Woolley (trainer of 50-to-1 long shot Kentucky Derby-winner, Mine That Bird), Don Haskins (who coached the first integrated college basketball team to a national title), and of course Marty Robbins. Rosa's spends most of its daylight hours as a restaurant, getting especially busy during the Sunland Park winter racing season. The evenings find Rosa's transformed into a traditional bar, hosting live bands from all over the country and a busy dance floor.

When you go, do keep in mind that despite its legacy this is still a locals' bar. One regular we talked to had been going there for lunch for 35 years. We asked him how often he hears the song by Robbins, and he shot us a look Clint Eastwood typically reserves for guys he's about to put an end to. If the place is empty, play the song. If it's crowded, abstain and wait for some other sucker to put the money in and draw the menacing stares from the locals.

THE FOOD

Rosa's kitchen is run by 30-year veteran Martha, who says the secret to making good Mexican food is love. If that is true, she must pour her entire heart into every meal she prepares: the food is great.

The most popular and most recommended plate is the Mexican Plate. The plate, both colorful and generous, gives you a wide range of excellent Mexican food, from tacos to enchiladas, along with beans, rice, and chips and salsa. It is a must-try when you stop in.

THE DRINKS

Until recently, Rosa's had a limited liquor license, which only allowed them to serve beer and wine. However, they now have a full liquor license and feature a full bar with most easy-to-make cocktails at the ready.

For a recommended drink we suggest either a Lone Star beer and/or a shot of Cuervo. These are the cheapest beer and shots you can get just about anywhere, and for that that reason alone, the idea is appealing.

NEARBY DISTRACTIONS

Sunland Park Racetrack & Casino—Website: www.sunland-park.com **Address:** 1200 Futurity Dr. Sunland Park, NM, 88063, (575) 874-5200 (operating hours vary by season, live racing occurs December-April). Though it's less than two miles from Rosa's Cantina, Sunland Park Racetrack and Casino is in a whole other city and state. Featuring live horse racing December to April and a casino open throughout the year, a stop here will help to give you the total Rosa's Cantina experience. 50-1 odds Kentucky Derby-winner Mine That Bird's trainer used to frequent Rosa's and the racetrack is located in what is considered the "Badlands" of New Mexico as described in Marty Robbins' song, "El Paso".

The State Line—Website: www.countyline.com/StateLine.html **Address:** 1222 Sunland Park Dr. Sunland Park, El Paso TX, 79922, (915) 581-3371 (Monday–Thursday 11:30am–9:30pm, Friday–Saturday 11:30am–10:00pm, Sunday 11:30am–9pm). Where else can you park in Texas, eat in New Mexico and pee in either? Less than two miles from Rosa's, and right next door to Sunland Park Racetrack, is the State Line Restaurant. Featuring tasty BBQ, Texas-sized helpings, and outstanding beef ribs while straddling New Mexico and Texas, it's a great place to stop if you are craving BBQ.

The Plaza Theatre—Website: www.theplazatheatre.org **Address:** 125 Pioneer Plaza El Paso, TX, 79901, (915) 231-1100 (operating hours vary by show, call or visit their website). Though it's a lengthy 25-mile drive from Rosa's to the Plaza Theatre, if you're in the area long enough it's worth the drive. Opened in 1930, no expense was spared in the creation of this legendary and lavish theatre: the largest theatre between Dallas and Los Angeles upon completion. Recently renovated, today it continues to be a must-see destination, hosting popular performances from all over the globe. Tours are offered weekly, so plan ahead if you'd like to attend.

WORLD FAMOUS KENTUCKY CLUB, JUAREZ, MX

Address: Av. Benito Juarez 643, Centro, 32000, Cd Juarez, Chih. Mexico, +52 (656) 632-6113
Video tour: https://youtu.be/8ddF5bSiG4Q
Food: Yes **Live Music:** No **Hours:** Monday–Sunday, 11am–2am **Type of Bar:** Dive **What to Drink:** Margarita **Why You Should Go:** Opened in the early 20th century and quenching the thirst of Americans across the border since prohibition, also maybe the birthplace of the Margarita.

THE HISTORY

Founded in 1920, the Kentucky Club was opened two years into prohibition. A wise move. Only a short walk from downtown El Paso, Texas, USA, Ciudad Juarez, Mexico was ready and willing to help thirsty Americans quench that thirst. And, apparently, the Kentucky Club was one of the finest, which is evident from the array of local and Mexican celebrities whose portraits line the walls, and who were kept tipsy here.

Picture after picture show smiling Matadors and members of the local Juarez baseball team of the Mexican League, all perched in dusty frames along the side wall above small, intimate booths. There were also a number of celebrities, from the 1920s on, who have visited this classy bar. A number of movies, especially cheaply made westerns, were shot in the area, and so, for thirsty movie stars it was an almost sure thing that they'd turn up at the Kentucky Club. The list includes the likes of John Wayne and Steve McQueen. We can picture them drinking here.

The place was well known to dignitaries passing through, especially after bartender, Lorenzo "Lencho" Hernandez created what became their signature drink, the Margarita, in the 1930s. This is one of about four Margarita-invention stories out there, and possibly the oldest, however, it's pretty unlikely that it was invented here (as opposed to Mexico City in the late 1800s as other urban legends claim). But in any case, the drink at the Kentucky Club is well made using the classic recipe of tequila, sweetened lime juice, and a bit of Grand Marnier and served in a rocks glass with a salted rim.

TODAY

To be honest we weren't sure what we'd find when we made the trek across the US-Mexico border to visit the Kentucky Club. The drug war this town saw in the years surrounding 2010 closed many of the businesses in the cross-fire: as the tourists stayed across the border, many slowly faded away. We were afraid the Kentucky Club was another casualty. Luckily though, it's persevered.

The look and feel of this place is all East Coast, big city cocktail bar—not border city cantina. You could take this place and drop it in Chicago, Boston or New York and it'd feel about the same—with the exception of the few nods to their Mexican heritage, like the giant, dust covered, stuffed Eagle perched facing the bar (it's has probably been there since opening).

Behind the long bar sits a rich, coffee-brown, ornately-carved bar back, stretching up to the ceiling, holding an array of tequila bottles and large, heavy mirrors. It was carved in France in 1935 specifically for the Kentucky Club, and then shipped to Juarez to be assembled here. It's graced the bar ever since.

The bar itself sits on a tiled floor that sports a pretty old feature—a trough running the length of it. If you're not familiar with these, they sit just above the floor, right below your feet if you're sitting. But understand there was a time when you didn't sit at a bar, you stood. And if you didn't want to leave the bar but had to relieve yourself, the trough was convenient. We didn't examine it too closely, but we don't think it'd been used in a while.

THE FOOD

We didn't try the food but they do have a full kitchen and it smelled great, plus there were a few people eating hamburgers or more locally-familiar dishes (like burritos and such).

THE DRINKS

Definitely have a Margarita. After all, this is one of the places where it was supposedly invented. They are strong and are traditionally-made, so think of lime-juice, triple sec, tequila, a splash of Grand Marnier, and that's it. Don't expect anything frozen or sugary, this is the real stuff. You'll also enjoy pretty inexpensive prices: we paid about $3.00 for a Margarita and a beer.

NEARBY DISTRACTIONS

Cathedral of Ciudad Juarez—Website: www.diocesisdeciudadjuarez.org
Address: Calle Venustiano Carranza y Vicente Guerrero, Av Vicente Guerrero 101, Centro, 32000 Cd Juárez, Chih., Mexico, +52 6155502 (Office open

Monday–Friday 930am–1pm, 4pm–6:30pm, Saturday 9:30am–1pm, check website for mass schedule). A Franciscan mission was erected here all the way back in the 17th century, and while the Cathedral that you see was constructed in 1957, it is still joined to that same, original mission. Inside, visitors find a beautiful cathedral with intricate and ornate alter, reminiscent of those found throughout Mexico and Spain. If you have the chance, attending a service here is moving, as the faithful from this huge border city flock into the church to pray the Rosary and listen to mass.

Mercado Juarez—Address: Av. 16 de Septiembre 611, Centro, 32000 Cd Juárez, Chih., Mexico, +52 656 349 9471 (Monday–Sunday, 8am–6pm). This lively and colorful market has been serving Juarez residents and visitors for decades if not longer. This is where you want to go for tourist knick-knacks of all kinds. If you can, bring someone to translate for you, as this is haggling territory. At the very least, never pay full price for anything.

CORN EXCHANGE AT LA POSTA DE MESILLA, MESILLA, NM

Address: 2410 Calle De San Albino, Mesilla, NM, 88046, (575) 524-3524 **Website:** www.laposta-de-mesilla.com **Video tour:** http://youtu.be/h2jUd60Tmuo **Food:** Yes **Live Music:** No **Hours:** Monday–Thursday 11am–9pm, Friday 11am–9:30pm, Saturday 8am–9:30pm, Sunday 8am–9pm **Type of Bar:** Saloon **What to Drink:** Fine tequila on rocks or a Chile 'Rita **Why You Should Go:** The sheer history of the place, stand in the footsteps of western legends, like Billy the Kid, Ulysses S. Grant and others.

THE HISTORY

La Posta dates back to the 1840s when it was a freight and passenger service station known as the Corn Exchange. It was located on the Pinos Altos stagecoach line and was owned and operated by the Bean brothers. In the 1850s it became a critical stop for the Butterfield Overland Stagecoach and featured the Corn Exchange hotel, one of the finest hotels in the Southwest during the 1870s and 1880s.

The hotel hosted such guests as President Ulysses S. Grant, who according to the original guest book, never paid for his room, frontiersman and Indian fighter, Kit Carson, Mexican revolutionary Pancho Villa, and—while it cannot be confirmed—it is rumored that the notorious outlaw Billy the Kid was a guest at the hotel as well. In addition to the hotel, the complex hosted a fine dining restaurant, the cantina—at that time called the Bean Saloon (so named for the original owners)—a blacksmith shop, a mercantile, a stable and even a local school house.

In 1939 local entrepreneur and niece of the owner, Katy Griggs Camunez, purchased the saloon and restaurant portion from her cousin for "one dollar and love and affection." She set up a small dining room on the dirt floor and began cooking and selling regional Mexican food. The small enterprise grew into the large restaurant and cantina found today.

TODAY

Today La Posta is the only building left from the original Butterfield Overland Stagecoach route and through years of growth and acquisitions it has expanded to occupy the entire original Corn Exchange complex of over 10,000 square feet. Upon entering the complex you will find yourself greeted by exquisite southwestern décor, tropical birds and, due to a new legislative measure, some of the last remaining piranhas in New Mexico.

We recommend you take some time to walk around the restaurant and bar to get a feel for the place, being careful to not get lost in the expansive and confusing halls and rooms. A couple of things to look for are the old (and for the most part, original) ceilings and adobe brick walls, the original blacksmith shop with fireplace still installed, the Bean Saloon and the original La Posta restaurant that is located just off of the bar.

Once you've explored the building, retire to the Corn Exchange Cantina for drinks and atmosphere. Remember that in this small room you'd be drinking with some of the most legendary characters from the old west.

The crowd at La Posta is as diverse as its history. You'll find college students, professors, farmers, tourists, locals, politicians, artists, musicians and everything in between. As a matter of fact, during our visit New Mexico Governor Susana Martinez arrived to have a working lunch with some of the local business owners and community leaders (sadly, we weren't invited to include our input).

THE FOOD

La Posta features a mainly Southern New Mexican menu with food made from scratch, served hot, quickly and includes generous portions.

We highly recommend the spicy shrimp cocktail—more of a Bloody Mary than a traditional shrimp cocktail, especially when ordered with a side-shot of tequila (added to the cocktail, not drunk).

Another highly popular menu item is the tostada compustas, three corn tortillas fried and shaped into small cups and then filled with an assortment of chile, including their famous red chile meat (which they make in a very traditional manner from local chile pods).

Finally, we also suggest the fajitas brought sizzling to your table with all of the garnishes and trimmings.

THE DRINKS

The featured drink at the Corn Exchange Cantina is the Chile 'Rita, a twist on the traditional Margarita. It's made with fresh squeezed lime juice, Patron's orange liqueur, Hornitos tequila, house sweet and sour mix, and a blackberry habanero sauce called Besito Caliente.

It's the habanero sauce that makes this drink so different and tasty. The drink is sweet to be sure, but tempered of course with the tequila. The unique part comes at the end of a drink, when the heat from the sauce kind of slowly drizzles down your throat. It is a great twist on a traditional drink.

Now granted Ulysses S. Grant and Billy the Kid wouldn't have had Margaritas. However, considering the proximity to the border, they would have been drinking what used to be known as mescal wine or mescal brandy—now known as tequila. The cantina features over 100 tequilas, enough to find something for even the most distinguished tequila connoisseur. Try one in a glass neat or on the rocks and sip it while taking in the history.

NEARBY DISTRACTIONS

Mesilla Plaza—Website: www.oldmesilla.org/html/the_plaza.html, Located in the heart of Mesilla and mere feet from the door to La Posta is Mesilla Plaza, which was originally created by the concentration of the town's population for defense against Apache raiders. You will find the San Albino Basilica, founded in 1851, and a monument celebrating the consummation of the Gadsden Purchase that took place here in this very plaza in 1853. You'll also find that many of the same buildings and structures that were built here in the 1800s still exist, but feature gift shops, galleries and restaurants. No trip to Mesilla is complete without visiting the Plaza.

Trinity Site—Website: www.wsmr.army.mil/PAO/Trinity, Visit website for directions to site (575) 678-1134 (open twice a year to visitors). The Trinity Site is where the first atomic bomb was tested during the early morning hours of July 16th, 1945. The event and the discovery of the atomic explosion led to a quick end of World War 2, a new age in electric production and a terrifying dynamic with Russia during the Cold War. Though it's a lengthy three-hour drive from La Posta and only open to the public two times per year, a visit here is a glimpse into America's scientific ingenuity and a world-altering discovery. Definitely worth the time if you're here when it's open.

EL PATIO, MESILLA, NM

Address: 2171 Calle De Parian, Mesilla, NM, 88046, (575) 526-9943
Video tour: http://youtu.be/vUSXiqApHYA
Food: No **Live Music:** Yes **Type of Bar:** Dive **Hours:** Monday–Thursday 4pm–2am, Friday–Saturday 2pm–2am, Sunday 12pm–12am **What Type to Drink:** Cheapest beer they have, preferably PBR **Why You Should Go:** Housed in a building from 1870 that's seen Billy the Kid through it, great Southwestern history, and is the quintessential dive bar.

THE HISTORY

Albert J. Fountain was a Colonel in the Union Army during the Civil War. Originally from San Francisco, he moved to Mesilla, New Mexico, after the war to run a newspaper and law office. He opened shop in an adobe building on the corner of Calle de Parian and Calle Princessa. In January of 1896, Fountain and his youngest son Henry traveled to Lincoln County, New Mexico to assist in the prosecution of a suspected cattle rustler. On Feb. 1st, 1896, they loaded their horse drawn carriage for the day's trip back to Mesilla. They were never seen or heard from again and the only things found were the horses, the carriage, shell casings and two pools of blood. They had just vanished.

Fast forward to 1934 and the Fountain family had maintained ownership of the building now housing El Patio. At that time a young Art Fountain was an up and coming engineering student at nearby New Mexico A&M (New Mexico State University today). While discussing his plans for the future with one of his professors, he was discouraged from pursuing a career in engineering due to his Hispanic heritage. Art took this rather racist advice and on the heels of Prohibition opened El Patio Bar in 1934.

From 1934 until today the bar has been owned and operated by the Fountain family while being passed on from father to son. The bar has always been a hot spot for local, national and international bands, and during the last 77 years it's hosted more than its fair share of celebrities, surprising given the bar's location in a small and out-of-the-way town. According to the current owner, celebrities like James Earl Jones, the Blues Brothers, and even Clint Eastwood have stopped by.

TODAY

Today El Patio can be described in two words: Dive Bar. The dark interior is a hodgepodge of mismatched tables, chairs, southwestern murals, mounted deer heads and even the quintessential Christmas-tree lights. The building itself, well over 125 years old, is authentic southwestern architecture and just seeing the exposed mud bricks is worth the stop.

There's a small stage that still features an assembly of bands that run the gamut from punk to ska and country. The crowd is similarly varied, with university professors, artists, students and professionals mixing it up together. The staff is no-nonsense and typically harried by the large crowds that can pour in on weekend nights.

Day or night though it is a great place to step into, breathe in that dive bar smell, enjoy a cold beer, check out the dozens of photos of all the great talent that has come through and catch some great bands. If you happen to run into Al Fountain, offer to buy him a beer and invite him to sit down; he has some great stories to tell about the history of the bar, the history of the town and most interestingly the history of Billy the Kid (who in his time would have walked through this building).

THE DRINKS

As with a lot of other dive bars, El Patio isn't really known for their specialty in a particular alcohol or mixed drink. They do have a full bar and some talented bartenders, but then again the place also serves a big college crowd. In other words think simple, like a beer and a shot over martinis or more sophisticated drinks.

Their beer selection also isn't that extensive, but it is cheap. Go with whatever is on special, or if nothing is on special then just go with the cheapest beer they have. It will be a fitting tribute to both the great history of the building and to the dive bar of dive bars that now resides there.

NEARBY DISTRACTIONS

White Sands National Monument—Website: www.nps.gov/whsa **Address:** 19955 US 70 Alamogordo, NM, 88310, (575) 479-6124 (operating hours vary and unexpected closures due to missile testing are to be expected, call or visit website) About an hour's drive east of Mesilla is the White Sands National Monument. Featuring over 275 square miles of white sand dunes, it's the world's largest gypsum dune field. It is also the last place that Colonel Albert J. Fountain (a onetime Billy the Kid lawyer and relative of El Patio's founder) and his eight-year-old son disappeared and are assumed murdered though the bodies were never recovered. White Sands is a fun and interesting place to visit, and if you can time your visit on a full moon night it's a once-in-a-lifetime experience watching the moon rise over the mountains and reflect off the white sand.

Gadsden Museum—Address: 1875 Boutz Rd. Mesilla, NM, 88046, (575) 526-6293 (operating hours vary, call ahead for hours or an appointment). Less than a five-minute walk from El Patio is the Gadsden Museum. Run by a descendant of Colonel Albert J. Fountain, it's described as "a charming trip back to the history of southern New Mexico and the Mesilla Valley." Be sure to call ahead to find out the hours or set an appointment as there are no official hours and no website.

Fountain Theatre—Website: www.mesillavalleyfilm.org **Address:** 2469 Calle De Guadalupe Mesilla, NM, 88005, (575) 524-8287 (screening daily at 7:30pm with matinees at 1:30pm on Saturday and 2:30pm on Sunday). Located literally around the corner from El Patio is The Fountain Theatre. Built in 1905 on the site of a Confederate Army barracks, it is New Mexico's oldest continuously running movie house and originally featured both cinema and vaudeville performances. Today it includes alternative, foreign and independent films and features geared towards seasonal cult classics like Rosemary's Baby close to Halloween. Check the schedule before you arrive and you may be able to view one of your favorite classic movies on the big screen.

EL PASO'S HISTORIC BARS

Pershing Inn—Website: www.pershinginn.com **Address:** 2909 Pershing Drive El Paso, TX, 79903, (915) 566-1331 (Monday–Sunday 12pm–2am). Opened in 1949 this bar claims to have one of the first and oldest liquor licenses in El Paso, Texas. We have no idea how that's possible, considering the bar that turned into Rosa's Cantina had been there since the early 40s, but nevertheless. The place is a well-loved dive bar, filled with locals and not many tourists or visitors. Their drinks range from specialty margaritas to their take on classic cocktails. Be safe, go with beer.

Aceitunas Beer Garden—Website: www.aceitunasbeergarden.com **Address:** 5200 Doniphan Drive El Paso, TX, 79932, (915) 845-2277 (Tuesday– Thursday, Saturday 4pm–2am, Friday 3pm–2am). It's kind of hard to think of an authentic beer garden in this dusty border city, but Aceitunas fits the bill perfectly. Featuring koi ponds, streams and tons of character, this El Paso staple has been serving the community for over 30 years. Their shtick is to be a beer garden, so expect loads of flowing beer, but they also feature a full bar (many of them in fact) so you'll be fine going for the Jagermeister instead of the PBR (assuming you are either a hipster or fraternity member).

Palacio Bar—Address: 2600 Avenida De Mesilla Ave, Mesilla, NM, 88046, (575) 525-2910 (Monday, 4pm–12am, Tuesday, 1pm–12am, Wednesday– Sunday 12pm–12am). In 1936, the building that currently houses Palacio's was a blacksmith shop owned by Pablo Salcido and his father. Then one day, Pablo's wife decided to have a dance and invite all of the locals from the nearby village of Mesilla, New Mexico. The success was so overwhelming they dropped the blacksmithing idea and opened a bar and dance hall. Today Palacio's is an important landmark of the community. During the day it's a quiet local's bar, and at night hosts live bands of all kinds. They serve cheap beers and strong pours. If you're in the area, this is definitely a worthwhile stop.

Chope's—Address: 16145 NM-28, La Mesa, NM, 88044, (575) 233-3420 (Tuesday–Saturday, 11:30am–8:30pm) The restaurant, Chope's, was founded by Longina Benavides in 1915 as a small, local Mexican restaurant that fed the locals. After prohibition they decided to open a small bar in the same building as the restaurant, which also happened to be the family's house. Longina's son, Chope, was a bit concerned, because the room that his three daughter's shared was behind the wall of the bar (where men liked to have "colorful" discussions). So, in the early 1940s Chope built a new, square building about 30 feet from the restaurant and placed the bar there. Today this bar is a favorite stop for locals and visitors. The beer is cheap and the margaritas are cold. Be sure to try the food while you're here.

HONOLULU, HI

When Captain Cook sailed past the small island of Oahu almost 250 years ago, he never could have imagined the metropolis that would slowly emerge like a volcano rising above the Pacific. The small region the king settled is today lined with mirrored high-rise hotels and condos, shops with the most luxe brands in the world, amazing, 5-star restaurants, and dozens of great bars. But we're not really going to talk about those places

Honolulu has a long bar history, and not all of it's good. Since the 19th century, the place has been thick with saloons and dives, opium dens, and brothels. At first, they opened to cater to the many sailors and migrant workers in the sugar plantations. But as the US military began placing its warships and bases here, the focus on clientele shifted to members of the US Marines and Navy. They were despised by some and loved by others, but entrepreneurs got wise and opened even more bars just to cater to them.

The booze and drinks here are also pretty special. Up until the end of World War 2, Hawaii was known for its native moonshine, Okolehao. This stuff is made from the root of the ti plant, which is native to the South Pacific (but brought to Hawaii by its original settlers about 300 AD). The ti plant root was first fermented by Captain Cook's crew back in 1778 to prevent scurvy. Then it took a wily escapee from the Australian penal colony to distill that "beer" into moonshine, and Hawaii has been soaked through with it ever since. The taste is one you'll never forget—earthy, funky, organic (made us think of what an earth worm might taste like).

Then there are the mixed drinks. This isn't a place you go to order an Old Fashioned or a Manhattan. The drinks here are colorful and adorned with fruit and tiny umbrellas. Surprisingly the most popular of those drinks—the Mai Tai—was actually invented in California in the 1930s, but you can find it everywhere now. There were plenty that were invented here though, like the Blue Hawaiian and the Tropic Itch. If you want authentic, you'll want to drink these.

Finally, we can't forget the beer scene. Hawaii used to be ruled by a single brewery, Primo. It was a beer not unlike the lagers found throughout the United States in the early 20th century. It was thin and a bit tasteless, but it was homegrown, and many identified it with Hawaii. Primo still exists, brewed as more of a throwback vintage, but tourists and locals alike are getting more of a taste for something a bit better. Like any other large city in the country, this place has its share of local craft breweries, like Waikiki Brewing Company, Honolulu Beerworks, and Aloha Beer Company to name a few. You'll find these on tap or in bottles or cans in most of the places you drink at, so be sure to order local.

There's a lot to Honolulu that most people don't ever see because they never get past Waikiki. But once you put all that mirrored glass in your rearview, you find a different side of paradise.

SMITH'S UNION BAR, HONOLULU, HI

Address: 19 N Hotel St., Honolulu, HI, 96817, (808) 538-9145
Video Tour: https://youtu.be/DEI2Yzb3QOY
Food: No **Live Music:** No **Hours:** Monday–Sunday 8am–2am **Type of Bar:** Dive **What to Drink:** Smith's Union Bar Cinderella Liberty Blonde or Hotel Street Pale Ale **Why You Should Go:** Oldest bar in the Hawaiian Islands, a throwback to when this section of Honolulu was the red-light district of the city, and most importantly the bar that the crew of the USS Arizona hung out at.

THE HISTORY

In the 1930s, Hotel Street in Honolulu was a really fun place (well, from our point of view). It was filled with opium dens, brothels, gambling halls, and bars. It was a favorite hangout of all sorts of unsavory people, from Chinese drug lords and gangs, to heavy-handed pimps and madams. And all of them had an interest in controlling a bigger share in what they did. Or, if not, they were at least quite interested in saving what they had. This was the red-light district in Honolulu, Hawaii, and it was every bit as exotic and dangerous as the Charlie Chan mysteries of the 1920s and 1930s tended to show.

It was in this environment that a tiny bar opened called the Seaman's Bar. In 1934, the name changed to Smith's Union Bar as a nod to the loyal patrons (smiths) who cashed their union checks here. According to the owner, the checks were often just applied to the customer's tabs, and a good time was then had by all.

What's interesting about this place is that it still exists. The red-light district, as you can imagine, was a pretty rough place for everyone. Stepping out of the light and into the shadows could cost you your life if someone decided your wallet was worth more. And there are dozens of stories of different bars, gambling halls and brothels "suspiciously" burning down. Even a moment's consideration will tell you it was probably a rival gang that did it. But Smith's miraculously, escaped all this. But how?

We speculate it's because they really weren't that much of a threat to anyone. You see, Smith's is small. Really small. You walk into a long, thin room with a bar to the right, a few tables to the left, and that's it. There's no room for a gambling hall, or a brothel, much less an opium den—hell not even a 3-piece band could fit in here. All they could do, ever since the beginning, is serve booze and beer to the people who wandered in. But we think that's why they survived. After all, how much of a threat could they be to all the other places that lined this area? Smith's never burned down because it was just a simple bar.

Then, in 1939, Smith's got a whole new collection of patrons to serve: the crew of the USS Arizona. 1939 is when the Arizona, along with a number of other ships, was transferred to the Pacific Fleet. Sailors had always prowled the red-light district in the past, but now the US Navy wanted to make sure they weren't causing problems (or having problems caused on them), so they became stricter about the places they allowed their personnel to visit. Each ship, such as the USS Nevada or the USS Maryland, had a bar that they would visit—and they would only visit that bar.

For the crew of the ill-fated USS Arizona, the bar they claimed as their own was Smith's Union Bar. This was their hangout when they were away from their ship. Nights would be spent here swapping stories, getting into fights, and drinking lots and lots of alcohol. It was a wonderful, innocent time, but it was all wiped out in just a matter of hours on December 7, 1941.

Smith's Union Bar survived all this, though. They survived the crime of the red-light district. They survived World War 2. They survived post-war Hawaii when tourists flooded the place. And they've somehow survived the conversion of so many of Honolulu's historic buildings into shiny, new businesses. This place should be on every visitor's list of historically significant memorials to visit. Sure, it isn't a memorial recognized by the Feds, but it is a memorial nonetheless. It's a memorial to all those young men on the USS Arizona who had their lives cut short in the blink of an eye. If you go to the USS Arizona Memorial you'll learn all about how these guys died. But if you have a beer at Smith's Union Bar, you'll learn about how these guys lived.

TODAY

In 2013, Smith's Union Bar was bought by Dwight Lockwood, a veteran of the US Navy and Army who decided that life would be well spent owning a bar in paradise. When he bought the place—after patronizing it for a while—he said his first job was to strip the bar of all the Tiki and Polynesian kitsch the previous owner had put up and replace it with period pictures of Hawaii and the military personnel that roamed the island back in the day. He wanted to transform the place back into just a bar—the kind that would have been enjoyed by the sailors of the USS Arizona circa 1939.

Then, one December day, in wandered an elderly man named Laruen Bruner. Lauren was a Fire Controlman on the USS Arizona, and was calling in coordinates of the enemy when the ship took a direct hit to the magazine. When she was torn apart by the explosion, Lauren was thrown from his post into the water. Despite burns to over 70% of his body, he was able to swim to safety and then spent the next nine months in a hospital recovering. He was one of the few survivors of the USS Arizona, and to him, coming back to Smith's Union Bar after over 70 years was like coming home. After talking to Lauren and showing him around the old place, Dwight knew he'd made the right choice in restoring the bar back to its former glory.

When you enter the narrow room, you see a long bar off to your right. Behind it are the usual beer signs, liquor bottles and such. Also on the wall are relics of the past, like pictures of sailors from the bar's early days. The same is true on the left. As you scan the walls you'll notice numerous pictures of Lauren Bruner, Smith's oldest regular. You'll also see a chilling image of the USS Arizona just as she exploded, with an arrow pointing to part of the ship and a note scribbled in marker that says, "my battle station" followed by Lauren's signature. Don't miss these relics, as they do a better job of telling this old bar's story than we ever could.

The bar sees different crowds throughout the day: locals and regulars from opening until about four or five, then the professional crowds come by after getting off work to have a drink before heading to dinner or home, then later at night, in comes the younger crowd looking to down some shots or beers during a bar crawl. They're all welcome here, though. The patrons we met seemed friendly and warm, as were the bartenders serving the drinks. They were quick to laugh at each other's jokes or poke fun at a regular.

The historical significance of this place cannot be overstated. It's every bit as important as any other historical marker that tells the story of what happened when Pearl Harbor was attacked. The difference, though, is that this place is still doing what it was doing when the attack came.

THE DRINKS

This is a shot and a beer place. They can make the classics for you—the Old Fashioned, the Rum and Coke, or Vodka and Tonic—but this isn't a cocktail lounge, so keep it simple. One thing we do recommend you order is one of the beers that Smith's itself is making: Hotel Street Pale Ale and Cinderella Liberty Blonde. The beer-names themselves have some significance. The Hotel Street Pale Ale is pretty easy to figure out considering the bar is on Hotel Street (which was thick with bars when the place opened in the early 1930s). But what about the other? A "Cinderella Liberty" is what they called a shore pass that allowed a sailor to go ashore from his ship (a liberty), but which ended at midnight (just like Cinderella's party ended at midnight). Funds from the sales of these beers also go the Lauren Bruner USS Arizona

Memorial Fund to keep alive the memory of the men who died that day. Have one…or ten, and toast Lauren and his brethren.

NEARBY DISTRACTIONS

Chinatown—Since you're at Smith's, you need only walk out the door to find one of the best cultural treasures of the city: Chinatown! Bordered by Beretania Street, Nuuanu Stream, Nuuanu Avenue, and Honolulu Harbor, this 36-acre area is recognized as the oldest Chinatown in the United States (formally established in the late 1800s). The place at one time harbored silk shops, Chinese grocers and produce stands, but also brothels and opium dens. This was the setting for the Charlie Chan films of the 1920s and 1930s, when the intrepid detective would chase ne'er do wells through the dark back allies and speakeasies. There are amazing, traditional eateries around every corner. Dim sum, noodle shops and other dishes are only steps away. You'll also find where most of the cities leis are made, and you can pick them up cheap. Definitely spend some time wandering around here.

Aloha Tower—Website: www.alohatower.com **Address:** 155 Ala Moana Blvd, Honolulu, HI, 96813, (Monday–Sunday 9am–5pm). Built in 1926, this historic lighthouse was usually the first thing that people would see of Hawaii as they steamed toward it by boat. Placed next to the pier where visitors would disembark their ships, Aloha Tower stood watch over hundreds of thousands of visitors through the years. Go to the top of the tower and you'll be treated with wonderful views of the ocean, the city and even the mountains. Take time to also stroll the pier and visit the shops and restaurants in the area. As a bonus, if you take bread or crackers, you can feed a myriad of tropical fish at the marina just to the east of the tower.

Iolani Palace—Website: www.iolanipalace.org **Address:** 364 S King St, Honolulu, HI, 96813, (808) 522-0822 (Monday–Saturday 9am–4pm). The history of the Kingdom of Hawaii and the United States is complex, and sometimes not very pretty. Nowhere is that more on display than in the palace of the last royal monarchs of the Hawaiian Islands, Iolani Palace. The only royal palace in the US, Iolani was home to David Kalākaua, the much-beloved world traveling Hawaiian monarch who ruled from 1874 until his death in 1891. Featuring beautiful craftsmanship and architectural features seen nowhere else in the world, this stately palace is open to visitor and tour groups. Here you get to see how the royalty of the islands lived during the latter part of the 19th century. However, you also get to learn about the overthrow of the sovereign Hawaiian government and the imprisonment of the last monarch of the islands. This place will make you think, and is so worth seeing. Book ahead of time to ensure you're able to tour the place.

TROPICS BAR & GRILL, HONOLULU, HI

Address: 2005 Kalia Rd., Honolulu, HI, 96815, (808) 949-4321
Website: www.hiltonhawaiianvillage.com/dining/tropics-bar-and-grill **Video tour:** https://youtu.be/27tu365s5As
Food: Yes **Live Music:** No **Hours:** Monday–Sunday 7am–10:30pm **Type of Bar:** Tiki **What to Drink:** Blue Hawaii or Tropical Itch **Why You Should Go:** Oldest bar on Waikiki and part of the original Hawaiian Village Hotel and Resort that started the building boom along the beach.

THE HISTORY

Henry J. Kaiser was one of the most enterprising men in American history. He oversaw the construction of the Hoover Dam. His shipyards built Liberty Ships during World War 2. He organized the Kaiser Permanente healthcare system, and he even founded an automobile company. In the early 1950s, though, he set his eyes on paradise.

In 1954, Kaiser, in partnership with a developer, built the Hawaiian Village Hotel out of almost 20 acres on Waikiki Beach. The hotel featured 70 rooms and three swimming pools along with a private lagoon. It was constructed and decorated with Polynesian touches, including bamboo and a thatched roof. The idea of the "Village" was to provide Hawaii to the guests while they were at the hotel so they never really had to leave. Everything they could do on the island was provided here for them instead. They could take in a hula show, a concert or a luau. They could go surfing and play all day on the beach, or they could dine at fine restaurants and go shopping. Kaiser provided it all.

Also in the Hawaiian Village Hotel, located steps from the beach, was a small cocktail lounge called the Tropics Bar. In here, guests could relax after a day in the sun and sip tropical drinks while listening to a live band. With the breeze blowing in off the Pacific and the palm tree swaying just outside, the

111

place must have seemed like heaven to the wealthy tourists that started flocking here after the hotel opened.

When the bar opened in 1955, Kaiser hired a young bartender named Harry Yee. Harry was a prodigy behind the bar. He was quick, both in filling a glass and with his wit, always drawing a laugh from the patrons. His customers loved him and he was quite popular, a favorite, in fact. And, even more important, he had a great imagination. He could come up with new and interesting drinks on the spot when his customers wanted something special or different.

The Banana Daiquiri was invented by Harry, and so was the Tropical Itch, a fruity cocktail that uses a bamboo back scratcher as the swizzle stick.

But he's best known for something he made as a favor.

One of the liquor distributors they bought from asked Harry if he could come up with something using his company's signature Blue Curaçao liqueur. Harry mixed the Curaçao with rum, pineapple juice and sweet and sour mix and served it up. To his delight, people loved it. Harry called his concoction, the Blue Hawaii. This drink is perhaps most identified with not only Hawaii, but also with the era of 1950s and 1960s Hawaiiana kitsch.

Oddly enough, it was in the Hawaiian Village that Elvis Presley stayed when he made his film, Blue Hawaii. They say there's no connection between the drink and the name of the movie, but we find it a bit hard to believe there'd be such a coincidence.

TODAY

Since its opening in 1955, the 70-room Hawaiian Village Hotel has slowly been replaced by the gargantuan Hilton Hawaiian Village. This is one of the largest hotels in the world (the 15th largest, in fact) and the largest in Hilton's portfolio. The 70 rooms have multiplied into over 3800, and the multiple buildings take up a full 22 acres with the largest swimming pool in Waikiki, 22 restaurants, a museum, shops, exotic animals and botanic gardens.

The original Tropics Bar was closed somewhere along the way, but was remodeled and reopened in 1985 at the same site. For all intents and purposes this is the same location and the same bar. However, it's far from the same place.

Instead of a Tiki lounge atmosphere complete with hula dancing and live shows, guests now find a long, u-shaped bar and tables strewn throughout. The décor isn't kitschy, but a bit upscale while staying true to its tropical theme. The place is elegant throughout, and also acts as a restaurant with Hawaiian-style plates and a lot of seafood. There's great seating outside either in front of the place or to the side, next to the beach and ocean. The views from this part of the bar are spectacular as you look over the Pacific and watch the sunset.

The bar itself is fast paced and features a thick book of tropical cocktails. Of course, at the center of these drinks are the concoctions that Harry Yee came up with over 60 years ago.

Getting a table isn't difficult, as the place has a lot of seating, and it's easy to come across an empty table when you want one. It's also easy to find an empty seat at the bar simply because it's so big. Once you settle in, the bartenders are on you promptly, and they're happy to answer any questions you might have about the different drinks they whip up here.

The crowd is pretty diverse, but there's really nobody here who isn't a tourist—locals usually drink elsewhere. If you're a bar aficionado or looking to connect with the Hawaii of your grandparents, this is the place to do it at.

THE FOOD

This is a Hilton, so you're not going to find many bargains here. However, if you're here for lunch we highly recommend the Loco Moco. This is a hamburger patty resting on steamed white rice, and then covered with two eggs and brown mushroom gravy. We know it sounds funky, but this is a traditional working man's meal that's been around for decades. If you get out of Waikiki, you'll see this on the menu of just about every café on the island, but if you're not going to go to those then you might as well try it here.

THE DRINKS

They pride themselves on their tropical drinks and are making them about as fast as they can for thirsty tourists. But if you make it here, you definitely have to try one of the Harry Yee originals. The two most popular are the Tropical Itch (complete with back scratcher) or the Blue Hawaii.

NEARBY DISTRACTIONS

Hawaiian Parasail—Website: www.hawaiianparasail.com **Address:** 1651 Ala Moana Blvd #600b, Honolulu, HI, 96815, (808) 591-1280 (Monday–Sunday 8am–6pm). This is probably something you need to do before you hit the bottle at Tropics Bar and Grill. Hawaiian Parasail is located only about a quarter mile from the bar, so you won't have to exercise too much for this distraction. Towed behind a boat just off Waikiki Beach this might be the absolute best way to see the skyline of Honolulu, Waikiki Beach and Diamond Head. Reservations are needed in advance.

Fort DeRussy United States Army Museum—Website: www.hiarmymuseumsoc.org **Address:** 2131 Kalia Rd, Honolulu, HI, 96815, (808) 955-9552 (Tuesday–Saturday 10am–5pm). The history of the military in Hawaii is a long and complicated one, and this museum, just off Waikiki Beach and about 1/2 mile away from Tropics Bar and Grill might provide a different perspective. The museum is housed in an old coastal artillery bunker first built to defend the Hawaiian coast. Exhibits include a history of warfare in early Hawaii, European warfare of the 18th century, and then the US military's presence through the 20th century.

Waikiki Gun Club—Website: www.hawaiigunclub.com **Address:** 2142 Kalakaua Ave, Honolulu, HI, 96815, (808) 922-6442 (Monday–Saturday 10am–11:15pm, Sunday 12pm–11:15pm). If you've ever wanted to shoot some of the world's most notorious and famous guns, you can do it here, just a few blocks from Waikiki Beach. The Waikiki Gun Club is an indoor shooting range that allows you to fire off rounds on everything from AK-47s to AR-15s to even a .50 caliber. Again, something you want to do before visiting the bars.

HONOLULU'S HISTORIC BARS

La Mariana Sailing Club—Website: www.lamarianasailingclub.com **Address:** 50 Sand Island Access Rd, Honolulu, HI, 96819, (Monday–Sunday 11am–9pm). Built in its original location in 1957, this is the oldest Tiki bar in Hawaii (and arguably one of the oldest in the United States). It was built originally as a small marina for locals but quickly became a popular destination for drinks and dinner after a day of sailing. Eventually they were forced to move to their current location, but luckily, they were able to haul everything with them—the décor, the bar, everything. There aren't many old Tiki bars left in this world, so when you come across one, you definitely need to savor it. Sure, there are a few that are older than the La Mariana Sailing Club, but none of them are located in Hawaii, which is pretty much what all the others are trying to recreate. Here you find hand-carved Tikis and Koa wood tables (if you aren't familiar with Koa wood, this is a Hawaiian-native wood that is both very expensive and very rare). You also find all the requisite tropical drinks, complete with pineapple and little umbrella. Come here for a true taste of old-school Hawaii, and perhaps the most authentic Tiki experience you'll ever have.

Café Anasia—Address: 2227 S Beretania St, Honolulu, HI, 96826, (Monday-Sunday, 2pm-2am). There's a reason this place is so loved by locals, students and late-night revelers. After all, with from-scratch Vietnamese cuisine alongside sports on the TV, pool tables, darts (the real darts), and lots of beer and booze, how can you possibly go wrong? This locals' dive is great for just relaxing and getting some grinds while catching a game. It looks a bit intimidating, but it's perfectly safe. The drinks are cheap, as is the food, which is authentic and filling. Be forewarned, the parking situation is miserable, so if you go after business hours, find a stall in a nearby place that's closed for the evening.

Anna O'Brien's—Address: 2440 S Beretania St, Honolulu, HI, 96826, (Monday–Friday 2pm–2am, Saturday 10am–2am, Sunday 10am–12am). Formerly known as Anna Banana's, this dive has been, and is still, the veritable college hangout for students and locals alike since the late 1960s. It was remodeled into an Irish pub-like bar over the last few years, but still retained its college-dive atmosphere. They feature Irish whiskey specials as a bonus, so that's good. They also have live music upstairs as well as pool, but then offer a place to relax and chill downstairs. All in all, it seems to work and is still a popular college nightspot even after it's Irish transition.

LAS VEGAS, NV

Really, are there any other cities that come to your mind when you think of having a good time, of drinking your cares away, of relaxing on the other side of a bar from a friendly bartender happy to serve you drinks and listen to your banter? If the answer is "yes, any city *but* Las Vegas," then you're a lot like us.

The truth is, Las Vegas is a terrible bar city. Sure, it has all the nightclubs and lounges you could want, but bars are a different story.

You wouldn't think so, would you? At one time Las Vegas was flush with great places to drink, meet friends and enjoy company. But, all of these places drifted away in favor of other, more trendy spots.

In fact, one of the coolest places in about a 50-mile radius closed up in early 2011. Atomic Liquors, with its famous neon and kitschy décor, started when Las Vegas was exploiting the nearby H-bomb tests, and remained unchanged for over 50 years. Luckily some loyal patrons re-opened it in 2013 and today it is doing great, but we almost lost it!

Simply put, traditional bars aren't flashy. They don't pull in the money like the $500 bottle-service places do. The celebrities don't go to bars when they go to Vegas, they go to nightclubs. That's where the money is.

And, just to be clear, we did cover one nightclub in this book—Mother's in Chicago—but that place hasn't changed in over 40 years. In Las Vegas? They change the décor, the music, the whole environment like a Kardashian changes her wardrobe.

And for those places that aren't nightclubs, that are actual lounges or bars, most all of them are attached to the casino, and hopes of conversation and peace are usually dashed quicker than our streaks at the blackjack table.

True bar aficionados find a tough time going to Sin City. Where can they go to escape Las Vegas itself (for, that's what a bar is after all, an escape)? Aside from jumping on the next plane and heading home, there are still a couple of options.

ATOMIC LIQUORS, LAS VEGAS, NV

Address: 917 Freemont St., Las Vegas, NV, 89101, (702) 982-3000
Website: www.atomic.vegas **Video Tour:** https://youtu.be/N_MgrS85lzI
Food: Next door. **Live Music:** No **Hours:** Monday–Wednesday 4pm–2am,
Thursday 2pm–3am, Friday 2pm–4am, Saturday 12pm–4am, Sunday 12pm–
2am **Type of Bar:** Dive **What to Drink:** Atomic Cocktail **Why You Should
Go:** The oldest freestanding bar in Las Vegas, home to the Rat Pack and
many other notable celebrities of the 50s and 60s.

THE HISTORY

   Founded when the Las Vegas we all know and love was in its infancy, and
withstanding the philosophy that anything older than five years old is too old,
Las Vegas' oldest free standing bar is a testament to a time long gone, but
(thankfully) forgotten no longer. Joe and Stella Sobchik originally opened
Atomic Liquors in 1945 as "Virginia's Café." It was at the end of World War
II and they quickly realized two things: rationing during the war limited their
access to quality and diverse food items, and Joe would rather make cocktails
than food. So, they began transitioning into more of a bar, and less of a café.

   And while this transformation was taking place, a nuclear testing site was
being built by the United States Army a mere 50 miles away. In this age of
innocence, it quickly became vogue to, on nights when the wind was just
right, grab an "Atomic Cocktail" and climb a ladder to the café's roof to
watch mushroom clouds on the horizon.

   Joe and Stella finally made the official switch from Virginia's Café to
Atomic Liquors in 1952, renaming it in honor of both the atomic testing

down the road, and the Atomic Cocktails Joe was known for making. They erected the beautiful sign that stands on Freemont Street not long thereafter.

Because of its geographic location-a short walk from the strip of popular casinos on Fremont Street (popular for the day)-Atomic Liquors quickly became a local's spot. Cocktail waitresses, dealers, pit bosses and casino performers would make their way to the bar after their shifts were over. Because it was away from the crowds of the casinos, celebrities were often spotted. Regulars included Barbara Streisand (she has an honorary stool there today), the Smothers Brothers, Frank Sinatra, Sammy Davis Jr., and Dean Martin (The Rat Pack). It's even rumored that Jimmy Hoffa was known to drop in from time to time (in fact, he may still be there).

Atomic Liquors was the essence of Vegas in the golden days of the 1950s and '60s. From the Atomic testing just up the road, the celebrity patrons of the day, casino workers, mobsters and law enforcement officers, it represented Vegas as it was: a melting pot of talent, dreams, criminals and the everyday working stiff.

But, then in the 1980s and '90s, the bar fell victim to the downturn of Fremont Street, the downturn in the economy, and general urban decay as vagrants replaced the stars and casino workers, and Atomic Liquors went from the "go-to" bar, to the bar to avoid.

TODAY

By 2011 Joe and Stella had both passed away, and the little bar the Rat Pack once enjoyed closed for good. Luckily though, it was purchased by a group of local businessmen who couldn't bear to see it close. They immediately set to restoring the gem, spending a significant amount of time, effort and money restoring this iconic bar to her previous glory. Atomic Liquors now features a remodeled but classic interior, a cocktail menu with a mix of both new and period cocktails, and a nod to her history and notoriety at every turn— including the rolling video of mushroom clouds above the urinals in the men's room (didn't check the women's rooms).

The location of Atomic Liquor's might discourage some from going. It's nowhere near the Strip, and it's even an intimidating distance from the relative safety of the madhouse that is the Freemont Street Experience, but it's worth the cost of the Uber to go. Sure, in the bars along Las Vegas Boulevard you might spot someone famous. No doubt if you hit one of the nightclubs there, you'll be drinking in a place where celebrities probably hang out. But you won't be drinking where the legends drank.

To sit at the bar that once hosted the Rat Pack, that once hosted mobsters and other *really* famous people is something entirely different. These are people in the history books. The others are people on the covers of those bargain-bin DVDs you find at Walmart. This bar is also one of the last bastions of history you'll find in Sin City, a city that gives itself a facelift every ten years or so.

So the next time you visit the Strip, get off the Strip as fast as you can, catch a cab or request an Uber and tell the driver to take you to Atomic Liquors on Freemont Street. Then spend a night soaking up the history of the city's past.

THE DRINKS

Ah, where to start! The bar serves old fashioned cocktails, the type that Sinatra's cronies would have ordered. We suggest, though, in honor of the place and of Joe and Stella, you order an Atomic Cocktail. If that doesn't suit your fancy, then try a Hunter S. Mash, named after Hunter S. Thompson who reportedly also graced the bar with his presence (and it's made with Old Crow, his favorite whiskey).

NEARBY DISTRACTIONS

El Cortez Hotel and Casino—Website: www.elcortezhotelcasino.com **Address:** 600 Fremont St, Las Vegas, NV, 89101, (702) 385-5200. This place was opened in 1941 and was, at the time, considered too far downtown to make any money. The owner, Marion Hicks and J.C. Grayson proved the naysayers wrong, however, as the place was so profitable that gangsters Bugsy Siegel, Meyer Lansky, Gus Greenbaum, and Moe Sedway paid them well over double what they had into it in 1945. This place really represents the segue into Las Vegas by the mob, and soon the profit from this place would lead Siegel to open the Flamingo, the first casino/resort on what's now the Las Vegas strip. To be honest the El Cortez used to be a dump, but recently went through a complete renovation, and is now not nearly as stinky. To soak in the original Las Vegas, perhaps the oldest in the city, come by here and have a beer at one of the handful of bars.

The Mob Museum—Website: www.themobmuseum.org, **Address:** 300 Stewart Ave, Las Vegas, NV, 89101, (702) 229-2734 (Sunday–Wednesday 9am–10pm, Thursday–Saturday 9am–12am). The mob has deep ties to Sin City, and some would say that when they were running things, the place was a lot more fun (corporations, we've been told, have taken the soul out of the town). The Mob Museum shines a light on the complicated relationship between the casino industry and organized crime through the decades. This museum, only a few blocks off Fremont, features great exhibits and an authentic view of Las Vegas when it was the crime families calling the shots.

SlotZilla Zip Line—Website: vegasexperience.com/slotzilla-zip-line **Address:** 425 Fremont St #160, Las Vegas, NV, 89101, (702) 678-5780 (Sunday–Thursday, 1pm–1am, Friday–Saturday, 1pm–2am). Glide above Freemont street, right underneath the lights of the Freemont Street experience. This has got to be one of the most fun activities you can do with your clothes on in the downtown area. The rush of zip lining over the heads of the cheering crowds below is not something you'll soon forget. For an even more thrilling rush, try it on your belly, Superman style, instead of in a harness. The prices aren't cheap, but it is most definitely a thrill. Make reservations in advance on line.

HARD HAT LOUNGE, LAS VEGAS, NV

Address: 1675 Industrial Rd., Las Vegas, NV, 89102, (702) 384-8987
Video Tour: https://youtu.be/SwCM5nsurUA
Food: Yes **Live Music:** Yes **Hours:** Open 24 hours **Type of Bar:** Dive/Lounge
What to Drink: Loaded coffee, mystery bag beer **Why You Should Go:** One
of the oldest bars in Vegas, surprisingly good food, Frank Bowers mural,
haunted

THE HISTORY

The Hard Hat Lounge was originally opened in 1958 as a simple restaurant.
But, after realizing there was more money to be made in the sale of alcohol, it
became a bar sometime in the early 60s (though rumors abound that alcohol
sales had been going on since the restaurant opened).

Shortly after opening, the bar became exceptionally popular with local
construction workers. The reason for this popularity can be traced to two
primary factors: you could wear your hard hat in the bar, and it was a
paycheck-cashing location. On the surface these factors may seem
insignificant, until you consider that wearing a hat indoors went against the
customary practice of removing your hat when inside a building during the
period (the bar did it to reduce the chance patrons would leave their hard hats
behind—an important and required piece of equipment on construction
sites). Secondly, you were given a free beer if you cashed your paycheck there,
which made it one of the most popular bars in the area on Friday nights. It
was this popularity with construction workers that eventually led to the
moniker, Hard Hat Lounge. It was also during these formative years that
noted painter, Frank Bowers, arrived to leave his mark on the storied lounge.

Frank Bowers was an artist known for two things: painting racy murals in bars, and painting said murals to pay off his bar tabs. Bowers arrived at the Hard Hat with his 4th wife, Vicki, and proceeded to exchange his services for room, board, and bar credit. The mural he and his wife painted is still present in the bar today, and is also the only Bowers painting known to be a "blacklight painting" (be sure to ask the bartender about it during your visit). The painting was completed in 1962 and Frank died in 1964, making it one of his last "bar works."

Throughout the following years, the Hard Hat remained a favorite of both the Las Vegas construction community and the city's residents. Through the ups and downs of the city, nation, and world, it's always kept its doors open, its prices cheap, and it's remained a welcome reprise from the glitz, glamor and heat located just outside the door. It's probably for those reasons that it became known as the bar that built Las Vegas.

TODAY

As you walk into the Hard Hat today you'll almost certainly feel like you have stepped into a local dive. It isn't overly dirty, smelly, or rundown, but instead simply has that divey feeling—dark, a little small, with cheap drinks, a well-worn bar, heavily used barstools, and an unpretentious atmosphere. None of this is really surprising when you consider it's been operating around the clock for over 60 years. Don't fret though, the place is welcoming, the bartenders friendly, the drinks priced well below the overinflated ones you'll find on the strip, the food good, and the classic Vegas pastime alive and well if you're willing to risk a few dollars in their video poker machines (gamble and you'll get free drinks).

The Hard Hat Lounge also sits in the shadow of the Las Vegas Strip, and about a half mile from Stratosphere hotel. It was recently acquired by local classic bar aficionado, Derek Stonebarger (who was also part of the team responsible for reopening Atomic Liquors). Derek, a self-declared history buff and bar lover, purchased the Hard Hat in the hopes of both returning the bar to its former glory, and to ensure it continues to operate for another 60 years.

The Hard Hat is the Yin to the Las Vegas Strip's Yang. Where the strip is loud, flashy, and geared towards tourists, the Hard Hat in many ways represents the exact opposite. It welcomes both tourists and locals equally, but it isn't looking to separate you from your money as quickly as possible. It has gambling, but it's an afterthought, not a focus. And, yes, it has alcohol, but not the whalebones or giant Eiffel Tower replicas you find on the strip. Its drinks are served in cans, bottles, and glassware. In short, the Hard Hat is where tourists should, and locals do go when they simply want a traditional bar in which to enjoy a few adult beverages, an interesting conversation, or a good laugh.

THE FOOD

The Hard Hat has a full-service kitchen that's currently hosting Sin City Soul Deli and Caribbean Barbeque. The must haves here are the Lobster Mac and Cheese and the Brisket Melt, both of which are exceptionally tasty. And while the kitchen isn't open around the clock, you'll always have a food option as the bartenders are more than happy to whip up a Southwest Chicken Tornado or some Fried Egg Rolls, just in case those late-night munchies roll around.

THE DRINKS

Since the Hard Hat has been a construction workers' bar since shortly after its opening, many of its drinks focus on coffee (who doesn't need a stiff cup of joe before heading in for the graveyard shift), and so a loaded coffee is a great start. Additionally, they have a mystery bag beer for the low price of $3.00. Just ask for it and you'll be served one of 16 possible beers.

NEARBY DISTRACTIONS

The Las Vegas Strip—We know, recommending something like the strip is a step out of our norm. But, if you've made the trip to Las Vegas and have yet to experience it, it's a must…at least once. The Strip is a 4.2 mile stretch of South Las Vegas Boulevard that is, ironically enough, not actually located in the city of Las Vegas (it's in the unincorporated towns of Paradise and Winchester). A short .6 miles from the Hard Hat, it's a crowded cacophony of electronic stimulation, bars, casinos, hotels, restaurants, and multiple channels of excess that have more ways to separate you from your money than just about any other place we've been. Give it a go, you might like it or you might hate it, but either way, it'll be memorable.

Stratosphere Tower Attractions—**Website:** www.stratospherehotel.com/Attractions **Address:** 2000 S. Las Vegas Blvd, Las Vegas, NV, 89104, (702) 380-7777, (Sunday–Thursday 10am–1am, Friday–Saturday 10am–2am). Just up the road from the Hard Hat, and easily viewable from the bar's parking lot, is the Stratosphere Casino and Hotel (a place we frequented during our poor college days). At the top of this unmistakable Vegas landmark are a few rides, like the Big Shot, Insanity, and Sky Jump, that are certain to appeal to the thrill-seeker or amusement park aficionado in your group.

Piero's Italian Cuisine—**Website:** www.pierocuisine.com **Address:** 355 Convention Center Drive, Las Vegas, NV, 89109, (702) 369-2305 (Daily 5:30pm–10pm). Less than 2 miles from the historic Hard Hat Lounge is Piero's Italian Cuisine, a piece of Las Vegas history. It was once a frequent hang out of the Rat Pack, and the linguine and clams hasn't changed since Frank Sinatra was a regular. It was even featured in the notorious Scorsese film, "Casino." The place has that often-copied-but-never-replicated historic Las Vegas feel, it's a perfect dinner-stop during your Vegas visit. Must-tries include the Linguine and Clams, Garbage Caesar, and Osso Bucco. We simply can't recommend this place enough if you're looking for that classic, Las Vegas dining experience.

PIONEER SALOON, GOODSPRINGS, NV

Address: 310 Spring Street, Goodsprings, NV, 89019, (702) 874-9362
Website: www.pioneersaloon.info **Video tour:**
http://youtu.be/zX0PimkvMSk
Food: Yes **Live Music:** No **Hours:** Monday–Thursday 9am–9pm, Friday–
Saturday 9am–10pm, Sunday 9am–9pm **Type of Bar:** Saloon **What to
Drink:** Shot and a beer **Why You Should Go:** The real history of the area
outside of Las Vegas, great bar with unusual gaming, and just to become a
full-fledged Asshole.

HISTORY

The Pioneer Saloon was founded in 1913 by entrepreneur George Fayle,
who came to Goodsprings, Nevada because of the boom it was experiencing
in the early 1900s. The boom reached its peak in 1910, with everything from
lead to zinc and copper being pulled out of the nearby hills.

After World War I, the price for these metals dropped because the demand
was simply no longer there. And so, like many towns in the Southwest,
Goodsprings just kind of faded away. Many of the buildings were actually
relocated to Southern California, and many others just sort of rusted into
nothing.

But when Fayle built his saloon to quench the thirst of the local miners, he
sought the help of a business that was actually commonly utilized in many of
the boom towns in the West: Sears and Roebuck, Inc.

Sears, in the early 1900s, sold just about anything you could think of
through its catalogs and that included buildings. In fact it would sell whole
houses, delivered to you on the railroad and then constructed at your

homestead. In this case though, Fayle purchased a tin building (actually, two of them, including the general store next door). The outside walls of the Pioneer Saloon are stamped tin to look like bricks, and the entire interior (except the floor) is also stamped tin.

You can imagine that with little humidity or wet weather the condition hasn't changed much since the day it was constructed.

And befitting its place in the West, the Pioneer has seen its share of rowdy nights. One such episode put a man—a cheater at cards—six feet under. Apparently the miner had been winning pretty regularly, so often so as to become irregular in fact. When the dealer called him on his streak the gambler lunged at him, prompting the dealer to stick a revolver in the gambler's face and tick off about three rounds. He died on the floor of the saloon. If you look on the wall towards the back of the bar you'll see the sun peeking through three, perfectly round bullet holes.

The Pioneer Saloon is also famous for being the place where the actor Clark Gable grieved over his wife's death after her airplane crashed into the mountain right behind the bar. He reportedly stayed in the place by himself, drinking for a full day and night while her body was being recovered.

TODAY

The Pioneer Saloon excels at being fun. From the Chicken Shit Bingo to their Asshole club, there isn't a thing about this place that isn't geared towards the smart-ass of the bar aficionados.

Maybe it's because they're so far away from the Strip they have to be as different as possible, or maybe it's just the result of 100 years in the hot sun. Whatever the cause the Pioneer Saloon couldn't be more different than the corporate blandness of the Las Vegas Strip.

When you visit, there are a few things you have to do. The first is to play the aforementioned Chicken Shit Bingo. Essentially the game involves placing a bet on one of many squares painted on the bottom of a small cage. Then a chicken is placed in the cage and whatever square the chicken shits on is the winner. Talk about a game of chance!

The second is to become an Asshole, a certificate certifying that status only costs five dollars. Once upon a time the small town council of Goodsprings was seeking toy donations for local charities. When they asked the mayor if he wanted to recruit the regulars of the Pioneer Saloon down the street, he replied that "they're just a bunch of assholes." The result was a huge toy drive by the regulars, and the tradition of calling themselves assholes—but with pride. Now, for a small sum you too can be sworn in as an Asshole (and your money still goes to helping out underprivileged kids).

Generally speaking, the place simply makes you feel welcome. At the same time it feels like being transported to the Wild West, when dealers still carried guns and popped off cheaters at their tables. And while you might spend an hour getting here, trust us, it's well worth it.

THE FOOD

In the next door General Store they have a kitchen that serves up basic pub grub: burger, fries and such. But, the really cool part about the place is the back patio lined with gas grills.

For no charge you can bring your own steak, burger, hot dogs or anything else you can imagine and grill your own food for free. Almost like bringing your own booze to a restaurant, but instead you're bringing the food to the booze joint.

So, on your way out of Las Vegas, stop by a grocery store and pick up a couple of steaks to throw on the grill and then enjoy them on the patio.

THE DRINKS

They don't really have a signature drink, though they have a full bar and make all the basics as expected.

It's probably best to stick to the basics, too, considering the history of this joint. Try the simple bottle of beer or (even better) a shot or two of a good American whiskey—something they would have been drinking at the table right *before* the gambler got caught and then, subsequently, plugged.

NEARBY DISTRACTIONS

Gold Strike Hotel & Gambling Hall—Website: www.stopatjean.com **Address:** 1 S. Main Street Jean, NV, 89019, (800) 634-1539 (Monday–Sunday 24hrs). The Gold Strike Hotel and Gambling Hall is only seven miles from the Pioneer Saloon and one of the few places out in this relatively desolate area. Featuring a hotel and full-service casino it is the perfect place to stop for the night if you have had a little too much to drink, are hungry or just have that gambling itch.

Sloan Canyon National Conservation Area—Website: www.blm.gov/nv, (for directions visit the BLM website). About 20 minutes from the Pioneer Saloon, and on the way into or out of Las Vegas, is the Sloan Canyon National Conservation Area. Featuring multiple hiking trails, the area's main attractions are its petroglyphs. Believed to have been created by native cultures there are over 300 rock art panels with 1,700 individual designs. A great stop to stretch your legs and enjoy a hike.

LAS VEGAS' HISTORIC BARS

Fireside Lounge at Peppermill Las Vegas—Website: http://www.peppermilllasvegas.com/ **Address:** 2985 South Las Vegas Boulevard Las Vegas, NV, 89109, (702) 735-4177 (Monday–Sunday 24hrs). If you were looking for a filming location to shoot the sleazy past of Las Vegas, this would probably be the first place you'd go. In fact, that's just what directors like Martin Scorsese have done. The place has graced the strip since 1972, and unlike most other places on the same street, they've refused to change. The décor is campy 1970s, which is cool now. The waitresses still wear dresses with slits up to their waists, which again are in style. In other words, this place didn't change, it just waited for the rest of the world to catch up to it. Have a Scorpion Bowl with a partner, and then take a cab to your hotel.

Decatur Tavern—Address: 4680 South Decatur Boulevard Las Vegas, NV, 89103, (702) 248-5332 (Monday–Sunday 24hrs). This is a local's bar, one of the last left in the city. It was founded in 1963, making it older than most anything else in the area—especially considering it hasn't had the face-lift that any of the others have had after being around longer than, say, ten years. A lot of the service-oriented professionals from the city come here when they get off, which means that this is the place to go on just about any given night. The specialty drink is cold beer, so be sure to order at least a couple and just enjoy what it must be like to live in the city everybody else in the world wants to travel to.

Four Mile Bar—Address: 3650 Boulder Highway Las Vegas, NV, 89121, (702) 431-6936 (Monday–Sunday 24hrs). Opened at some point in the '40s (memories seem to lapse when you ask precise questions), this dive well away from the strip is a combination Cheers and truck stop. It has one of the most loyal followings of regulars we've ever seen and their karaoke is legendary. The beer is phenomenally cold and the service is warm. All in all, this is the type of bar cities are built on.

Champagne's—Website: http://www.champagnescafe.vegas/ **Address:** 3557 S Maryland Pkwy, Las Vegas, NV, 89169, (702) 737-1699 (Monday-Sunday 24hrs). Known as Champagne's Café until 2016, when Bar Rescue changed the name to simply Champagne's, it originally opened in 1966 and was a known mobster and Rat Pack hangout. Don't let the name or history confuse you though, most of the mobsters no longer frequent the bar (although one is still known to make an appearance on occasion), food is no longer served, and it is nothing like the typical "champagne" room many of you are probably familiar with. Today it is a local and tourist favorite, known for its wallpaper (ask about it during your visit), karaoke, and drink specials.

LOS ANGELES, CA

You know, with such a large city, you'd expect an equally impressive history concerning the city's bars and the drinking in general. And in general, the City of Angels is one of the foremost cities to drink in—there's something for everyone here.

The city's history is tied to the rich Spanish heritage of the area. After all, the first brewery to be built in California was built under Spanish rule.

However, interestingly enough, not much remains of those earliest settlers, at least not where drinking spots are concerned. In L.A. we don't find the 150-year-old saloons like we do in the northern part of the state.

And, oddly enough, we also don't find any evidence of the Spanish linked to the city's bars either. There aren't any cantinas or old watering holes left.

But what we do find is a greatly diverse mix of 20th-century bars that run the gamut from speakeasy to Tiki bar to dive. Los Angeles has one of the best mixtures of bar types, even if they're not as old as what you'd find in perhaps New York or the Washington D.C. area.

If you're going to take the Bucket List Bar™ tour of L.A., take the whole thing. The different styles of bars, the history in and around them, and the different ages that each of them represent make this one of the best historic pub crawl in the book!

FROLIC ROOM, HOLLYWOOD, CA

Address: 6245 Hollywood Boulevard, Los Angeles, CA, 90028, (323) 462-5890
Video tour: http://youtu.be/a9jmCNiTDjQ
Food: No **Live Music:** No **Hours:** Monday–Sunday 11am–2am **Type of Bar:** Classic/Dive **What to Drink:** A martini or a PBR **Why You Should Go:** Last true bar on Hollywood Boulevard, celebrity sightings, and the Black Dahlia history.

THE HISTORY

There is no concrete evidence that we could find about how the Frolic Room got its start or its name, but the current owner, Robert L. Nunley, gave us his take on how it all started. With that information and a little digging on our own, we think we have come up with a little insight into the Frolic Room and its storied past.

In 1930 the Pantages Theatre was built to host live vaudeville performances as well as first-run movies. At the time of its construction, Prohibition was still in full swing and would be for another three years. As is evidenced by the still remaining stairs and a bricked-in entrance, the area that houses the Frolic Room today was at one time attached to the Pantages Theatre. Many believe this was the only door leading in or out of the Frolic Room. It's rumored that an individual by the name of Freddy Frolic was the host of the room, which he set up so actors, actresses, and distinguished guests would have a place to enjoy a cocktail or two after the show.

Much of this is speculation, but we do know the Frolic Room formally became a bar in 1934, and in 1949, Howard Hughes bought the attached

Pantages Theatre. Hughes moved his personal offices into the second floor and the theatre hosted the Academy Awards from 1949 until 1959. More rumors suggest Hughes hosted many private parties in the Frolic Room and we imagine the place saw more than its fair share of famous patrons during that time.

On the other side of all the glitz and glamour of the Frolic Room's past exists a darker and more twisted story. On January 15th, 1947, Elizabeth Short's body was found in the Leimert Park neighborhood, gruesomely mangled, disfigured and cut in half. Elizabeth would come known as the Black Dahlia and the Frolic Room was one of the last places she was ever seen alive. Her murder to this day remains unsolved, though plenty of speculation is provided in books and movies as to who is responsible for the disturbing act. One thing that has remained constant in all the speculation is that the Frolic Room was one of Elizabeth's favorite bars.

During the 1970s and 1980s the Frolic Room and the surrounding area became caught up in the seediness and decay that infected many of America's cities. The area was known more for pimps, hookers, the homeless, drug addicts, and dealers than today's array of restaurants, clubs and boutiques. But the Frolic Room resisted both decay and change as Los Angeles and Hollywood Boulevard evolved into the tourist destination it's become today.

TODAY

Located right in front of Gary Cooper's star on the Walk of Fame, the Frolic Room remains an iconic and original part of storied Hollywood Boulevard. The interior dates back to 1963 when the last remodel was completed. The Al Hirschfeld mural on the wall is likely the only one of its kind and is truly reminiscent of Hollywood's golden age. Befitting its classic status, the bartenders still wear vests and bow-ties, and the bar features a no-nonsense list of cheaply priced and stiffly prepared drinks (an all-time favorite is still the martini).

Gita Bull, longtime bartender at the Frolic Room, said that their crowd depends on what is playing at the theatre next door or at other shows nearby. But, she also told us that "you can be sitting next to a homeless person on one side and Kiefer (Sutherland) on the other."

It will get packed at night, especially during the weekend, oftentimes by those going to a show, but frequently by regulars. Those regulars, according to Gita, are more the hipster set. But don't let that detract from wanting to go; it's a piece of Hollywood history that's just too rare to miss.

THE DRINKS

They don't have a signature drink per se at the Frolic Room. They do have a full bar and the bartenders are pretty old-school, so they can mix up just about anything you want.

If you go for a mixed drink, make it something classic. We suggest a martini, just because it seems to go with the era this place is based in.

If you're looking for a beer then go with a PBR; you'll blend in with the skinny-jean-wearing crowd trying to get in the door.

NEARBY DISTRACTIONS

Hollywood Walk Of Fame—Website: www.walkoffame.com, Running east to west on Hollywood Boulevard from North Gower Street to North La Brea, the Hollywood Walk of Fame is 1.3 miles long. That stretch includes the sidewalk in front of the Frolic Room, making a visit to this historic landmark a requirement to get into the bar itself. However, a visit to the Frolic room isn't complete without spending some time walking Hollywood Boulevard viewing the shops, restaurants, interesting characters lining the street and, of course, the Walk of Fame.

Grauman's Chinese Theatre—Website: www.chinesetheatres.com **Address:** 6801 Hollywood Blvd. Hollywood, CA, 90028, (323) 461-3331 (open seven days a week for tours; call ahead as hours change; movie show times vary). Grauman's Chinese Theatre is an iconic landmark along Hollywood Boulevard and one that almost anyone would recognize though few could tell you its name. Opened in 1927, the theatre cost $2,000,000 to build and even today it is often considered the most lavish and sought-after theatre in Hollywood for studio premieres. It also features nearly 200 celebrity footprints and autographs scribed into the concrete at the theatre's entrance. Less than a mile from the Frolic Room, it's a must-see during your walk along Hollywood Boulevard.

Pantages Theater—Website: www.broadwayla.org **Address:** 6233 Hollywood Blvd. Los Angeles, CA, 90028, (323) 468-1770 (operating hours vary by show). Literally connected to the Frolic Room, the Pantages Theatre opened in 1930 and was built to host vaudeville performances and first-run movies. Throughout its years it's had multiple owners, including Howard Hughes, and even hosted the annual Academy Award ceremonies. Today it's one of L.A.'s leading venues for live performances and a great place to catch a show before, after, or in between visits to the Frolic Room.

Hollywood Bowl—Website: www.hollywoodbowl.com **Address:** 2301 North Highland Avenue Los Angeles, CA, 90068, (323) 850-2000, (operating hours vary by season and show). Built in 1919, the Hollywood Bowl is the world's largest natural amphitheater and has played host to a long list of world-famous symphonies, operas, ballets, presidential addresses and concerts. Today it continues the same tradition of summertime events enjoyed under a starlit sky with most people arriving early to enjoy a picnic with family and friends (you can bring your own picnic basket or even arrange to have one waiting for you). With ticket prices sometimes as low as $1, the Hollywood Bowl is definitely worth looking into during your trip to the area.

TOWNHOUSE (DEL MONTE SPEAKEASY), VENICE, CA

Address: 52 Windward Avenue, Venice, CA, 90291, (310) 392-4040
Website: www.townhousevenice.com **Video tour:**
http://youtu.be/7FrRpjtDrgA
Food: No **Live Music:** Yes **Hours:** Monday–Thursday 5pm–2am, Friday
2pm–2am, Saturday–Sunday 12pm–2am **Type of Bar:** Speakeasy **What to
Drink:** Manhattan **Why You Should Go:** The speakeasy downstairs, the
feeling of drinking in a 1920s saloon, and the craft cocktails.

THE HISTORY

Originally opened in 1915 by Italian immigrant Cesar Menotti, the
Townhouse is the oldest continuously operating bar in the Los Angeles area.
At the time of its opening it was called Menotti's Buffet, and Venice Beach
was a very different place than the veritable commune of hipsters, artists,
street performers and bums it is today.

In 1915, Venice Beach had luxury hotels, an elegant promenade, plans for
an opera house and the Abbot Kinney Pier. The Pier, larger and more
extravagant than the current Santa Monica pier, was located at the end of the
same street the Townhouse is located on today and contained an amusement
park, an aquarium, a hotel, restaurants and a grand dance hall.

Overnight, Prohibition changed the face of Venice, California, as many of
the elegant hotels had to stop serving. However, it didn't do much to slow
down the Townhouse.

Ever the entrepreneur, Cesar Menotti didn't miss a step when he turned his
upstairs bar into a grocery and the basement into a chic and popular

speakeasy. To get in and out, customers had to be raised and lowered by a small, two-person hand-operated elevator.

Menotti was able to keep his speakeasy well-stocked by using a steam and utilities maintenance tunnel running from the base of the Abbot Kinney Pier to Menotti's place, and then into other parts of the city. Because during Prohibition the territorial waters of the US only extended out three miles, ships would come down from Canada and anchor offshore. Small boats would then ferry the booze from the larger vessels anchored offshore to the base of the pier where it was carried to Menotti's speakeasy (as well as others in the area).

TODAY

When current owner Louie Ryan bought the Townhouse in 2007, he brought in world-famous interior decorator Nathalie Chapple to renovate and redesign the bar and speakeasy. The goal was to bring the place back to its original luster and, simply put, they were extremely successful.

Today the upstairs bar is more traditional, with just a hint of period accents. But it's the downstairs portion—The Del Monte Speakeasy—that is the true gem of the Townhouse. The speakeasy exudes a different atmosphere altogether, with a dress code, small-band music and access to the more sophisticated side of the cocktail culture.

The trip down the stairs into the speakeasy is like a short journey back in time to the roaring twenties. When you reach the bottom of the stairs you almost expect to look up and see Cesar Menotti sitting at the bar with a drink.

During our visit we were lucky enough to spend time with two fantastic bartenders, Brandon Ristaino and George Czar-necki, both great mixologists and both devoted to their craft.

Brandon is a throw-back to a time when barmen were true artisans. Responsible for the Townhouse's monthly drink rotation, their move to using fresh juices, house-made syrups and hand-cut ice, he is to cocktails what DaVinci was to art.

George, a fixture at the Townhouse for years, can give you all of the history we weren't able to cover. A favorite among the patrons, he has a million dollar voice that's perfect for telling the stories of the Townhouse and Venice Beach.

THE DRINKS

If the ambience of the bar itself doesn't make this one of the best saloons you've ever seen, then surely the drinks will make you fall in love with the place. The passion they pour into their period cocktails is both astounding and inspiring. From their devotion to the perfect ice—they use a custom-made, extra dense ice specially created for them—to their custom-blended Buffalo Trace Bourbon, they take the art of making traditional cocktails to a whole new level.

There are two drinks they make here—both whiskey-based—that really should be your selections when you visit. The first is the Old Fashioned, especially if you can have Brandon make it for you.

The second, the one to choose if you're facing George, is the Manhattan.

Both drinks are traditional, period drinks that use the best ingredients they have, from the hand-cut, dense ice to their own whiskey. They are mixed with devotion and effort that most just don't put into their drinks.

NEARBY DISTRACTIONS

Venice Beach—Website: www.venicebeach.com **Address:** 1800 Ocean Front Walk, Venice, CA, 90291. The Townhouse is literally steps away from the Venice Beach Boardwalk, so why not spend some time exploring one of the most unique destinations in Los Angeles, if not the entire planet. The Boardwalk is more of a shop-lined sidewalk than an actual boardwalk and features restaurants, food stands, shops, street vendors and street performers. Be prepared for some unusual sights and sounds, depending on where you're from, as the area continues to wear its tradition of liberal social change as a badge of honor. Though an alien and strange place to most, it's still worth a visit as it will give you a chance to experience a culture available in few, if any, locations in the world.

Santa Monica Pier—Website: www.santamonicapier.org **Address:** 200 Santa Monica Pier, Santa Monica, CA, 90401. A short three miles up the beach from the Townhouse is the Santa Monica Pier. Built in 1909 it was originally built as a Municipal Pier with a pipeline running under its 1,600-foot length that ran treated sewage out to the ocean, a practice that stopped in the 1920s. Today the pier is a destination for locals and tourists alike featuring an amusement park, restaurants, an aquarium and a bar. Time your visit to watch the breathtaking sunset.

The Proud Bird—Website: www.theproudbird.com **Address:** 11022 Aviation Blvd. Los Angeles, CA, 90045, (310) 670-3093 (Monday–Thursday 11am–9pm, Friday–Saturday 11am–1pm, Sunday 9am–9pm). A short five mile drive from the Townhouse is the Proud Bird restaurant and bar. Located adjacent to one of America's busiest runways and airports (LAX), it gives diners the unique experience of enjoying a meal in the open air while literally being feet from landing aircraft. Consider it a stop on your way to or from the airport or just as a purely unique dining experience.

TONGA HUT, NORTH HOLLYWOOD, CA

Address: 12808 Victory Blvd., North Hollywood, CA, 91606, (818) 769-0708
Website: www.tongahut.com **Video tour:** http://youtu.be/WwRylBIgvoE
Food: No **Live Music:** Yes **Hours:** Monday–Sunday 4pm–2am **Type of Bar:** Tiki **What to Drink:** DB Punch or the Rhumboogie **Why You Should Go:** Oldest existing (original) Tiki bar in the L.A. area, great décor, killer drinks, and the Loyal Order of the Drooling Bastard.

THE HISTORY

In 1958, twenty-four years after Don the Beachcomber opened, brothers Ace and Ed Libby opened the Tonga Hut in North Hollywood, CA, inspired by their travels through the South Pacific and the growing popularity of Tiki bars. Ace and Ed found their perfect location and brought in a builder and designer to transform it into a Polynesian oasis. Using no more than a piece of chalk and the floor as his canvas, the designer drew the life-size layout for seating, the front and back bar and decorative concepts. Impressed by the ideas, the brothers gave the go-ahead and the Tonga Hut was born.

After opening, the bar quickly became a staple and a favorite escape for the citizens of the San Fernando Valley. The "Hut," as it was referred to became "The" Tiki bar in North Hollywood throughout the late 1950s and 1960s until Tiki culture fell out of favor sometime in the 1970s (f***ing disco). Through the 1980s and 1990s the bar continued to be a favorite local hang out but the "Tiki" ness slowly faded away. The fountains stopped working and the bar eventually turned into a dive/sports bar featuring TVs, dart boards and plenty of taxidermy. The current owners took the place over in

2005 and quickly began restoring the Tonga Hut "sports bar" back to the Tonga Hut "Tiki bar."

TODAY

Today the Tonga Hut is owned by Amy Boylan and Jeremy Fleener. Fleener, guitarist for SX-10 (and formerly of Cyprus Hill), originally fell in love with the Tonga Hut upon his initial visit back in the 1990s. They purchased the bar in 2005 and immediately set about restoring it to its original luster. The video games, neon beer signs and sports memorabilia that were a part of the dive/sports bar were immediately torn out and replaced with traditional Tiki décor. This included the repair of long-broken fountains, the reintroduction of Tiki mugs, multiple traditional Tikis and some custom risqué velvet paintings of beautiful island women painted by local artist Jasin Sallin.

When you step out of the bright California sun and into the Polynesian oasis that is the Tonga Hut, it is immediately apparent that owner's love for the place and hard work has paid off. The atmosphere is pure island and leaves little to be desired as far as Tiki bars are considered. The décor is simple, the atmosphere relaxed and the liquid aloha flows heavily into some of the finest concoctions. When you stop by, simply kick back with a few island-themed drinks (more on those shortly,) listen to some jams on the jukebox, talk with the bartenders, locals and regulars, or spend your time just taking it all in.

And if you happen to find yourself in the Tonga Hut during happy hour you'll notice a "RESERVED" sign on the bar. It was placed there in honor of Dottie. But who is Dottie and why does she have a reserved seat?

Dottie and her husband started coming to the Tonga Hut in 1961 during the heyday of Tiki bars and quickly became regulars, showing up every day of the week (except Sundays, of course). Every day they ordered the same things: Brandy Alexander for Dottie and Scotch and soda for her husband. Dottie's husband passed away in the early '80s, but Dottie continued the tradition and arrived every weekday at 4pm to enjoy happy hour. She continued to order her usual as well as a scotch and soda with a lemon twist and water back in honor of her husband.

Dottie was a staple at the Tonga Hut and it's said she could tell you anything about the bar, its customers, owners, and employees. Sadly, in February of 2010, she passed away at 87 years young. In homage to Dottie and her 49-year presence at the Tonga Hut, her very seat and place at the bar is reserved everyday during Happy Hour. Please don't try to sit there.

The Tonga Hut also features a rite of sorts called the Loyal Order of the Drooling Bastard, which they created to commemorate the long lost art of the Tiki cocktail as outlined in the *Grog Log,* a book by Jeff Berry that has become the bible of exotic tropical drinks. Berry spent years immersing himself in Tiki culture while tracking down the founding recipes of Tiki-themed cocktails. His resulting record resurrects the drinks and the craft bar tending that goes into making island-inspired cocktails.

If you choose to accept the challenge of becoming a Bastard, you must finish every cocktail contained in the Grog Log (at your own pace). Once finished you receive your name on the Drooling Bastard plaque and a life-long discount on some of the Tonga Hut's signature drinks.

THE DRINKS

Tiki bars are notorious for their island-themed drinks and the Tonga Hut didn't disappoint. We tried a few and came out with two winners.

First up was the "Rhumboogie," made with Sailor Jerry Spiced Rum, a secret mix of tropical juices and a 151 rum float. This drink packs both great flavor and the one-two punch of Sailor and Bacardi 151. The Tonga Hut says "It'll boogie on your brain!" and we can't agree more.

Second up is the "DB Punch" which contains Appleton Rum, Ginger liqueur, Blood Orange liqueur, and a mixture of juices. Designed specifically for The Loyal Order of the Drooling Bastard, this stuff is dangerously tasty and easy to drink. Perfect for a hot Southern California day to help numb the mind.

NEARBY DISTRACTIONS

Universal Studios—Website: www.universalstudios.com **Address:** 100 Universal City Plaza Universal City, CA, 91608, (800) 864-8377 (open year round, hours vary by season, check website). Only six miles away from the Tonga Hut, Universal Studios has become a world-renowned attraction. Featuring some of the all-time greatest show and movie-themed rides as well as the world's largest working movie studio, this place is fun for any age. Keep in mind it is usually busiest over holidays and the summer, making a Front of Line Pass worth the money.

Griffith Observatory—Website: www.griffithobs.org **Address:** 2800 East Observatory Road Los Angeles, CA, 90027, (213) 473-0800 (Wednesday–Friday 12pm–10pm, Saturday–Sunday 10am–10pm). Only 12 miles from the Tonga Hut is one of the most famous and visited landmarks in southern California: the Griffith Observatory. The observatory features public events almost daily, like the L.A. Astronomical Society's Public Star Party, and has been featured as a backdrop in a long list of movies and shows. Admission is free to the Observatory building and grounds but there is a nominal charge to see shows located in the Samuel Oschin Planetarium.

Hollywood Sign—Website: www.hollywoodsign.org **Address:** N. Highland Ave and Hollywood Blvd. Los Angeles, CA, 90028 (the view is always open). No landmark or sign screams Southern California, L.A., show business, or Hollywood like the Hollywood sign. If you are interested in getting a great view of the sign, head over to the intersection of N Highland Ave and Hollywood Boulevard. Here you will find the Hollywood and Highland Center. Designers of the center made it a point to make the distant sign the centerpiece of their structural composition and as such photo opportunities are plentiful throughout the facility.

COLE'S P.E. BUFFET, LOS ANGELES, CA

Address: 118 E. 6th St., Los Angeles, CA, 90014, (213) 622-4090
Website: www.colesfrenchdip.com **Video tour:**
http://youtu.be/UhSgAC_HhCg
Food: Yes **Live Music:** No **Hours:** Monday–Wednesday 12pm–12:00am,
Thursday–Friday 12pm–2am, Saturday 11:00am–2:00am, Sunday 11am–
12am **Type of Bar:** Café **What to Drink:** Red Car Named Desire **Why You
Should Go:** Real, genuine Los Angeles history (not a lot of that around
anymore), superb craft cocktails, and the tasty French dip.

THE HISTORY

Cole's P.E. Buffet owes its start to the Pacific Electric Railway, also known
as the Red Car. The Red Car was a mass transit system in Southern California
that used streetcars, light-rail, and buses interconnected throughout cities in
Los Angeles and Orange County. At the center of the Red Car was their main
depot, the Pacific Electric Building, which was located at 6th and Main
Streets in downtown L.A. The depot became L.A.'s version of New York's
Grand Central Station and it's here that Los Angeles' oldest, still-operating
restaurant and saloon was started.

Founded by Henry Cole in 1908 on the ground floor of the Pacific Electric
Building, Cole's was built to serve the 100,000-plus residents that passed
through every day. Henry was an innovator, initially using varnished doors of
retired Red Cars as table tops, and shortly after opening started L.A.'s first
check cashing service from the bar. The check cashing business was so
successful that in 1936, records show they cashed 176,000 checks for a value
of $7,150,000.

The establishment quickly became a cornerstone of the Pacific Electric Railway's main terminal, and vastly popular among hardworking men and women of the area. Of course it probably didn't hurt that customers could grab a meal, a drink, and cash their payday checks all at a location conveniently situated on the way to and from work.

Cole's operated continuously for decades, but as the interstate road system was built in the 1950s and 1960s, the Red Cars eventually disappeared. The last train ran in 1961, after over a half-century of service.

With the closing of the Red Car service and, eventually, the hub upstairs, Cole's P.E. Buffet lost much of its clientele. To make matters worse, many businesses relocated out of downtown L.A., and the area fell into decline and seediness. By the 1980s and 1990s, the oldest bar in the city was teetering on the brink of closing, flirting with the titles of "dive" or "dump" and quickly gaining a bad reputation.

TODAY

Luckily in 2008 Cole's was purchased by 213 Hospitality, a company led by Los Angeles' own nightlife king and visionary, Cedd Moses. Cedd and 213 are considered proprietors of historic downtown L.A. bars and purchased the thread-worn saloon intending to both preserve it and return it to its previous glory.

After a year of renovations, Cole's re-opened in December of 2008 bringing back the traditional feel and look of the place from 1908. The décor and pictures throughout look to have come from all corners and periods of Southern California's history and if you look through the peep holes in the hall leading to the bathrooms, you can even spy a scene dating back to the early 1900s.

THE FOOD

Though its location and claim of the oldest restaurant and bar in the city of Los Angeles give it clout among some of the most historical places across the nation, it is Cole's greatest gift to the nation (invention of the French Dip Sandwich) that it is most known for today.

Though it is an ongoing debate with Philippe's (who also opened in 1908 and claims to be the inventor of the French Dip) Cole's claims that Henry Cole first dipped a roast beef sandwich into the drippings at the request of a customer with recent dental work. The customer stated the French bread was too hard to eat without causing discomfort and requested it be dipped in juice to soften it. Henry, always willing to please his clientele, was happy to oblige and dipped the sandwich. It was an immediate hit as other customers saw what Henry had done and requested he do the same for them. And so from a man with recent dental work, some hard French bread, the caring heart of a bar owner, and the hungry eyes of his patrons, the French Dip was born.

So what is Cole's P.E. Buffet's French Dip like? Amazing, to put it simply. The beef itself is outstanding, but throw in some horseradish sauce, au jus,

and an atomic pickle on the side and you have the must-try plate at Cole's …
maybe even in all of downtown L.A.

THE DRINKS

Cole's has taken a spare-no-detail traditional approach to their cocktails and
it shows with one of their most popular drinks, "The Red Car Named
Desire!" The Red Car was created by one of Cole's bar managers and is a twist
on the historic Manhattan containing a couple of the traditional ingredients
and a few nontraditional ones like Cynar (an Italian bitter liqueur) and
Luxardo Cherry Liqueur.

Watching the bartender make the drink is like watching one of the great
artists paint, with no attention to detail spared. The drink is a pleasure to the
senses, visually striking, aromatic and a great mixture of flavor. It is the must-
try drink at Cole's.

NEARBY DISTRACTIONS

Staples Center—Website: www.staplescenter.com **Address:** 1111 S. Figueroa
Street Los Angeles, CA, 90015, (213) 742-7100 (operating hours vary by
event, no tour offered). At just 1.6 miles from Cole's, the Staples Center is
literally just right down the road. Often considered the sports and
entertainment center of the world, it hosts a very long list of sporting and
entertainment events. Have a free night in L.A.? Check out the Staples
Center, it's almost guaranteed to have something going on.

Santa Anita—Website: www.santaanita.com **Address:** 285 West Huntington
Drive Arcadia, CA, 91007, (626) 574-7223 (simulcasting goes on year-round,
live racing runs September-November). Twenty miles and what seems like a
world away from downtown L.A. and Cole's is horse racing's Santa Anita
Park. Traditionally associated with the film and television industry (legends
like Bing Crosby and Shirley Temple were known to be regulars) it's probably
best known for hosting one of the greatest race horses in America's history:
Seabiscuit. The track is open to tours every Saturday and Sunday of live
racing season. The tour offers a rare behind-the-scenes glimpse into this
storied track and the sport of horse racing.

LOS ANGELES' HISTORIC BARS

Ercoles Bar—Address: 1101 Manhattan Avenue Manhattan Beach, CA,
90266, (310) 372-1997 (Monday-Sunday 10am-2am). Since 1927 this
Manhattan Beach gem has been a study in modesty. Not one ounce of
pretense is to be found in this classic dive bar. They have basic beer on tap—
Coors included—and some really great drink specials for some really great
classic wells, like whiskies and gin. The food is dive-bar-basic: hot dogs and
burgers and the like. The crowd is diverse and pleasant, and like the bar,
humble and authentic.

Barney's Beanery—Address: 8447 Santa Monica Boulevard West
Hollywood, CA, 90069, (323) 654-2287 (Monday–Friday 10am–2am,

Saturday–Sunday 9am–2am). Opened at this location in 1927, Barney's is a beloved sports bar that's been serving the city continuously since it opened its doors. It's been in a slew of movies and has had a cast of notables and celebrities through its doors. On one particular night Jim Morrison, three sheets to the wind, pulled down his pants and took a leak right on the bar. He was immediately booted out of course, but a plaque honoring the event is clearly in place. Take a picture next to it for the album!

The Roost—Address: 3100 Los Feliz Boulevard, Los Angeles, CA, 90039, (323) 664-7272 (Monday–Sunday 12pm–2am). This Hollywood dive is known for two things: cheap drinks and popcorn. It's been around since the 1960s and from the looks of the décor it hasn't changed much in that time (the interior has been said to resemble the inside of grandma's house). It attracts a fairly diverse crowd composed of hipsters and old local regulars.

Formosa Café—Address: 7156 Santa Monica Boulevard, West Hollywood, CA, 90046, (323) 850-9050 (Monday–Friday 4pm–2am).Opened in 1925 this small café is a Hollywood landmark (seriously, it was declared a landmark in the 1990s). It's located directly adjacent to one of the most famous studio lots in the city—now Samuel Goldwyn Studio. Movies have been filmed there since the early 1920s and are still filmed there today. Because of its location, it's been a frequent watering hole for dozens of celebrities over the past century, from Humphrey Bogart to Brad Pitt.

MINNEAPOLIS-SAINT PAUL, MN

It really doesn't make sense to separate these two cities, so we'll tackle them both together in one chapter. If you've ever been here you'll understand, because it's pretty easy to lose track of which one you're in as you drive through the metro. And honestly, does it really matter? There's an abundance of great bars to visit in this area so you're going to have a great time no matter which one you're in.

This is the grain belt! Minnesota is one of the nation's leaders in both corn and wheat production. If you go in just about any direction from Minneapolis-Saint Paul you'll probably be in a grain field of some kind. That's a good thing if you're making beer. In fact, Grain Belt, the beer, has been brewed here since 1893, so they have a pretty good history when it comes to boozing it up in the Twin Cities.

Not all of that grain was fermented though. This city is also the birthplace of both Pillsbury and General Mills. Both of them started as mills that were turned by the Mississippi River, and each one turned the wheat that was grown nearby into flour. This was big business in Minneapolis. Near the city, mills, over thirty of them, were found all along the river in the late 1800s. As a side note, another big business in the area was the production of artificial limbs. Apparently, for many, milling was a dangerous occupation.

Minneapolis is a hard-working town with a long history of thirst. The timber industry was another one of the earliest sources of work here, and 17 sawmills were found along the river in the 1800s. So, imagine, a city full of farmers, millers, and lumberjacks, all immigrants from Ireland, Germany and Poland. What do you think were they going to do in their spare time? If you said "drink" then you're on the right track. The problem was, however, that not everyone enjoyed this past time. In fact, a new, large group of Scandinavian immigrants who arrived in the late 1800s just happened to be teetotalers. You can imagine that the two butted heads almost immediately.

As a compromise, the city set up special zones (called Liquor Patrol Limits, or LPLs) where liquor, beer and wine could be sold. Much of the zoning allowing booze was in areas where the Irish, German and Polish had settled, so they were happy with the arrangement. Within these zones, you could find just about any kind of drink you wanted, but everything outside of the LPLs was dry.

The attitude against liquor and bars still exists somewhat, and though the LPLs were eliminated through a citywide vote, it's still tough to open a liquor store or bar in the area, and restaurants often can't sell liquor at all, only beer and wine. Saint Paul wasn't as restrictive as Minneapolis was, but it still has some laws that cap the number of liquor licenses a city ward can have (as well as the type of alcohol that restaurants can sell).

In all though, there are some great old gems to drink at in these two cities. Both have wonderful saloons where you can tip back a few and talk to the locals.

140

NEUMANN'S BAR, NORTH SAINT PAUL, MN

Address: 2531 7th Ave E, North St Paul, MN, 55109, (651) 770-6020
Website: www.neumannsbar.com **Video tour:**
https://youtu.be/3J1NCmvIwWI
Food: Yes **Live Music:** Yes **Hours:** Monday–Sunday 10am–1am **Type of Bar:** Dive **What to Drink:** Hamm's **Why You Should Go:** One of the oldest bars in Minnesota with a beautiful, original bar and speakeasy past.

THE HISTORY

Neumann's Bar started out life in 1887 as what used to be known as a "tied" house. Back in the day, breweries would build a bar to sell just their beer. Then, after the bar was built, they'd find some local to run the place. Eventually, they'd sell the bar—building and all—to the loyal barkeep. And that was the case here in North Saint Paul. William Neumann was a nearby farmer, but became the operator of the Hamm's saloon in 1887. He ran the bar until the early 1900s when it was taken over by his son, Jim Neumann, who then operated the place until his death in the 1940s. Following Jim's death, it was taken over by his son-in-law and then finally would up in the hands of local customer, Mike Brown.

Founded in 1865 by German immigrant, Theodore Hamm, Hamm's brewery was located in Saint Paul and was the second largest brewery in Minnesota by the time Neumman's Bar was founded. Like all breweries in the country, Hamm's stopped making beer during prohibition but kept itself alive by making soft drinks and other, legal products. As soon as prohibition ended, though, Hamm's quickly expanded and by the 1960s had breweries in Baltimore, Houston, Los Angeles and San Francisco. Unfortunately, like many of the old breweries found throughout the country, the bigger breweries proved too tough to fight and, after a being bought and sold a number of times, the Saint Paul brewery closed for good in 1997. You can still find Hamm's on the shelves (and in Neumann's), but it's now made by MillerCoors.

While the bar was opened by William Neumann, it was Jim Neumann that really made the place fun. He was known to be a character and had a colorful approach to running the bar that his father left him. For starters, he refused to stop selling after prohibition started. Instead, he just moved the party upstairs and put in a bait shop on the ground floor. While there was no phone in the place that connected outside of the bar (more on that in a bit) there was a single phone at the ground floor that had a line running to another phone upstairs at the top of a staircase. If someone wanted a drink they could ring the upstairs phone and be let up. The downstairs phone is long gone, but the upstairs phone is still mounted on the wall. And there's even a small window at the top of the stairs where visitors could be identified before being let in. They use the upstairs speakeasy for special events and parties. Ask and maybe Mike will give you a tour if you're nice.

After prohibition, the place got back to business and Neumman's once again became a saloon, though one that was no longer tied to Hamm's. This was when Jim Neumann started many of his antics, like placing fake spiders in the light fixtures that could be dropped onto unsuspecting guests by the push of a button. The unsuspecting guests were usually women. These women were also the reason the bar did not, as mentioned above, have a phone. In fact, up until the 1980s the bar had no outside phone at all. Jim wouldn't allow it because he thought that if he did have a phone, wives would be calling and asking their husbands to come home. He didn't want to lose business so he simply never got one installed.

Another item that Jim added was a large aquarium in the front window. To this aquarium he then added a few gigantic bull frogs, courtesy of a customer in the 1920s. The frogs had their own pond, lamp for warmth, and a big rock to perch on. In the pond swam a few catfish, small but big enough to avoid being eaten. The frogs have been there ever since (or newer ones as the older frogs passed on), happily sitting on their warm and cozy rock, munching earthworms or whatever else they can be fed (we're told they eat pretty much anything).

TODAY

We're pretty sure Jim Neumann would still recognize his place if he walked in. It's not overly divey, and retains the charm that you can only find in saloon that's over 130 years old. The bar to your right is long and beautiful, an original that has been here since day one. The bar back itself is beautifully carved, and one of the most attractive, authentic bars from the late 19th century you'll ever see. To your left on the wall are mounted numerous dead things, like deer and even a moose. These apparently were bagged by Jim's sons, so they've been keeping watch over patrons for years. At the end of the small but cozy saloon is a stage for live music, which they feature pretty often.

The aquarium is still there, too. When we visited, they had two bull frogs about as wide as soccer balls. Mike, the owner, said he didn't know how old they were, but they'd been there since he bought the place and thinks they might pushing 20 years old. They have a good life, that's for sure.

Throughout the small bar are a scattered number of tables and chairs, and at any given time you'll see regulars wander in, grab a seat and then sip a beer or grab a bite to eat. Though known as the oldest bar in the state, it still heavily caters to locals. In fact, they put on a number of events just for the locals, and take part in everything from motorcycle rides to a classic car show right outside their door every summer.

The food here is pretty good. It's classic bar faire—hamburgers and such—but it's quality. We ate a burger and some deep-fried cheese curds (a must if you visit Minnesota) and were happy and full by the time we left. They also have soups and sandwiches, chili and wraps. If you swing by in the morning you can also get a hearty breakfast to start your day of boozing.

There's an outside patio with bar where you can sit during the warm summer months. It's especially nice when the car show is going on because you can have a drink and watch the crowds that flow into North Saint Paul to look at the classic cars. This is prime people watching territory, but it's also nice just to enjoy the warm weather when you can get it.

As mentioned before, the crowd is composed of locals but they do get many visitors, owed to their legacy and age. Oftentimes you might see a local sports celebrity hanging out here as well. And when there's a game on, the place gets really crowded. When there's live music on the stage (Thursday–Saturday nights), the crowd gets even bigger. The bands are typically playing classic rock tunes, so nothing too obnoxious. All in all, this is a must-see bar when you're travelling through the Minnesota-Saint Paul area.

THE FOOD

Burgers, burgers, and more burgers. Neumann's is known for their hamburgers in all sizes and flavors. Their standard burgers are a quarter-pound but they also have the half-pound o' beef option. Check out their website for daily specials, like $1 hamburgers on Mondays (you read that right) or Coneys on Tuesdays. Whatever you pick you're going to be happy, though (this isn't complicated stuff so it's hard to go wrong on any of it).

THE DRINKS

They have great happy hour specials throughout the week, so you're sure to find something inexpensive and tasty. We went all nostalgic and had a Hamm's since that's this place's legacy. But they also make great cocktails as well and have a large beer selection, including many craft beers on tap. Most of the craft beers are also local, so it's a sure thing that you'll get to taste something you've never tried before.

NEARBY DISTRACTIONS

Antique Shopping—Yeah, we know, we can't believe we're suggesting it either, but here we are. While we were waiting for Neumman's Bar to open, and since we had nothing else to do, we wandered into the antique store next door. Then we had a revelation. Amongst the glassware and doilies, dolls and trinkets, were some of the best vintage beer and booze memorabilia we've ever seen. We found beer signs from long-closed breweries, like Hamm's and Blatz, and from currently operating regional breweries like Grain Belt. Antique stores are found throughout North Saint Paul, so you should be able to find some great items for the man cave. There's even one of the most renowned vintage military collectibles stores nearby (www.vdgmilitaria.com, 2564 7th Ave E, North St Paul, MN 55109).

History Cruzers—Website: www.historycruzer.com, downtown North St. Paul on 7th Avenue, between 1st Street & Charles Street (essentially, in front of Neumann's Bar), (651) 261-8031 (seasonal on Fridays from June–September). One of the biggest car shows in the state, every Friday during the warm-weather months, dozens of classic or new exotic cars turn out on 7th Avenue in North Saint Paul. There's a party atmosphere complete with DJ's, food trucks, booths and venders. The local bars feature drink specials and live music and there's generally large crowds moving from saloon to saloon. This is a great, festive, event that really turns out locals and visitors alike. Get to Neumann's early and grab a table, then go out and wander around the amazing, vintage cars.

Life Bridge Brewing Company—Website: www.liftbridgebrewery.com **Address:** 1900 Tower Dr W, Stillwater, MN, 55082, (888) 430-2337 (Monday–Thursday 3pm–10pm, Friday–Saturday 12pm–10pm, Sunday 12pm–6pm). You can't visit this part of the Minneapolis-Saint Paul metro without visiting a nearby brewery (there are plenty as you get closer to the city, but this one gets you out of the city a bit to see the surrounding area). Lift Bridge features experimental beers, plus brewery tours and picnic tables in a beautiful outdoor setting. Going here will get you into a more rural part of Minnesota that will quickly help you understand why so many people want to live here.

THE SPOT BAR, SAINT PAUL, MN

Address: 859 Randolph Ave, St Paul, MN, 55102, (651) 224-7433
Video tour: https://youtu.be/e3sy7uUUnuM
Food: Yes **Live Music:** No **Hours:** Monday–Saturday 10am–1am, Sunday
10am–1am **Type of Bar:** Dive **What to Drink:** Grain Belt **Why You Should
Go:** Great, dark dive, one of the oldest in the state, with darts, pinball, and
cheap beer.

THE HISTORY

The old bar that's now called The Spot was founded by German immigrant,
Engelfried Wittmer, in 1885. When it opened, it joined a total of 39 other
saloons in the neighborhood where you could get a beer (and that's not even
including the 6 nearby breweries). At the time, Saint Paul (and nearby
Minneapolis) was seeing an influx of immigration from Germany and Poland,
and so any place that sold beer became really popular, really quickly. The
Spot, called Wittmer's at the time, hosted thirsty farmers, millworkers and
steelworkers for two decades before Wittmer himself died in 1915. After his
death, the bar was bought and continued running, but under a different
name.

During prohibition, The Spot, like most every other bar in the city, turned
into a café and sold near beer. However, also like most every other bar in the
city, it (reportedly) still sold booze. This was a common practice, and it makes
sense considering Canada is only separated from Minneapolis-Saint Paul by a
two-hour drive and Lake Superior (where lots of rum-running boats liked to
navigate).

After prohibition, it opened once more as a bar, and apparently never lost its appeal or popularity. However, it also never quite found another owner like Wittmer. In fact, after his death in 1915, the bar went through 12 different owners (and likely went through 12 different names changes as well). Eventually, though, the bar was bought in 1983 by Mike O'Toole, and it's been in the O'Toole family ever since (Mike passed away in 2012 but his daughter and wife are the current owners).

Mike turned the little neighborhood bar into a destination for people throughout the city. He started hosting events, like a pig roast during the first weekend of October. Mike would stay up for 24 hours and roast a whole pig, then throw open the doors to invite regulars and visitors alike to join him in a day-long celebration. He'd also get his customers together and take bus trips to Milwaukee or Chicago for baseball games (he believed, rightly, that baseball should be played outdoors). And then there was Mike himself, who was funny, warm and sincere. He was the kind of bartender you wanted if you were having a bad day. He is missed, but the bar he helped keep alive is still going strong.

TODAY

Thanks to the hard work of Mike, and of course due to the ambition of Engelfried Wittmer, The Spot is now a beloved destination for locals from all across the Twin Cities. On any given day, you can find a handful of regular customers, throwing darts or sipping beer. The low-slung bar is minimal, but functional, and the drinks are cheap and strong. Beer is especially cheap here and they do serve pizza (frozen, not from scratch), so you can get by on just a few bucks. That makes this place very popular with the blue-collar crowd, who also appreciates the fact that they open early.

The inside is decorated with paintings and pictures that give you a glimpse of the bar's past. Above the back bar is a beautiful stained glass picture of The Spot that was created by a local artist (that's how much people love this place). To the right as you enter you have a number of booths to choose from, and they also have a backroom with chairs and tables for crowds to sit and chat. There's a single TV above the corner of the bar, and it's usually tuned to sports of some kind. They also have an array of table top games you can play, or pinball or even darts (the real kind), so there's plenty to do.

The bar is still immensely devoted to the community. On various occasions they host a vintage clothing sale provided by a local entrepreneur who spends the year scouring the area's thrift stores. When he finds nice clothes in great condition, he buys them, washes them and travels around the region reselling them at certain destinations, one of which is The Spot. When we heard about this, the owners noted our raised eyebrows (as we found this a bit strange), but then told us why they allow it. The bar is home to a solid working-class group of people. Those customers, we were told, love the fact that they can find nice, inexpensive clothing and look forward to the sales when they happen. Not too many bars go out of their way so much for their customers like this place does.

They also still hold the pig roast in October, and have dubbed it the Mike O'Toole Memorial Pig Roast in memory of Mike. It's still a big event, and it also draws a large crowd, though many of them didn't find The Spot until after Mike had passed, and so don't really know the person the event is honoring. But, we don't really think that would have mattered to Mike O'Toole, instead we think he probably would have just wanted them to enjoy the roast, and to enjoy his bar.

There is one thing they do here that, apparently, is commonly found in bars in Minnesota: a meat raffle. Yes, you read that right. On Friday evenings (when we happened to show up), The Spot raffles off meat from a local butcher shop. The raffle tickets go for a buck each, and that gives you the chance to win anything from sausage to steaks. If you don't win on the first wheel spin, they spin again for a beer. It was a very cool event that was more fun than we thought it would be, even though we never won any meat. In any case, this is a friendly, warm and welcoming landmark that you owe it to yourself to find if you ever come to the Twin Cities. Stick around for a while if you do stop by, and chat with the locals. You'll soon learn how important this bar is to them, and to the city.

THE FOOD

They do have food, but we're talking toaster over-prepared stuff (think frozen pizzas and such). If you're hard up for something to eat, then this is certainly an option. But if not, then you might want to just drink some cheap beer instead.

THE DRINKS

They carry both Hamm's and Grain Belt, each one a locally-brewed, historic beer. Most importantly they're also very cheap. Other than that, they do carry a number of other beers and have all the standard liquors behind the bar. They can make most basic cocktails, but remember that the place isn't a cocktail lounge, it's a bar.

NEARBY DISTRACTIONS

James J. Hill House—Website: www.mnhs.org/hillhouse **Address:** 240 Summit Ave, St Paul, MN, 55102, (651) 297-2555 (Wednesday–Saturday 10am–4pm, Sunday 1pm–4pm). It was the Gilded Age, and barons of industry ruled the country. As rewards for their enterprise, they built themselves huge mansions, America's answer to the castles of Europe. Few men were ever as wealthy as James J. Hill, nicknamed the "Empire Builder" after connecting his railway in Minneapolis-Saint Paul to Seattle. In 1885, his railroad was worth 25,000,000.00. Adjusting for inflation that is over 600 million dollars today. The James J. Hill House was his castle. Tours are given at the amazing 3-story stone mansion that overlooks the Mississippi on Summit Ave. Visitors can explore 36,000 square feet of living space that included bedrooms, offices, drawing room, and living areas. This place makes modern mansions look like the slums.

Summit Brewing Company—Website: www.summitbrewing.com **Address:** 910 Montreal Cir, St Paul, MN, 55102, (651) 265-7800 (Thursday–Friday 2pm–9pm, Saturday 12pm–9pm). Founded in 1986, way back before craft beer was even a thing, Summit Brewing Company is one of Saint Paul's most loved breweries. Their different varieties can be found on tap and in cans and bottles throughout the region and beyond. They make numerous different beers, plus seasonal and small, experimental varieties as well, so you're sure to find one you like. They serve beer on the brewery patio and give tours three days a week, but it's worth it to sit on their patio overlooking the Mississippi river and sip some delicious, freshly-made beer. They also typically feature live music or other entertainment in their beer hall, and have food trucks parked outside. This is great place to waste away an afternoon or two.

Historic Fort Snelling—Website: www.mnhs.org/fortsnelling **Address:** 200 Tower Avenue, Saint Paul, MN, 55111, (612) 726-1171 (Open seasonally June–September, Tuesday–Friday 10am–4pm, Saturday–Sunday 10am–5pm). The US Army first built a fort here in 1819, back when the area was completely unsettled and a wild frontier. The original purpose of the garrison was to protect the Northwest Territory from encroachment from the British and Canadians, but eventually they were also tasked with protecting settlers from Native Americans. Named after the architect of the current structure, Colonel Josiah Snelling, who was also its first commander, this historic fort was used off and on by the military all the way up to 1946, and even afterwards was used for US Army Reserves and other offices. It was designated a National Landmark in 1960, and attempts ever since have been made to restore it. Today, during the summer months, you can tour the grounds, visit its museum, and learn first-hand about life on the frontier from costumed docents.

MINNEAPOLIS-SAINT PAUL'S HISTORIC BARS

Palmer's Bar—Website: www.palmersbar.net **Address:** 500 Cedar Ave S, Minneapolis, MN, 55454, (612) 333-7625 (Monday–Sunday 10am–2am). A church for the down and outers, and those who romanticize them, Palmer's Bar has been serving thirsty neighbors since 1906. Not even prohibition could shut this place down, instead, they just served illegally like most all other places did (there was reportedly a tunnel to another nearby bar during the 1920s). Originally, it was opened and owned by Grain Belt Brewing company (or, rather, it's predecessor), like many other saloons around town. With a brothel upstairs during the 1930s, Palmer's has served the city one way or another for over a century, and it's earned the respect of locals and visitors alike. The crowd is diverse and composed of a cross-section of the people who live here. You get the hipsters and art crowd, you get the students and degenerates like us, but you also get professionals from all over the place. Business suits (with ties loosened of course) and medical scrubs are just as common a site as cut off shorts and flip flops. Palmer's Bar should definitely be on your list for a night in the Twin Cities.

Gluek's Restaurant and Bar—Website: www.glueks.com **Address:** 16 N 6th St, Minneapolis, MN, 55403, (612) 338-6621 (Monday–Saturday 11am–2am, Sunday 12pm–8pm). Gluek's Brewery was founded (though under a different name), by German immigrant Gottlieb Gluek in 1857. At one time, it was one of the largest breweries in the region, and as the region (full of thirsty German and Polish immigrants) grew, so, too, did Gluek's. In 1902, the company built a beautiful, three-story saloon and beer hall to serve its product in the warehouse district of Minneapolis. But, as usual, prohibition came along and fouled everything up. Though Gluek's survived prohibition and started brewing again afterwards, they sold the beer hall to Charles Fransen, who worked closely with Gottlieb. Gottlieb passed away not much later, and the brewery was consumed by a fire, all but ending the original Gluek's beer. The recipe and rights to the name were sold a number of times afterwards until eventually it was a cheap knockoff and virtually unrecognizable as the beer that was so loved throughout the region. As for the beer hall, the Fransen family has owned and operated it ever since it was sold to them in 1933. In the 1970s, as a nod to their humble beginning, they changed the name to Gluek's Restaurant and Bar, and the family has even bought the rights to Gluek's Beer and has started brewing it again. This is a great place to experience some wonderful Twin Cities history.

Monte Carlo—Website: www.montecarlomn.com **Address:** 219 3rd Ave N, Minneapolis, MN, 55401, (612) 333-5900 (Sunday–Thursday 11am–10pm, Friday–Saturday 11am–11pm). The Monte Carlo in Minneapolis has been serving food and drinks for decades, but it wasn't always like that. When it originally opened, it was much more like a saloon than anything else, and back in those days it only allowed men inside. When the current family purchased it in 1964, they started serving food, and they've been a landmark destination ever since. The booths are lined in vinyl and they wallpapered throughout, but the bar is a beautiful, copper-topped work of art where you can get an ice-cold martini, or just about any other drink you can think of. The menu is pretty extensive, and the offerings fall somewhere in between pub grub and full-on restaurant. They serve steaks and oysters, but of all the fine-dining options, they're best known for their chicken wings, which they've been making for a half a century now. Take some time to study the portraits of celebrities—local and otherwise—who've bent an elbow here. They can make just about any drink you can order, so don't feel like you're stuck with the simple classics here. Oh, and they do allow women now.

19 Bar—Address: 19 W 15th St, Minneapolis, MN, 55403, (612) 871-5553 (Monday–Friday 3pm–2:30am, Saturday–Sunday 1pm–2:30am). This is the oldest gay bar (that we're aware of) in the state of Minnesota, and one of the oldest gay bars in the country. Opened in 1952 by life partners Everett Stoltz and George Koch, 19 Bar has been sheltering a local gay crowd for over half a century. This is pretty significant, considering that when the place was opened it was officially illegal to be gay in many places throughout the United States. Often, many bars that "allowed" gay people to gather openly charged them exorbitant prices for their drinks in exchange for giving them room to be themselves. 19 Bar, however, was different. It was a place where this community could find welcomed shelter. Today, as with many other bars in the Twin Cities, it is a much beloved institution. How much is it loved? Well, in 1986, arsonists set fire to the old saloon. The loyal patrons rushed to save it and it was back open within a week. This is a wonderful bar to enjoy some pool, old school video games, and some cheap drinks. Go with friends and learn the real history of Minneapolis-Saint Paul in one of their best bars.

MILWAUKEE, WI

Milwaukee is and always has been a thirsty city. In 1860, owed to an influx of German immigrants, Milwaukee had 35 breweries. Some of them you might be familiar with—Miller, Schlitz, and Pabst to name just a few. Between the fresh water of the lakes and the millions of acres of wheat close at hand, brewing was an easy enterprise to get into. But not only that, places that served that beer were also pretty easy to find. In the mid 1800s there was one saloon for every 40 residents (255 saloons in 1850) compared to 47 churches. Finding a place to wet your whistle was easier than finding a house of God.

The combination of all that beer and all those bars made the place quite lively. But it needed to be. These were hard working people who spent their days in foundries and machine shops, factories and farms. Not to mention the fact that most all of them either immigrated from or were descended from immigrants from the various German or Eastern European states and countries.

Of all the breweries here, the biggest had to be Schlitz. After the Chicago fire of 1871 destroyed much of Chicago's brewing industry, Schlitz sent 10,000 gallons of beer to the thirsty residents and gained a strong foothold there. It then opened saloon after saloon throughout Chicago to make sure it sold plenty of beer in the Windy City. The plan worked, and by the time prohibition shut it down, Schlitz was the biggest brewery in Milwaukee.

But even after prohibition, Schlitz and Pabst fought for the rights to call themselves the largest. Schlitz won the battle, but in the end, lost the war. They began to artificially speed up the aging process of their beer in the late 1960s. This affected the flavor and even made the beer a bit hazy (forcing them to dump about 10 million bottles in the mid 1970s). They finally closed their Milwaukee plant in 1981, and were sold off completely in 1982.

Ultimately, the only one that really survived was the Miller Brewing Company, which has since been bought and sold and is now owned by a conglomeration that also owns Coors and Molson. However, they still brew in Milwaukee at the original brewery (and give a pretty decent tour).

Many of the old saloons that used to be found all over town have also closed down, though they have been replaced by a thriving craft brew scene. Small brewpubs are popping up throughout the neighborhoods, replacing the classic bars that told the story of the city. But, a few good saloons can still be found here if you know where to look (luckily, they're all in this book, of course).

A good day in Milwaukee is spent touring these old saloons and then stopping at a German restaurant for some sausage and beer. You can also tour the city's small distillery if you've got time. Needless to say, you'll find plenty of distractions when you visit.

THE UPTOWNER, MILWAUKEE, WI

Address: 1032 E Center St, Milwaukee, WI, 53212, (414) 702-6798
Website: www.uptownerbar.com **Video tour:** https://youtu.be/ht3eH27py3E
Food: No **Live Music:** Yes **Hours:** Monday–Sunday 12pm–2am **Type of Bar:** Dive **What to Drink:** Schlitz **Why You Should Go:** Oldest bar left in Milwaukee and an absolute melting pot of people. Live music, cheap beer and a warm and welcoming atmosphere.

THE HISTORY

Opened in 1884, this small bar was originally a Schlitz saloon, or "tied" house in the beginning. A tied house was a saloon that served only a single type of beer, the beer made by the brewery that built the saloon (hence, it was "tied" to that saloon). It's said that Joseph Schlitz himself picked out this corner location. There's no way for us to be sure about that, but whether or not he did, we're sure the place was popular. In a city full of thirsty European immigrants yearning for the type of beer they'd get back in their home countries, a saloon like The Uptowner was definitely welcomed.

The building that houses the bar also held a number of other businesses in the early days. At one time, there was a barbershop and a candy store here (the barber shop we can see, but the candy store not so much). During prohibition, the place turned into a soda fountain and a drugstore. This was the greatest of all scams. Here you could legally purchase prescription alcohol if you were directed to by your physician. Luckily, many physicians were prescribing it at the time, and often they could be found in the drugstore itself (talk about convenience).

And if you didn't have a prescription there was still a pretty good chance you were taken care of anyway.

After prohibition, the bar opened once more, but as a private saloon not connected any longer to Schlitz (tied houses became illegal). Around 1950 the bar was bought by a charismatic, semi-pro baseball player named "Chic" Giacalone who changed the name to The Uptowner, supposedly as a nod to Uptown New York, where the wealthy and high society would mingle and drink the night away. It must have been his wish to have such a crowd, but in a city of blue collar workers we're not sure how well that worked out for him.

Instead, Chic's clientele was a cross-section of the working class of the city, and he took care of them well, with a warm atmosphere and decent drink prices. He also gave a lot back to his community, including sponsoring many different baseball and bowling teams in the area.

In 1985, The Uptowner was bought by its current owner, Steve Johnson, a Milwaukee native who owned another bar down the street at the time. He's had this place ever since.

TODAY

The bar today probably looks a lot like it did when it first opened. It's simple, unadorned, utilitarian. There's the beautiful long bar and back bar just ahead of you when you enter. Then, to the left, a long room with pool table, and a single TV hanging up in the corner to your right. Below you is an ancient, scarred, hard-wood floor, and above you is a tin ceiling. Back beyond the bar are a couple of pinball machines (they have tournaments), and a door that leads to the back patio. There are also a few tables strewn about, but that's really about it.

The walls, though, are something else entirely. Whereas you'd expect a place like this to be heavily adorned with neon beer signs (and there might be a couple), Steve instead put up artwork—fantastic artwork. Steve has always appreciated fine art and paintings, and so when artist Mike Fredrickson began working for him and offered to sell him some of his portraits, Steve was happy to oblige. The pieces can be seen throughout the place and are really impressive. There are other local artists' work hanging as well, and Steve would be happy to tell you about them.

They also have a back patio—complete with priceless iron work fencing (ask the owner Steve about that). This is a nice little area outside that lets you sit, relax, and think about what the place looked like over a hundred years ago when it opened.

The bar serves cheap beer and strong drinks, but definitely try a Schiltz, as that's kind of what started The Uptowner in the first place. They're especially known for their live music, which they feature throughout the week, including a long-lasting hip-hop night. The Uptowner gets crowded during the live shows, so get her early to get a bar stool.

The customers are a mixed bag of neighborhood locals, hipsters, blue-collar workers and the occasional riffraff like us. They're young, old, tattooed, bald, hairy, black, white and everything in between. In fact, it's the crowd here that makes The Uptowner so special—they're more of a family than just a bunch of barflies. The motto here is "the home of the beautiful people," and if you get a few drinks deep into conversation with them, you'll agree that's just what they are—beautiful people.

THE DRINKS

They're pretty upfront about what they can and can't serve. They can serve cheap, local beer. One of the most popular craft breweries in town is called Lakefront Brewery so give that a try. Also, as mentioned before, a Schlitz makes sense too. They can make cocktails, but not specialty cocktails, so stick the traditional drinks.

NEARBY DISTRACTIONS

Miller Brewing Company—Website: www.themillerbrewerytour.com **Address:** 4251 W. State St, Milwaukee, WI, 53208, (414) 931-3880 (Monday–Friday 10am–5pm, Saturday 10am–5:30pm). Brewery tours are always fun, no matter how big or small, because they often include at least a small sampling of the product being brewed. Touring the Miller Brewing Company is a great way to connect with the city, learn a little about big brewing, and taste a little beer while you're at it. The tour shows you around the historic brewery and takes you through their operations, ending in a brief exploration of the caves that Miller used to keep his beer fresh. For a great comparison, you can also tour Milwaukee's most popular craft brewery, Lakefront Brewery (www.lakefrontbrewery.com).

North Point Lighthouse—Website: www.northpointlighthouse.org **Address:** 2650 N Wahl Ave, Milwaukee, WI, 53211, (414) 332-6754 (Saturday–Sunday 1pm–4pm). This restored historic lighthouse built on the shore of Lake Michigan has been serving the city and the sailors of the Great Lakes since 1888. Inside, there is a museum that provides a great perspective about the importance of these lakes to industry and the economy of the country in 19th and early 20th century. It's only open for visits and tours briefly on Saturday and Sunday, but it's worth seeing.

Pabst Mansion—Website: www.pabstmansion.com **Address:** 2000 W. Wisconsin Ave, Milwaukee, WI, 53233, (414) 931-0808 (Monday–Saturday 10am–4pm). The wealth accumulated by the early beer barons is almost unthinkable today. The money they were making from the seemingly unquenchable thirst of the nation bought all sorts of luxuries, and this certainly included their homes. Completed in 1892, this mansion is a wonderful example of the gilded age, when the Rockefeller's and the Vanderbilt's of the day spent on extravagance unheard of today. Come see what brewing beer can get you! Tours available daily.

MILWAUKEE'S HISTORIC BARS

Holler House—Address: 2042 W Lincoln Ave, Milwaukee, WI, 53215, (414) 647-9284 (Tuesday–Thursday 4pm–12am, Friday 3pm–12am,

Saturday 2pm–12am). Opened in 1908, the Holler House's claim to fame is that it has the oldest, sanctioned bowling lanes in the entire country. The lanes were installed when the bar was first built and feature wooden lanes and manual pinsetters (called, "pinboys," be sure to tip them). Bowling was popular in Europe in the 19th century, and so when Mike Skowrenski opened his bar, originally called Skowrenski's, it made sense to him to use the basement for the lanes since most of the residents in Milwaukee were from Germany or Poland. Since that time, the bar has become a beloved place for locals to gather and drink the night away. They don't serve beer on tap, instead everything is bottled (except for Schlitz, the only one served in cans). They also have a full bar and can make a great Gin Ricky. The bowling shoes are a bit suspect so you might want to bring your own (you'll also be keeping score manually by scratching it out on paper, so bring a calculator too).

Landmark 1850 Inn—Address: 5905 S Howell Ave, Milwaukee, WI, 53207, (414) 769-1850 (Sunday–Thursday 2pm–2am, Friday–Saturday 2pm–2:30am). Just south of Mitchell International Airport, this place lays claim to the oldest bar in Milwaukee. Built in 1847, the place was originally called the New Coeln House, and served as the public house for the small German settlement of New Coeln. Here, mail was delivered, rooms were rented upstairs, and beer was served. They don't rent out rooms anymore but they do still serve the beer, a pretty impressive lineup of over 20 taps, in fact. Inside, you'll find a massive space with huge bar, tin walls, and period pieces throughout. They have a menu with bar food (hamburgers and such), as well as a complete bar. It gets noisy here between the crowds and TVs, so you might be shouting to have a conversation. During game nights, the place is really popular. The crowd is made up of locals and employees of the airline industry (which makes sense, considering the proximity to the airport). Overall, it's a warm, welcoming slice of Milwaukee that serves up some great regional history along with frosty drinks.

Puddler's Hall—Website: www.puddlershall.com **Address:** 2461 S St Clair St, Milwaukee, WI, 53207, (414) 747-9005 (Monday–Thursday 3pm–2am, Friday 3pm–2:30am, Saturday 11am–2:30am, Sunday 11am–2am). This place, the second oldest bar in the city, opened in 1873 as a union hall for the steelworkers of the local Milwaukee Iron Company. It was sold 20 years later to the Falk Brewery and became a tied house to serve Falk Beer. Unfortunately, the Falk Brewery burned down and they had to almost immediately sell it to Pabst, which then made it a Pabst tavern that lasted until prohibition. When the 18th amendment closed it down, the place was sold again and became a dancehall and reportedly a speakeasy, complete with underground tunnels. It started serving again after prohibition and remained in the same family until 1971, when the family sold it off and it entered a string of new names and owners—but through it all it remained a bar. It was sold the last time in 2011 to owner Casey Foltz, who, as it turns out, is a bit of a history buff. In honor of the people who would patronize the place when it was first opened, Casey renamed it Puddler's Hall (a 'puddler' was a steelworker involved in the process of making iron). The place has been beautifully restored and could probably pass as the union hall the steelworkers visited so long ago. They serve food here (pizza), so you won't go hungry (and during a Packer's game, the food is free). Plus, they have a great beer list with cheap options and can make up any drink you need. Also, check their website for special events, like concerts or table tennis tournaments.

This Is It!—**Website:** www.thisisitbar.com **Address:** 418 E Wells St, Milwaukee, WI, 53202, (414) 278-9192 (Monday–Thursday 3pm–2am, Friday 3pm–2:30am, Sunday 1pm–2am). This bar has been serving continuously under one name or another since 1936. In 1968, it was bought by Catherine "June" Brehm and her business partner, Michael Latona (whom June bought out two years later). When they acquired the place, they began openly welcoming the gay community, and ever since then the bar has been the premiere gay bar in Milwaukee. In fact, it's the oldest gay bar in the state. But more than that, if you consider that bars where the patrons were openly gay were being raided by the police up until the early 1970s, you'll realize the significance of this bar. You'll also admire the courage it took to own this place—in many cities the owners themselves would have been thrown in jail. They were careful, of course. The door and front window were the smallest allowed by law so it was difficult to peer inside, and they allowed patrons to use the back door if they chose so nobody would see them enter. In return for doing all this, the owners and the bar came to be much loved and celebrated by the community. Today, This Is It! is a warm, friendly and welcoming bar for anyone who steps through the door (the front door, that is). Inside, it's cozy and you'll feel like you stepped into the 1970s. They're known for their great bartenders who take the time to talk to their patrons and really get to know them. They serve excellent cocktails and have a complete bar with skilled mixologists manning it.

Wolski's Tavern—**Address:** 1836 N Pulaski St, Milwaukee, WI, 53202, (414) 276-8130 (Monday–Thursday 2pm–2am, Friday 2pm–2:30am, Saturday 12pm–2:30am, Sunday 12pm–2am). Opened in 1908 by Bernard Wolski, and still run by his great-grandchildren today, this legendary bar at the end of a twisting, winding street, is a place that you must visit when you visit Milwaukee. Known for its general convivial nature, Wolski's has never taken a break or closed, except once. Back in the early days, Bernard was forced to move locations, so the smart Polish bar owner picked up the entire place—the whole damned building—and moved it to its current location on Pulaski St. But it hasn't closed since. The place is crowded with locals and tourists alike, with salty popcorn and cheap beer flowing at all hours. There are a number of little quirks that make this place a one-of-a-kind. For example, there's the men's room sink, mounted outside of the bathroom, so everyone can publicly shame you for not washing your hands. Or there's the steel-tip darts and bristle dart boards that are pretty uncommon sites in bars nowadays (switched in favor of the cheaper, and safer, electronic boards). But perhaps what they're most well-known for are their signature bumper stickers

156

with "I Closed Wolski's" emblazoned on them. You'll see these everywhere in the city, from signposts to car bumpers. The way to get one? Stay until the place closes at 2am and they'll hand you one on the way out. If you peruse the many pictures on the wall you'll see fans of the bar have taken them everywhere in their travels, from China to England and everywhere in between (they give out over 20,000 of these every year). Be sure and get your bumper sticker when you come by!

Mader's Restaurant—Website: www.madersrestaurant.com **Address:** 1041 N Old World 3rd St, Milwaukee, WI, 53203, (414) 271-3377 (Monday–Thursday 11:30am–9pm, Friday–Saturday 11:30am–10pm, Sunday 11am–9pm). Okay, you got us, this isn't a bar, strictly speaking. This is a German restaurant, and one of the oldest in the country (certainly the oldest in Milwaukee). But, we're including it here because, owed to German tradition, beer is a huge part of its history and it has a beautiful bar from which it's served. Opened in 1902 by German immigrant Charles Mader, this sprawling restaurant has become a landmark in a city already full of landmark saloons. It serves traditional and classic German cuisine, like pork shank or schnitzel with sauerkraut and spätzle. There's also an amazing amount of authentic knight's armor from the old world. The walls are adorned with broadswords and shields, and suits of armor stand at attention, as if ready to be called into battle. These are all authentic and date back centuries—in fact, this is one of the oldest and most expansive private collections of historic armor there is. As you tour the place you'll see picture after picture of all the celebrities who've dined here, including presidents, actors, singers and famous writers (which excludes us). But it's the bar that we were drawn to. Standing large and impressive at the center of the restaurant, the Knight's Bar (as it's called) features tap after tap of fresh, German beer. They sell it in sizes ranging anywhere from small glasses to huge boots—so whatever your level of thirst is, they're sure to quench it. When you're in the neighborhood, which is likely because Old World 3rd Street is one of the tourist havens of Milwaukee, definitely swing by here for dinner and lots, and lots of bier!

NEWPORT AND PROVIDENCE, RI

Newport and Providence, Rhode Island were founded in 1639 and 1636, respectively. Both were settled for more or less the same reason—religious freedom. You see, despite the promise of such freedom in other colonies, Massachusetts specifically, it wasn't always to be found. Settlers here weren't allowed to practice their desired faith in Massachusetts, so fled to Rhode Island. Subsequently they both became important regions for religious dissenters.

From the start, these cities had a major impact on the future of the country. These were amongst the first to engage the British before the American Revolution (Newport men attacked and burned a British customs ship in 1772), and Rhode Island was the first colony to disavow loyalty to the Crown. Later, they became two of the most influential regions in the new country. Newport was the center of the whale oil industry, and later, sadly, the slave trade. Providence, conversely was one of the primary manufacturing centers, with factories churning out everything from silverware and jewelry, to machinery and textiles.

These cities were shaped by war. During the American Revolution, Newport was occupied by the British until 1780 when French and American forces regained the city and used it as a springboard to Providence and Yorktown, Virginia. Then, during the Civil War (though there was significant internal bitterness over slavery and the money that had been made off it by locals) the quota for Union Troop volunteers was always met or exceeded.

The US Navy also had (and has) a significant presence here. In 1861 the US Naval Academy was temporarily located in Newport, and then in 1952 a portion of the US Atlantic Fleet was also located here. Today it still hosts a number of Navy training centers, such as the US Navy War College and the Naval Education Training Command.

In all, these two cities have great history and are wonderful places to visit. And, for the purposes of this book, they offer some great watering holes that likewise have some great history.

WHITE HORSE TAVERN, NEWPORT, RI

Address: 26 Marlborough Street, Newport, RI, 02840, (401) 849-3600
Website: www.whitehorsetavern.us **Video tour:**
http://youtu.be/c3ZcmgmXU6o
Food: Yes **Live Music:** No **Hours:** Monday–Thursday 11am–9pm, Friday–
Saturday 11:30am–10pm, Sunday 11am–9pm **What do drink:** Dark and
Stormy™ **Type of Bar:** Tavern **Why You Should Go:** Oldest bar in America.

THE HISTORY

Constructed in 1652 as a lavish two-story residence for the Brinley family, it was sold to William Mayes Sr. and converted into a tavern in 1673. Stop for a moment and consider that: this place was a tavern over 100 years before the US was a country.

Besides a tavern, the establishment was also used for large assemblies, as a courthouse and even as city hall during the early years of Newport's existence.

William Mayes Jr., a notorious pirate, took over operation in the early 1700s after returning home with bounty rumored to have come from his adventures on the high seas. Hated by and a constant embarrassment to local British officials, he was loved and protected by the townspeople. Rumor has it the tavern played host to a multitude of pirate gatherings, rum trades and other illicit activities.

Eventually the establishment was sold to Jonathan Nichols who is responsible for naming the tavern "The White Horse Tavern."

During the Revolutionary War it was used by British troops for quarters. Rather than stay with Hessian mercenaries, Walter Nichols (son of Jonathan and owner at the time) fled with his family. Once the war ended, they promptly returned to set up shop.

The tavern was finally turned into a boarding house in the late 1800s and quickly fell into a state of disrepair. In the 1950s the Van Beuren family made a sizeable donation to the Preservation Society of Newport County for the purpose of restoring the building to once again be used as a tavern and restaurant. The White Horse reopened and has been in constant operation since 1957.

TODAY

Today the White Horse Tavern continues its rich tradition, serving great drinks and fine food on both of its floors. The building itself, though it has some modern additions, still retains its classic and traditional feel. From its large fireplaces to its antique furniture, period paintings and prints, this place feels like it's straight out of the late 1600s. It's easy to imagine colonials and even pirates stepping through its front doors, grabbing a drink at the bar and then sitting at the fireplace to warm up from the cold outside.

Though the building is predominantly a restaurant, the bar is still a prominent feature. In fact there are two of them, one upstairs that resembles more of a traditional tavern-style bar, and the bar downstairs—the main bar—that has a few scattered tables, stools and is flanked by a huge fireplace, at one time used for kitchen duty. This room is where you should make your stand.

THE FOOD

The White Horse is really about fine dining, and we have to admit, it's pretty good. Their clam chowder is outstanding, their Georges Bank Scallops are grand, but the must-try is their Individual Beef Wellington. Wrapped in a puff pastry, the seared prime tenderloin melts in your mouth and is exceptionally delicious.

THE DRINKS

The White Horse features a full bar with a long list of outstanding cocktails, but their most popular is the Dark and Stormy™.

Consisting of ginger beer, a float of Myer's Rum, and garnished with a lime and served in a highball glass, the drink is a popular classic in many British Commonwealth countries. Its appearance as the dark rum slowly sinks into the ginger beer is similar to what one may see as the sun sets on a dark and stormy night, hence the name. It is a must-try on your visit to the White Horse.

NEARBY DISTRACTIONS

12 Meter Charters—Website: www.12metercharters.com **Address:** 49 Bowen's Wharf 3rd Floor Newport, RI, 02840, (401) 851-1216 (operating hours vary by season and charter types). Have a few hours to kill and want to give sailing a try? If so, then check out 12 Meter Charters just half a mile from the White Horse Tavern. Featuring multiple former America's Cup sailboats and requiring no prior sailing background, it will give you a chance to experience New England sailing at its finest.

Newport History Tours—Website: www.newporthistorytours.org, (401) 846-0813 (operating hours and locations vary by tour and season). Interested in taking a step back into Newport's past and discovering where pirates lived, criminals were punished, riots took place, remarkable entrepreneurship occurred and what life was like for Newport's original settlers? If so, check out the Newport Historical Society's long list of historical tours. They'll help put the area into a better context and get you in the right frame of mind for drinks later at the White Horse Tavern.

Fishing Charters—Website: www.flippingoutcharters.com (401) 529-2267, **Website:** www.newportriwatersports.com (401) 849-4820, **Website:** www.flahertycharters.com (401) 848-5554. If you're in town for more than a night you might want to try your hand at catching some of New England's legendary fish. There are a number of charters to choose from, but for starters give one of the local fishing charters listed here a try. In the waters off of Newport you'll have the chance to hook into a shark, squid or a legendary striper.

NEWPORT & PROVIDENCE'S HISTORIC BARS

Cappy's Hillside Café—Address: 8 Memorial Blvd W, Newport, RI, 02840, (401) 847-9419 (Monday–Sunday 12pm–1am). Opened in 1938, Cappy's has been serving Newport locals cheap drinks and friendly service since day one. If you happen to like the New York Giants, you'll find a welcome home here (the one friendly outpost surrounded by New England fans). According to legend, they were the favorite of founder, John "Cappy" Cappuccilli, and the couple who bought the old dive in 1987 kept things as is, including the Giant's memorabilia. You'll find dark paneling, pool tables, and plenty of character surrounding you. Like most all dives they serve cheap beer, and they also serve a few things from the kitchen (like hot dogs and pizza on Fridays).

Murphy's Providence—Website: www.murphysprovidence.com **Address:** 100 Fountain St, Providence, RI, 02903, (401) 621-8467 (Monday–Thursday 11am–1am, Friday 11am–2am, Saturday 9am–2am, Sunday 8am–1am). This Providence staple was opened in 1929 as a café, but then became more of a delicatessen in the 1950s. Finally, Murphy's merged with the next door Keyhole Lounge in the 1960s to start the combination bar and deli found today. The menu is pure New York, with corned beef and Rueben sandwiches, sour pickles and chips, the whole 9-yards. They also serve decently priced beer—domestics plus seasonals—a whole range of booze, seasonal cocktails and wine.

Nick-A-Nees—Address: 75 South St, Providence, RI, 02903, (401) 861-7290 (Sunday–Thursday 3pm–1am, Friday–Saturday 3pm–2am). This is the most popular dive you'll find in Providence, with free live music and great drink specials. Open for over 20 years, Nick-a-Nees is one of the few dog-friendly dives in the area. They also have a great jukebox and pool table if you get bored with the TVs. They get crowded—very crowded—when there is live music, so get here early to find a spot. The crowd is diverse and represents a good cross section of the city, but they're friendly and welcoming. The service is fast and the drinks are cheap, what more do you need to know?

NEW ORLEANS, LA

When someone says New Orleans, most people's minds wander to things like the French Quarter, Bourbon Street, Creole cooking, Hurricane Katrina, swamps, and even alligators. But there is much more to the Crescent City than all of this.

New Orleans' history reads, in some ways, as a story you'd find in the National Enquirer. The area was discovered by French explorers in 1682, who then quickly claimed the land for France. Later, in 1718 France wanted to develop the area but was close to bankrupt, so they enlisted the help of entrepreneur, Mike Law, who created a company with the supposed mission of settling the area for France (the company was nothing more than an early form of a pyramid scheme). France quickly tired of Law, his questionable business practices, and his upset investors, and secretly passed ownership to Spain. Then, the US took over ownership via the Louisiana purchase in 1803. This is just a bit of the city's tumultuous history.

Here are just a few additional historical highlights of one of America's best-loved cities: In the early 20th century, the city was terrorized when a man utilized a straight-razor and axe to murder 6 residents and wound 6 more. He later penned an open letter telling local citizens they would be left alone if they were playing jazz in their houses, rumor has it the dance halls were full that night. In 1977, the New Orleans Jazz was the first and (still) only NBA team to draft a woman (alas, she declined the offer). In 1991, the state governor's race had a widely utilized unofficial slogan, "Vote for the Crook: It's important" when a notoriously corrupt Edwin Edwards ran for governor against a former KKK Grand Wizard. And, finally, who can forget the notorious Hurricane Katrina of 2005? A storm that almost wiped the city off the map.

But New Orleans isn't all doom, gloom, and stacked with oddities. As a matter of fact, the city has a spirit that you can feel as you explore it. From the classic bars dotting the neighborhoods to the parades, people and the food, you can feel the life of the city in every corner of it. No matter what it, and its people, have been through (and it's been a lot), they never give up. New Orleans is always pushing forward and makes the best of it all. And this spirit is reflected in her bars.

TUJAGUE'S, NEW ORLEANS, LA

Address: 823 Decatur Street , New Orleans, LA, 70116, (504) 525-8676
Website: www.tujaguesrestaurant.com **Video tour:**
https://youtu.be/1grlpGK7kpI
Food: Yes **Live Music:** Yes **Hours:** Monday–Sunday 11am–2am **Type of Bar:** Dive **What to Drink:** Grasshopper, Ramos Gin Fizz, Pimm's Cup **Why You Should Go:** Second oldest dining institution in New Orleans, where "Brunch" was invited, oldest stand-up bar in America, where the Grasshopper was invented.

THE HISTORY

Tujague's started life as a traditional restaurant when Guillaume and Marie Abadie Tujague, French immigrants, opened it in 1856. The restaurant served breakfast and lunch to the local dock workers, market laborers and seamen, all ever-present on the riverfront. Lunches at the restaurant were a grand affair, featuring seven courses, and beers were purchased for a paltry 4 cents. Guilliaume Tujague sold the restaurant to Phlibert Guichert shortly before his passing in 1912.

Just up the road from Tujague's was an establishment known as Begue's, Tujague's closest and, some say, fiercest competitor. It was originally founded and ran by Madame Begue, who is credited with creating the occasion of brunch (to accommodate additional guests slightly later in the day due to her small dining room size) we have all come to love and adore. Begue's was also known for lavish and extraordinary meals and it is a commonly held belief that Madam Begue also ran a successful brothel on the second floor of the restaurant (it is debated amongst those in the know which was more profitable, the brothel or the restaurant). Madam Beque died in 1906, leaving the restaurant (and brothel) to her daughter and son-in-law, the Anouilies. Later, in 1914, Begue employee Jean-Dominic Castet and Philiber Buichert (owner of Tujagues) purchased Begue's from Begue's widowed daughter and combined the two restaurants changing the name from Begue's to Tujagues and relocating both restaurants to Begue's location.

Following the combining of the two establishments, Tujague's would remain a center point of New Orleans culinary extravagance and have profound effect on the world of cocktails with the creation of the Grasshopper. The story goes that in the year 1919 (or maybe just prior to it), Guichet invented the cocktail during a New York City cocktail competition. The drink won second place in the competition and Guichet brought the cocktail recipe back to New Orleans and dubbed it "Grasshopper" due to its bright green color.

Tujague's passed from owner to owner over the years but the tradition and spirit remained. It even operated as one of the worst-kept secret speakeasies during prohibition (which can actually be said for the entirety of New Orleans). Local businessman Steven Latter took the place over in 1982 and immediately set about researching and restoring the restaurant and bar to its earlier glory. He brought in period furniture, photos, news clippings, and other forms of memorabilia relating to Tujague's colorful and proud past.

TODAY

Today Mark Latter, Steven Latter's son, owns and operates the establishment and has continued the tradition of outstanding cooking as well as traditional New Orleans craft cocktails, such as the Grasshopper, Ramos Gin Fizz, Pimm's Cup and Sazerac. The establishment is separated into two distinct areas, the restaurant and the stand-up bar.

The restaurant is a more formal affair than the bar, but that isn't to say it isn't a classic. Walk in today and you'll be swept away to the Tujague's of old, with picturesque balconies, ornate antique's, ceiling fans and continued creole culinary traditions, instilled by both Madam Begue and Tujague. The dining experience from the Tujague's of old is also alive and well with traditional five-course meals available with any entrée.

While the restaurant is truly something special to see, and to enjoy, the bar is no slouch. When you walk in today you will immediately notice the historic bar itself, dating back to 1856. Look closer and you'll see the absence of bar stools. That is because Tujague's features one of the oldest stand up bars in the US (stand up bars are believed to have been created to give weary horseback travelers a place to stretch whilst drinking.) This is where you want to start your evening, or, if time is short, hop in for a quick Grasshopper, Ramos Gin Fizz, or Pimm's Cup (we tried them all and honestly couldn't pick a favorite, each has its own unique place on our cocktail list).

The place is also believed to be haunted. As current owner Mark highlights, there are multiple ghosts that can often be heard banging around on the building's third floor.

Tujague's is simply one of the most beautiful and ornate bars we have had the pleasure of visiting.

THE FOOD

Tujague's has kept the creole cuisine traditions of Madam Begue and Guillaume Tujague alive and well. With menu items like Shrimp Remoulade, Trout Amandine, Crawfish and Wild Mushroom Gnocchi, and Tujague's Brisket, the food simply won't disappoint. The one thing we recommend is turning your entrée of choice into a five-course meal, giving you the feeling of Tujague's of old.

THE DRINKS

Tujague's revels in historic craft cocktails, focusing on New Orleans classics, like the Grasshopper–which was invented here, the Sazerac, making their own Pimm's for their Pimm's Cup—a long and arduous ten-day process—and utilizing real egg whites in their Ramos Gin Fizz. You can't go wrong with any, so consider trying them all.

NEARBY DISTRACTIONS

Steamboat Natchez—Website: www.steamboatnatchez.com **Address:** 1 Toulouse St., New Orleans, LA, 70130, (504) 586-8777 (3 cruises per day, 11:30am, 2:30pm, 7pm). The Steamboat Natchez is the last truly classic Mississippi steamboat operating out of New Orleans (that is to say it is the last steam-powered steamboat–most of the rest are powered by electric motors). We took this tour on a whim and thoroughly enjoyed the sights of both the river and the classic boat. For a truly unique experience hop on for the 7 pm cruise which includes traditional New Orleans jazz and dinner.

Cajun Encounters Tour Company—Website: www.cajunencournters.com **Address:** 55345 Highway 90 East, Slidell, LA, 70461 (tour times vary, check online). New Orleans is surrounded by swamps. As a matter of fact, besides Bourbon Street, Mardi Gras, and Drew Brees, it's usually one of the first things we think of when we think of the Crescent City. So why not get *out* of the cramped city and check it out? Cajun Encounters host's a multitude of swamp tours including VIP and nighttime excursions. We highly recommend the night tour as it gives you a chance to check out some of the wildlife prior to the sun going down (i.e., feeding marshmallows or hotdogs to alligators), enjoy a beautiful sunset, and see how the swamp and its active creatures change from day to night.

HENRY'S UPTOWN BAR, NEW ORLEANS, LA

Address: 5101 Magazine St., New Orleans, LA, 70115, (504) 324-8140
Website: www.henrysbaruptown.com **Video tour:**
https://youtu.be/jqPg4eSpNUo
Food: Yes **Live Music:** Yes **Hours:** Monday–Tuesday 3pm–?, Wednesday–
Friday 12pm–?, Saturday 10:30am–?, Sunday 10am–?, and these hours are
subject to change, we recommend calling ahead. **Type of Bar:** Dive **What to
Drink:** Bottled beer, shot **Why You Should Go:** 4th oldest bar in New
Orleans, oldest bar outside of the downtown area.

THE HISTORY

Located in (you guessed it) New Orleans' Uptown, Henry's is considered
the city's 4th oldest bar, and the oldest bar outside of the downtown area. It
was opened in 1900 by Irish immigrants James and Margaret Tully Lee. The
Lee's handed the bar down to their daughter and son-in-law, Edward and
Dorothy Crone, at which point in time the bar became known simply as
Crone's (it's unknown what the bar was called prior to that). Later, Edward's
daughter Dorothy, married a gentleman by the name of Henry Gogreve who,
upon his return from World War 2, took over the bar.

Henry was known to be quite the character. He was good-nature and no-
nonsense, and created a fiercely loyal group of patrons who still come to the
bar today. Henry was also known to hold a daily court with his World War 2
buddies right up until his passing in 2010 at 91 years old. Tim Thomas, the
bar's manager as of our visit, described the banter between Henry and his
buddies as some of the greatest and most entertaining he has ever heard
(watch the video if you want to know more, it's worth it).

Henry even had a run-in with one of America's most notorious characters of the 1960s: Lee Harvey Oswald. Oswald, whose house was a mere two blocks away, was known to have visited the bar a time or two to have a cold beer or stop by the adjacent market. It was during one of these visits that he and Henry got into it. Oswald wanted to change the channel from baseball to a news report that featured him. Henry told him no, the TV is for baseball. Oswald disagreed, and Henry proceeded to promptly escort him from the bar. Later, after Oswald Assassinated JFK, Henry was even questioned by the FBI.

Henry's has been loyally serving up drink for over 113 years, or "serving beer before you were born" as their slogan claims. In that time, the bar has seen more than its fair share of ups and downs, including Hurricane Katrina. Following the storm came rolling blackouts, and Henry's, wanting to keep the bar open and the community's spirits high, used a generator to power a beer cooler and a karaoke machine for days after the storm had subsided. If you happened to show up, you got free shots of tequila until you thought you could sing karaoke. And that spirit is what has made Henry's, New Orleans 4th-oldest bar, the spirit of community, dedication and support. Something lacking in many of today's bars.

TODAY

Today Henry's is a modest neighborhood bar known for its cheap beer, stiff drinks, televised sports and darts (rumor has it that Josh Brolin was recently asked to leave for misusing darts, were not exactly sure what "misusing" darts mean, but there you go). When you walk in you will immediately notice it's a step back from the loudness and sensory overload that is New Orleans. The décor is simple, the furnishings old but sturdy, and the photos and memorabilia dotting the walls celebrate past and present patrons and celebrities that frequent the place. In a word, Henry's is simply…comfortable.

It is that comfort that made Henry's successful, and continues to keep it that way. It's a place where you walk in for a cold beer, strike up a conversation with the bartender, or some other patron, and before you know it, the day is over and your significant other is wondering where the hell you've been all day. And for the most part, that's how Henry's gets along, for most of the year.

The bar does get rolling on Saints game day or during the Mardi Gras parade (the bar is located on the parade route). But on those days, you don't find a crowd reminiscent of Bourbon St. Instead you find multiple generations from the real city, hanging out, enjoying the festivities as judges belly up next to history professors, police officers, students and anyone who happens to be in the area. "Henry's is everybody's living room" according to one regular.

Henry's is without a doubt an unpretentious neighborhood bar, a throwback to the time when bars were located in the middle of neighborhoods instead of pre-planned, pre-zoned commercial development area. The sad part is that bars like this are becoming a rarity.

THE FOOD

Henry's has a Big Cheezy located inside of it which serves up "grown up grilled cheez." And whilst we were a little apprehensive at first, we must admit, it is pretty stinking tasty. We grabbed an Original, a Crawgator, and tomato basil soup, and found it a perfect complement to our cold beer and shots of whiskey.

THE DRINKS

You won't find the craft cocktail selections or rich sugary drinks New Orleans has become so well known for. Instead, you will find heavy-handed mixed drinks, bottled beer, and shots. You can't go wrong with any of them.

NEARBY DISTRACTIONS

Lee Harvey Oswald's House—Address: 4905 Magazine St., New Orleans, LA, 70115 (Open 24 hours, but don't disturb the neighborhood). Lee Harvey Oswald, the unscrupulous and psychotic Marxist who assassinated JFK, was from New Orleans, and rented this small house in 1963 for himself and his small family. This is, of course, the same year he assassinated Kennedy, and where he resided up until that fateful day. You can cruise by and take a gander at his once residence (we did simply out of curiosity), but we ask that you be respectful of the tenant and neighborhood.

The Prytania—Website: www.theprytania.com **Address:** 5339 Prytania St, New Orleans, LA, 70115, (504) 891-2787 (Show times vary, check their website to see what's showing and when). Built in 1914, this is the oldest, continuously running movie theater in the south, and one of the oldest in the entire country. This is a classic, single-screen theater, the kind that was built with majesty back in the early 20th century. They show a single current release movie, but that's not what you come here for. Instead, you want to take in one of their classic movies, shown throughout the week. This is a great spot to spend a couple of hours away from the heat and humidity, or maybe just to sober up. In either case, it'll be a memorable experience.

ARNAUD'S FRENCH 75 BAR, NEW ORLEANS, LA

Address: 813 Bienville St., New Orleans, LA, 70112, (504) 523-5433
Website: www.arnaudsrestaurant.com **Video tour:**
https://youtu.be/PKELVJ2dxew
Food: Yes **Live Music:** Yes **Hours:** Sunday 10am–2:30pm and 6pm–10pm,
Monday–Thursday 6pm–10pm, Friday–Saturday 6pm–10:30pm **Type of
Bar:** Saloon **What to Drink:** French 75, Sazerac, Rebennack **Why You
Should Go:** One of New Orleans oldest and largest bars, it has been around
for over 100 years, has a Mardi Gras museum and is haunted.

THE HISTORY

The year was 1918 when the customers of a vivacious wine merchant bet
him that even he, as outgoing and popular as he was, couldn't open a
successful restaurant in New Orleans. The man was Count Arnaud (his real
name was Arnaud Cazenave, but he decided to give himself this moniker),
and he immediately set out to prove them wrong by opening his very own
restaurant, which he called, fittingly, Arnaud's.

Count Arnaud quickly moved his restaurant to the forefront of the New
Orleans fine-dining scene with a tasty and expansive menu (featuring, for
example, over 50 seafood entrees). The place defined French-Creole cuisine
and provided a location where people could come to show off to guests,
celebrate, hold business meetings, stage a grand ball, or just grab a casual
dinner. He quickly proved his doubters wrong, and won the bet in the
process.

Arnaud's was so successful, in fact, that the Count was able to buy up 13
adjoining buildings, some of which were reputed opium dens and brothels,

that took up most of the block. He renovated and shaped the rooms to serve his and his customers' needs as he expanded, creating large expansive rooms capable of hosting grand balls, and even small private rooms perfect for a private and intimate dinner.

When prohibition became law, Arnaud's was setup perfectly considering its expansive size, complex floor plan, and intimate rooms. Combine the place's layout with the count's philosophy, that wine and spirits were natural companions to good living and good food, the fact that alcohol was illegal was a minor inconvenience. This led to the creation of the Richelieu Bar, a bar with no windows and where patrons could get spiked coffee during prohibition. His philosophy worked, for a while, but the law eventually caught up with him and he was imprisoned for a short time. He didn't let his imprisonment slow him down, though. On the contrary, he turned his experience into promotion, which helped make Arnaud's THE fine dining restaurant in New Orleans during the 30s and 40s.

Arnaud successfully ran the bar for 30 years before passing it on to his free-spirited daughter, Germaine. Germaine was herself larger than life and some consider her lifestyle to have been extreme, even by today's standards. She epitomized the spirit of not only Arnaud's, but of New Orleans itself.

After 30 years of running the restaurant, Germaine sold it to Archie Casbarian. It is believed that while she had many offers to purchase the restaurant on the table, it was Archie's similarities to her father that persuaded her to select his offer. The restaurant and bars remain in the Casbarian family today, and while Archie is no longer with us, his son and daughter continue to maintain the high standards established by Arnaud himself.

TODAY

After Archie Casbarian took over in 1978, he set about painstakingly restoring the establishment to its former glory. To help him achieve this goal, and gain additional insight into what the place was like in the past, Archie sent out numbered skeleton keys to past patrons. The skeleton keys worked on the Richelieu bar's street entrance, pretty much the only place in the building that didn't need work, and when the selected patrons stopped in for a visit or a cocktail he would do everything he could to garner additional information about the place, to find out what was missing, and to understand how best to return it to its original self.

Today the restaurant and Richelieu bar have been fully restored and simply emit classic New Orleans cool. Walk into either and you'll instantly feel like you've entered a time warp back to the early 20th century. The restaurant feels classy and high-end, but not overly pretentious. To get a real feel for the place head over to the Richelieu bar (this is where you could get Arnaud's spiked coffee). You'll notice a nondescript street entrance, supposedly one of the worst-kept secrets during prohibition, a lack of windows to help keep the prying eyes of the law out, and even a "stoopie bench," which was used by over-imbibers who needed a nap. This bar is a verified prohibition speakeasy, and you can feel it when you walk in.

The other bar located in Arnaud's is the French 75 Bar. Where the Richelieu bar emits that quiet speakeasy feel, the French 75 bar suggests pre-prohibition, when cocktails were celebrated as an art form. In the early days of Arnaud's this area was a male-only grill room, but was then transformed into the Grill Bar, was then renamed The Arnaud's Bar, and then finally christened the French 75 Bar. It features a warm and inviting atmosphere, with classic furnishing and décor throughout. The bartenders, clad in white dinner jackets, are dedicated to the art of cocktail making, and the bar features one of the best cocktail menus we have ever come across. In short, it is a real treat to any classic cocktail aficionado.

Arnaud's remains a staple of the French Quarter and one of New Orleans' finest dining establishments. This place simply can't be missed during a trip to New Orleans.

THE FOOD

Arnaud's serves up some of the finest creole inspired cooking we have had the pleasure of experiencing, and you simply can't go wrong with many of the menu choices, like the speckled trout for example. But at the top of the list we have to put the Souffle Potatoes. Light, airy, pillowy, and simply delicious, a must-have with anything you order!

THE DRINKS

Arnaud's aims to provide patrons a balance between old-school cocktails and cocktail-making, and the new-school craft cocktail movement, a goal they achieve exceptionally well. Their classics, like the French 75 and Sazerac, are some of the best the city has to offer, while their new offerings, like the Rebennack, are not to be missed.

NEARBY DISTRACTIONS

Museum of Death—Website: www.museumofdeath.net **Address:** 227 Dauphine St., New Orleans, LA, 70112, (504) 593-3968 (Open daily 10am–7pm). It has always seemed that New Orleans has had a kind of infatuation with death. We aren't saying it's a good or bad thing, we just feel it's there. So, what better place to put the Museum of Death? Be warned, though, this place is not for the faint of heart. It features shrunken heads, one of Dr. Kevorkian's suicide machines, hair recovered from the O.J. crime scene, videos of actual death, and tools of torture. There is a bright side though, rumor has it if you faint you get a free t-shirt that reads "I passed out at the Museum of Death…and lived to talk about it."

New Orleans Historic Voodoo Museum—Website: www.voodoomuseum.com **Address:** 724 Dumaine St., New Orleans, LA, 70116, (504) 680-0128 (Open daily 10am–6pm). It's hard to think of New Orleans without thinking of Voodoo in some form (curses, dolls, donuts, etc.). This museum will give you the opportunity to explore not only some of the legends, traditions and mysteries surrounding voodoo, but the way in which it has shaped the city and its people.

PAT O'BRIEN'S, NEW ORLEANS, LA

Address: 718 St. Peter St., New Orleans, LA, 70116, (504) 525-4823
Website: www.patobriens.com **Video tour:**
https://youtu.be/1WM0udqAQQY
Food: Yes **Live Music:** Yes **Hours:** Monday–Thursday 12pm–2am, Friday–
Saturday 10am–4am, Sunday 10am–2am **Type of Bar:** Pub **What to
Drink:** Hurricane **Why You Should Go:** Invented the Hurricane, epic piano
bar, flaming fountain.

THE HISTORY

Pat O'Briens was opened in 1930. Stop and think about that for a minute: it was opened during prohibition. That means it began life as a speakeasy and then went legit. It's only surprising until you consider that it was located in New Orleans, probably one of the wettest cities in the US, and probably second only to Detroit in the amount of alcohol available (it's estimated that at least 70% of the illicit alcohol that came into the United States during prohibition either originated or passed through Detroit).

Pat O'Briens was founded by Benson Harrison O'Brien (known as Pat), who opened the original speakeasy not far from the current location. To gain entrance you simply knocked on the door, whispered the secret phrase "storm's a brewing," and then entered. Later, at the end of prohibition, Pat moved the bar to a new location directly across the street from the speakeasy. The reason behind the move? Pat wanted to separate himself from his notorious days as a speakeasy proprietor.

Pat O'Brien's quickly grew in popularity, and Pat, with the help of a new partner by the name of Charlie Cantrell, moved the bar to its current location

173

in 1942. The new building, built in 1791, was a sprawling location that gave the establishment the room they needed to host two bars and an expansive patio. Pat O'Brien's continued to grow over the next couple of years and became the go-to location for New Orleans residents and visitors alike, right up until World War 2.

As the United States became more and more involved in the war, many of the everyday items citizens took for granted, like sugar, flour, wood, tires, and even booze, became harder and harder to come by. Thus, liquor distributors had an exceedingly small supply of high-demand liquors (like Scotch), and a seemingly endless supply of rum (due to very low demand in the US). To solve the problem, distributors would force bars to purchase upwards of 50 cases of rum for every case of Scotch, bourbon, or other high-demand liquor.

Pat O'Brien's wasn't immune to the "tariff," and so accumulated a huge stockpile of rum they needed to get rid of. Pat, being a wise businessman, held a bartending competition with the goal of creating a drink that would help move the massive quantities of rum he had on hand. The drink that won the contest featured 4 oz. of rum and would eventually become known as a Hurricane, named for the hurricane glass they served it in. Initially, the bar gave the glasses away with every drink, making it even more popular with tourists and even locals.

Pat O'Brien's continued to grow and innovate throughout the years. They were one of the first bars to feature dueling pianos, and are considered home of the original flaming fountain. A new owner, Sonny Oechsner, bought the bar in 1978, and proceeded to expand its locations to Mexico, Florida, Tennessee, and Texas. But throughout its growth, it's always remained an integral part of New Orleans and its culture.

TODAY

Today, Pat O'Brien's remains in the same expansive building it moved into in 1942, and while the years have ticked by, not much has changed in the bar.

As you make your way in via their carriage entrance, the first bar you come to on your left is known as the main bar. You'll almost immediately notice that this place feels more like a local's bar than a globally famous destination just steps away from Bourbon Street. You'll find televisions featuring local sporting events, photos of customers from different eras of its expansive history strewn across the wall, a jukebox belting out jazz tunes, and that local-bar ambiance you just can't commercialize. This bar alone makes it worth the stop.

As you move deeper into Pat O'Brien's you come across the piano bar (opposite the main bar), which is one of the most popular of its type in the country. It features dueling copper-topped baby-grand pianos and a variety of excellent pianists constantly cranking out new and classic hits, college fight songs, and even military tunes. It's worth a stop just to take in the scene. Write the name of a song on a napkin and pass it up (be sure to include a tip) if there's a tune you'd like to hear.

As you continue on, you arrive at the courtyard: an oasis away from the busy hustle and bustle of Bourbon Street just on the other side of the wall. It's here you'll find the famous flaming fountain, reportedly the first of its kind, surrounded by local and exotic tropical plants. This is also where you can take a second to catch your breath, order a hurricane and grab a bite to eat.

Despite its feverish growth throughout the years, ownership changes, millions of visitors, and multiple franchises, Pat O'Brien's has always remained an integral part of the New Orleans community. According to Shelly Oechsner Waguespack, Pat O'Brien's Vice President, "even though millions of people visit Pat O's every year, locals are the reason the doors stay open." It's that dedication to the community, and the community's dedication to the bar, that's continued to make Pat O'Brian's a must-visit destination bar during your next trip to Bourbon Street.

THE FOOD

We were lucky enough to try a few of Pat O'Brien's food offerings during our visit, and suggest you do the same. Stick to the Cajun/creole influenced items, like the alligator bites, popcorn crusted oysters, shrimp creole, crawfish étouffée, gumbo, jambalaya, and/or red beans and rice. Not a big Cajun/creole fan? That's ok, the menu is expansive and have dishes to satisfy most.

THE DRINKS

Pat O'Brien's has a full-service bar, so you can get pretty much any drink you want. But this place invented the Hurricane, to start off with anything but that would be a travesty.

NEARBY DISTRACTIONS

Saint Louis Cemetery No. 2—Address: 300 N Claiborne Ave, New Orleans, LA, 70112, (504) 482-5065 (Monday–Saturday, 9am–3pm, Sunday, 9am–12pm). While Saint Louis Cemetery No. 1 is off limits to the public and only available via tour guides, nearby Saint Louis Cemetery No. 2 is open to the public. It was founded in 1823 and features the above-ground tombs typical to New Orleans. There are also a number of statues and carved gravestones. And, like any other cemetery you'll visit in this city, it has a definite creep factor.

Haunted History Tours—Website: www.hauntedhistorytours.com **Address:** 723 St Peter St, New Orleans, LA, 70119, (504) 861-2727 (Sunday–Friday, 8am–11pm, Saturday, 8am–10:30pm). You need to go on at least one ghost tour in New Orleans, and this company is the biggest and highest rated. They offer a number of different tours around the city, with different themes throughout the day. If you want something that'll give you chills, then definitely try to book a ghost tour towards the end of the day.

SNAKE AND JAKE'S CHRISTMAS CLUB LOUNGE, NEW ORLEANS, LA

Address: 7612 Oak Street, New Orleans, LA, 70118, (504) 861-2802
Website: www.snakeandjakes.com **Video tour:**
https://youtu.be/8ijMRTJiobQ
Food: No **Live Music:** Yes **Hours:** Daily 7pm–? **Type of Bar:** Dive **What to Drink:** Schlitz and a Possum Drop **Why You Should Go:** Best dive bar in New Orleans, maybe in the US.

THE HISTORY

Put simply, Snake and Jake's history is vague. Dave, the current owner, grew up in the area and remembers it being there in the 50s, but we haven't been able to officially verify that. He believes the structure was originally a coal depot (where locals would swing by to pick up coal to be used for cooking and/or heating) and later an auto shop of some sort—its shape and structural attributes make both of these scenarios viable and likely.

The bar was put up for sale in 1992 and Dave, a bar musician at the time, felt he just had to buy it. A little short on money at the time, he went to every one of his friends and asked to borrow money and was turned down by all except one. That one friend offered to give him 20% of the bar's asking price, which, Dave felt, would be an insult to the seller. But, having scraped together all his personal monetary resources and exhausting all potential investors he made the low-ball offer to the sellers, who, surprisingly, accepted it. But, it wasn't all smooth sailing from there.

Dave worked in the bar around the clock, at first making less than nothing, then breaking even, and then finally turning a profit. He remembers when the first night the bar turned a profit, he called his business partner and exclaimed "we made ten bucks tonight!!" That was the turning point for Snake and Jake's, and is owed in part to its late hours. Local musicians, finishing up gigs at other bars, would head down to the bar to enjoy a late-night drink or six. Word spread, and Snake and Jake's continued to gain popularity. Today, it is a New Orleans' late night institution, and deservedly so.

TODAY

As you walk into Snake and Jake's today, you will be greeted by a small, dark room—lit only by Christmas tree lights—with a few scattered tables and a narrow bar extending into the red and green glowing depths of what you'd swear is little more than an old shack. One thing that will strike you quickly is the place's ability to stave off the outside world and provide you with a timeless, windowless pocket in which to immerse yourself. It is almost like there's a bubble of protection surrounding the bar and its inhabitants from the outside world. Stock market crash? Zombie apocalypse? None of it gets in or matters at Snake and Jake's.

Snake and Jake's just simply has "it." And by "it," we mean that special characteristic that makes its patrons simply love the place with an admirable loyalty. Maybe it's the darkness of the place that lets you walk in and get lost from the outside world, or maybe it's your problems you need to escape from. Maybe it's the friendliness of the owner and bartenders, or the revelry and near-collegiality between the other drinkers. It could also be the "I don't give a f!@#" personality of the place, but whatever "it" is, Snake and Jake's has it.

Stories of epic nights at Snake and Jake's are wide spread and plentiful. Anthon Bourdain filmed an episode of "The Layover" at this bar. George Clooney and some of his buddies crashed the place one night and no one ever noticed (apparently, no one noticed due to the lack of lighting until shortly before he left for the night). At one point in time, there was a rumor floating around that if you showed up naked, you drank for free. Some college fraternity brothers gave it a try only to find out it was nothing more than a rumor (and they locked their keys in the car so had to wait for AAA in the buff).

Put simply, people love Snake and Jake's. They love telling stories about their experiences, love talking about the ridiculous things they've seen here (like a possum falling out of the ceiling an onto a customer's head). The place is dark, almost too dark, but in a city like New Orleans, a place the Snake and Jake's is needed to balance out what's going on in the French Quarter. The place is similar to Atomic Liquors in Las Vegas: it is a placed removed from the circus on the other side of town.

Here you drink, you relax, you talk, and you laugh. You do this with the other shadowy figures around. And when you're done, the world is still there waiting for you on the other side of the door, but the brief reprieve makes the trip worth it.

THE DRINKS

This is a dive bar, so leave thoughts of high end craft cocktails at the door. Stick to the classic's, or, even better, stick to the bar's specialties, like Fish Water, Possum Drops, or an ice-cold Schlitz.

NEARBY DISTRACTIONS

Tree of Life—Address: East Dr., New Orleans, LA, 70118, (Open 24 hours). Simply put, this is a big, old tree. The age of this gnarled old oak is guessed at anywhere from 100–500 years old (the experts aren't really sure). With its massive trunk, moss hanging off it, and long, arm-like branches, this is a popular destination for photos. It's also popular to climb, and the secret of the tree is that is backs up to one of the walls of the zoo right next to it. On the other side of that wall are the zoo's giraffes, so after a short climb, and with no money spent, you can get a great selfie with a genuine *Giraffa Camelopardalis*.

Rock 'n' Bowl—Website: www.rocknbowl.com **Address:** 3016 S Carrollton Ave, New Orleans, LA, 70118, (504) 861-1700 (Monday–Thursday, 11:30am–12am, Friday–Saturday, 11:30am–2am). Grown up bowling is the best! Come by this bowling alley if you're looking for a fun activity that involves adult beverages and loud music. Rock 'n' Bowl is a great escape from the noise of the city (and the humidity if you visit during the summer).

Lafayette Cemetery No. 1—Address: 1416-1498 Washington Ave, New Orleans, LA, 70130, (504) 658-3781 (Monday–Sunday, 7am–3pm). You know all those images of New Orleans cemeteries and tombs? Chances are, many of them were taken here. This is an authentic, creepy, old New Orleans cemetery from the 19th century, complete with above-ground tombs, statues, moss and dreary decay.

NEW ORLEAN'S HISTORIC BARS

Jean Laffite's Blacksmith Shop—Website: www.lafittesblacksmithshop.com **Address:** 941 Bourbon St, New Orleans, LA, 70116, (504) 593-9761 (Monday–Sunday, 10am–3am). The building that houses what's now called Jean Laffite's Blacksmith Shop is one of the oldest in the city, built approximately 1761. However, much of its history is legend, and much more is rumor, though most is accepted without question, despite little evidence found really for any of it. Jean Laffite, the notorious New Orleans pirate, was said to have owned this building and to have used it as a blacksmith shop as a front for his nefarious deeds. There has also reportedly been a bar in the building since it opened, which would make it the oldest bar in the city (sadly, however, we have found zero evidence proving this). It's obvious this place it old. The fireplace especially suited for a blacksmith stands solidly at the front entrance of the place. The old bar is the only thing lit by anything other than candle light, which is how they illuminate the rest of the rooms. Drink offerings here range from beer on tap to the New Orleans staple, the Sazerac. It's also reportedly haunted by Jean Laffite himself as well as a sobbing woman upstairs. It's a fun place to visit while on Bourbon Street, and while thoroughly a tourist destination it's still fun and more preferable to the dozens of neon-lit clubs you'll pass to get here.

Absinthe House—Address: 240 Bourbon St, New Orleans, LA, 70112, (504) 523-3181 (Monday–Wednesday, 9am–3am, Thursday–Saturday, 9am–5am). The building housing Old Absinthe House was constructed in 1806 at the dawn of the United States. Before drugs like opium and cocaine were used widely in the 1800s, Absinthe was wildly popular for its supposed hallucinogenic effects. The drink was originally given to Napoleon's troops as a field-treatment for malaria. They brought back a taste for this "medicine" and it quickly became associated with the Bohemian culture. In 1846, the Alexis Coffee House opened where the modern day Old Absinthe House now stands. At the time a coffee house was the phrase used for a bar—if you wanted coffee you actually went to a café. Interestingly, a "coffee house" is where pot is sold in Amsterdam and if you want coffee you likewise go to the café. In any case, the Coffee House employed a skilled, Spanish mixologist named Cayetano Ferrer who took over the place in 1874 and changed the name to the Absinthe Room—thereby associating the bar with the spirit of 19th century hipster set. The bar lasted for years until Ferrer passed away in 1890 and his heirs took over and began calling the place the Old Absinthe House.

Carousel Bar—Website: www.hotelmonteleone.com **Address:** 214 Royal St., New Orleans, LA, 70130, (504) 523-3341 (Open daily, 11am–12am). The Carousel Bar is a New Orleans classic. Located in the Hotel Monteleone, the bar is literally a carousel that has been spinning in place since 1949. The unique bar, exceptional craft cocktail menu and grand view of the historic Royal Street makes this place exceptionally popular, but well worth the visit. It's definitely worthwhile to stop in here for either a well-made classic cocktail, or a new cocktail that puts their unique twist on the classic. In either case you will not be disappointed!

NEW YORK, NY

No city in the United States boasts more history—as it concerns alcohol and drinking—than New York. The very first brewery in the new world was founded here in 1612 by a couple of Dutch immigrants named Adrian Block and Hans Christiansen. Its first distillery, probably making hard apple cider (called applejack), was founded in 1640 on Staten Island. The first US gin distillery—Anchor Gin—was built here in the early 19th century.

Even things we take for granted today started out related to New York's booze industry. Take paved streets for example. The very first paved street in America was the street in New York City that fronted the many breweries. *Brouwer Street,* now known as Stone Street in the Financial District, was paved in 1658 to keep the wagons, heavy with kegs of beer from the breweries, from sinking into the mud.

Then there are the drinking places. New York City, filled with immigrants since its founding, has seen an immense number of bars, alehouses, porterhouses and grog shops. In fact, one of the most booze-soaked areas in the nation in the late 19th century was New York City's own Bowery. In this area the city's street gangs clashed and controlled gambling and prostitution. Flophouses and cheap booze were everywhere, and the value of a man's life was less than the cost of a quart of rum.

As for bars, this is one of the best destinations in the country for historic and truly unique places. The saloons in this area are some of the oldest in the nation, and a decent Bucket List Bar™ pub crawl could be made here.

MCSORLEY'S OLD ALE HOUSE, NEW YORK, NY

Address: 15 East 7th Street, New York, NY, 10003, (212) 474-9148
Website: www.mcsorleysnewyork.com **Video tour:**
http://youtu.be/t6ThJe3Foyc
Food: Yes **Live Music:** No **Hours:** Monday–Saturday 11am–1am, Sunday
1pm–1am **Type of Bar:** Pub **What to Drink:** McSorley's Ale **Why You
Should Go:** Sheer history, artifacts lining the walls, little changed in 150
years.

THE HISTORY

The history of McSorley's is a bit confounding. If you talk to the bartenders
and read their website you'll learn that John McSorley (the founder) was born
in 1827, arrived in the US in 1851 (making him 23 years of age upon arrival)
and opened his bar in 1854.

But contradicting this is a New York Times article taking issue with
McSorley's claims. According the article McSorley didn't appear in city
directories until 1862. Also, the article claims the building the bar occupies
was built no earlier than 1858. And finally, a census taker who visited
McSorley in 1880 recorded 1855 as the year McSorley arrived in the US.

Whatever the case may be, we'll go with what we were told. McSorley's was
founded by Irish immigrant John McSorley, who was born in Tyrone,
Ireland, in 1827. In 1845, when John was approximately 18 years old, the
Irish Potato Famine began, eventually killing one million and displacing a
million more who emigrated to the US.

John arrived in the US in 1851 and three years later opened a tavern called
"The Old House at Home." Like many taverns at the time it was a

gentleman-only space, which eventually led to a motto they became famous for: "Good Ale, Raw Onions, and No Ladies."

In 1875 John apprenticed his son, Bill McSorley, in the running of the bar. Bill took over the bar in 1905 only to be fired by his father after he began selling liquor. Up to that point they had only sold the ale John himself created and brewed in the basement.

When Prohibition began in 1920, McSorley's survived by serving Near Beer, created during Prohibition with an alcohol level below .5%.

In 1936, Bill McSorley sold the bar to Daniel O'Connell, a patron and NYC policeman, who was the first non-McSorley to own the bar. Bill passed away in 1938, shortly followed by O'Connell in 1939, who left the bar to his daughter, Dorothy. Dorothy had made a promise to her father to not change or manage the bar, much to the patrons' relief, and her husband, Harry Kirwan, stepped in and managed the bar until his death.

In 1964 while visiting Ireland Harry Kirwan's car broke down, and he was picked up by a Good Samaritan by the name of Matthew Maher. Harry told Matthew that if he ever decided to come to America and was in need of work, to come by the bar. Matthew took him up on the offer shortly after their meeting and worked as a bartender, waiter, and manager at McSorley's until 1977, when he bought the place from Harry Kirwan's son, Danny. Mathew still owns the bar today and chances are you'll find him sitting in the back enjoying a sandwich and laughing it up with his employees.

McSorleys is known for its motto, "Good Ale, Raw Onions, and No Ladies." Yes, it serves great beer (its own recipe still, but now made offsite), yes, it serves raw onions with practically everything, and yes, for well over 100 years they didn't allow women. In fact, the men-only policy was such a part of the bar that not even the female owner in 1954 would go in during normal business hours (only on Sundays when the bar was closed).

That all changed when on January 9th, 1969, two women, Karen DeCrow and Faith Seidenberg, attorneys and members of the National Organization for Women ("NOW") entered the bar, seated themselves, had multiple requests for service denied, and were finally escorted out by the bartender.

According to DeCrow, a man at the bar initially bought them a round when their requests were ignored. She stated that while the patrons did not turn on them, they did in fact turn on the gentleman who offered to buy them the beer. She claims he was forced out bodily with his face covered in blood.

The case against McSorley's went all the way to federal court, and in 1970 DeCrow and Seidenberg won. Shortly afterwards the New York mayor signed a bill barring discrimination in public places, which would have ended McSorley's men-only policy anyway.

McSorley's did seriously consider becoming a private club to prevent women from being allowed but ultimately decided against it. So on August 10th, 1970, the bar officially opened to women. Rumor has it that then-owner Danny Kirwan wanted his mother to be the first woman served, but she refused saying she would not break the promise made to her father.

TODAY

Today McSorley's is one of the most well-known historic bars in New York City. It's a great example of the Irish-owned saloons that peppered the Bowery in the 1800s and has a charm and class reserved for those very respectable but aged examples of what's not made any more, like a '57 Chevy, or maybe Robert DeNiro.

The crowd is composed of business professionals at lunch or after work, along with locals and a college crowd making the rounds. Interject these groups with a steady stream of never-ending tourists from across the globe, and you have a lively and rambunctious atmosphere.

The bartenders are no-nonsense and put on a show of glib toughness, but they are all heart (one guy who hadn't been in for over a year stopped in while we were there, and the bartender asked how his daughter was—she had been sick the last time the guy was in).

Take the time to slowly walk around and view all of the artifacts hanging on the walls. You'll see the original newspaper announcing Lincoln's assassination, JFK's death certificate and countless other priceless objects that should be in a museum (and arguably are).

Take a moment to study the gas lamp immediately in front of the bar. Hanging from the light fixture you'll notice a bunch of old and dusty wishbones. Legend has it that McSorley would give an ale and turkey dinner to soldiers preparing to head off to war. As they headed out the door, they'd hang the wishbone on the lamp in hopes of returning. If the soldier did return he would remove the wishbone. Those hanging are from soldiers who never returned. In a way, these bones are their memorial.

THE FOOD

The food at McSorley's is not only reasonably priced, especially for New York City, but it's also delicious. Their two traditional sandwiches, liverwurst and corned beef, are must tries. The corned beef is moist and tender, and the liverwurst has just the right amount of spice. Served on Jewish rye with thick slices of liverwurst and thin slices of raw onion, it's tasty, filling, and the perfect start to an evening of ale. Also, a must try is their spicy house Dijon mustard. We recommend you spoon some onto almost anything, as it has great flavor and a nice spicy kick.

THE DRINKS

McSorley's has stayed true to John's wishes and serves only ale, light and dark. The original recipe was created and brewed by John McSorley himself, but as demand for it increased he sold the recipe to a brewery called Fidelio. From there the brewery itself and recipe changed hands numerous times. Breweries such as Rheingold, Schmidt's, and Stroh brewed McSorley's Cream Stock Ale and Lager until it finally found a home at Pabst Brewing Company.

NEARBY DISTRACTIONS

Empire State Building—Website: www.esbnyc.com **Address:** 350 Fifth Avenue New York, NY, 10118, (212) 736-3100 (Monday–Sunday 8am–2am, the last elevator up is at 1:15 am). Once the tallest building in the world, and still one of the most recognizable, the Empire State building is as New York as Apple Pie is American. This is the perfect stop on your way to or from McSorley's, about a mile and a half away, and we highly recommend going up to watch the sunset and the city lights come on. Pay the extra money to get the VIP pass (otherwise you could easily stand in line for an hour or more) and enjoy the breathtaking views from this iconic skyscraper.

Artichoke Basille's Pizza—www.artichokepizza.com, 328 East 14th St. New York, NY, 10012, (212) 228-2004 (Monday–Sunday 10am–5am). If you're in the mood for some outstanding NY pizza then look no further than Artichoke Basille's Pizza. Only about a half mile from McSorley's, and open until 5am, they're famous for their artichoke pizza, which has been described as "more addictive than crack." Be forewarned, it's popular, so there's probably going to be a wait.

Katz's Delicatessen—www.katzsdelicatessen.com, 205 East Houston Street New York, NY, 10002, (212) 254-2246 (Monday–Wednesday 8am–10:45pm, Thursday 8am–2:45am, Friday–Sunday 8am–10:45 pm). Less than a mile from McSorley's sits the fabled Katz's Delicatessen. Opened in 1888 and featured in movies like "When Harry Met Sally" ('I'll have what she's having…' fake orgasm scene) and in the cult classic, Donnie Brasco, this place is as legendary as NY pizza. The food is outstanding and the pastrami and corned beef sandwiches are made to epic proportions.

SAM FRAUNCES TAVERN, NEW YORK, NY

Address: 54 Pearl Street, New York, NY, 10004, (212) 968-1776
Website: www.frauncestavernmuseum.org **Video tour:**
http://youtu.be/3bP2YxPTigc
Food: Yes **Live Music:** Yes **Hours:** (Museum) Monday–Friday 12pm–5pm,
Saturday–Sunday 11am–5pm, (bar) Monday–Sunday 11am–2am **Type of
Bar:** Tavern **What to Drink:** Craft beer or an Irish whiskey **Why You Should
Go:** One of the oldest bars in America, where George Washington partied
when the British left New York.

THE HISTORY

The building was originally built as a residence for the Delancey family, one
of the wealthiest families in New York at the time (though the family never
actually lived here). The building was eventually sold to a tavern keeper by the
name of Samuel Fraunces in 1762. Fraunces set about immediately turning
the building into the immensely popular "Queen's Head Tavern."

In colonial America, the local tavern was a place that commoners went to
read newspapers (if they could read), listen to newspapers being read aloud,
get reports of local goings-on, retrieve their mail, and, of course, to have a
meal and enjoy a drink or two. Jennifer Patton, Fraunces Tavern Museum
Education Director, summed it up nicely to us when she described them to be
like today's message board found at almost every Starbucks across the country.

Fraunces founded the "Queen's Head Tavern" during the very turbulent
times leading up to the American Revolution. At the time New York City
found itself divided into two groups—the Loyalist and the Patriots—and
most taverns reflected the cultural divide.

Fraunces was a Patriot bar. One could even say that Fraunces' was the Patriot tavern headquarters, as none other than George Washington and John Adams frequented the establishment and discussed, debated, and some even say plotted the beginning of the Revolutionary War.

Though it is unclear as to what occurred in the tavern during the time the English occupied the city, Fraunces Tavern played a significant role in the celebrations that occurred on November 25th, 1783, also known as "Evacuation Day." Evacuation Day was the day the British soldiers left New York for good, signaling the end of the war. And it was on this day George Washington paraded back into New York City and headed straight to Fraunces Tavern where a grand celebration was held. During the celebration George Washington himself, armed with hot-buttered rum, made 13 toasts to everyone from the American Army to the Kings of Sweden and France.

TODAY

Today the tavern is more museum than tavern, with the top floors serving as a museum and the bottom floor currently leased out to the Porter House Company, which operates a colonial-themed restaurant and bar. It is also considerably larger, with renovations that include three surrounding buildings.

The Queen's Head Tavern ceased to exist over 200 years ago, but what stands today is a reminder of what we are, where we came from and who we became. If you find yourself in New York and have the time to visit, then stop by Fraunces Tavern, spend some time thoroughly going through the museum, paying particular attention to the Long Room (which is where Washington gave most of his speeches and toasts) and the artifacts that let you get a glimpse of life during the formative years of our country.

Don't forget, this is the place where George Washington and John Adams would have discussed the revolution, what we would be as a country, and schemed and planned against England. It's also the place Washington himself came to celebrate after winning the war. You could say this is where the revolution started and ended.

After your museum visit take a few minutes to absorb everything while enjoying a cold one in the bar on the bottom floor (it is also called Fraunces Tavern). They offer a full menu of traditional Irish faire that would be perfect for a crisp autumn day or cold winter night.

They also feature a huge beer selection, both on tap and in bottles. Right beyond the front entrance is also a whiskey bar, for tasting and sampling many of the exclusive Irish whiskies they carry.

THE FOOD

The food selection at the Porter House Restaurant features upper-end classic pub grub, especially of the Irish kind. Expect fish and chips, shepherd's pie, and many of the other usual menu items.

THE DRINKS

They have an extensive Irish whiskey collection, many from tiny distilleries you'd never find in a typical liquor store here in the states. Their whiskey tasting room is pretty overwhelming, but they're patient and spot-on with recommendations.

They also have a huge assortment of taps flowing with craft beers from here and abroad. It would seem fitting to get a Guinness but don't: go with something you can't get anywhere else.

NEARBY DISTRACTIONS

World Trade Center Memorial—Website: www.911memorial.org **Address:** 1 Liberty Plz #20 New York, NY, 10006, (212) 312-8800 (tickets can be purchased online prior to your visit and we recommend you do so well in advance). A memorial to honor the nearly 3,000 innocent victims of the infamous 9/11 attacks, few places in the world are more hallowed than this location. Only a mile from Fraunces, this should be a required stop as part of your historical journey.

Statue of Liberty—Website: www.statuecruises.com, Liberty Island, New York (open every day except Christmas though hours change by season). To the world she's both a beacon and a symbol of freedom and democracy. Lady Liberty is one of America's most iconic land marks. To get to Liberty Island you will need to take one of Statue Cruises ferries, the only company that has access to the island. They leave from Battery Park, which is less than a half mile from Fraunces.

Ellis Island—Website: www.statuecruises.com, Ellis Island, New York (Open every day except Christmas, though hours change by season). Today it's a museum, but at one time it was the gateway to America for millions of immigrants. As a matter of fact about half of the current US population can trace their lineage back to an ancestor who passed through Ellis Island. If you plan on going to the Statue of Liberty, Ellis Island is a short ferry ride away and included with the same ticket.

OLD TOWN BAR, NEW YORK, NY

Address: 45 East 18th Street, New York, NY, 10003, (212) 529-6732
Website: http://www.oldtownbar.com **Video tour:** http://youtu.be/0UpDJo-4uow

Food: Yes **Live Music:** No **Hours:** Monday–Friday 11:30am–1am, Saturday 12pm–2am, Sunday 1pm–12am **Type of Bar:** Pub **What to Drink:** A martini or other classic cocktail **Why You Should Go**: Immaculate bar, conversation, urinals.

THE HISTORY

Sitting on East 18th Street in New York City and widely considered a writer's bar, Old Town Bar originally opened as a popular German establishment called Viemeisters in 1892. During Prohibition the bar renamed itself Craig's Restaurant, became a speakeasy and was supported, frequented, and protected by members of the nearby Tammany Hall.

Tammany Hall was a Democratic Party political machine that is rumored to have used its power to control and manipulate New York City and State politics while helping immigrants, mainly Irish, rise in the American political system from the 1790s to as late as the 1960s. So while Tammany Hall supported Craig's Restaurant, it had little to worry about.

During Prohibition, Old Town Bar (Craig's Restaurant) took advantage of a special feature built into its booths, a feature still present today. The top of each booth can be opened to reveal a convenient hiding spot. The booths and their hiding places got their 15 minutes of fame when they were featured in the film "Izzy & Moe," which was directed by Jackie Cooper, starred Jackie Gleason and Art Carney and focused on the era of Prohibition.

After Prohibition ended, the bar reopened as the Old Town Bar and was owned and operated by the German-American Loden family. At the time the neighborhood consisted mainly of German immigrants and their families, and as such, it specialized in German food. The Loden family owned it until the 1960s when Larry Meagher took over the day-to-day operations. Larry had unsuccessfully tried his hand at bar ownership in Brooklyn before finding himself running Old Town Bar. He eventually purchased the bar at a time when the surrounding area and New York City were awakening from their 1960s economic and cultural slump. Luckily for Larry and his family, he seemed to have found his calling at this place.

TODAY

Featuring an impressive 55-foot mahogany bar; some of the oldest, still operating dumbwaiters in New York; dozens of photos of visiting actors, writers, and politicians; giant urinals, and 16-foot pressed tin ceilings, walking into Old Town Bar is almost like walking into vintage New York. The place is quiet, low-key class with clientele ranging from tourists to college students, to local businessmen, writers and actors.

We asked current owner and operator Gerard Meagher to describe The Old Town bar today and feel he summed it up nicely when he said, "*We* celebrate writers, and *this place* celebrates conversation."

Frequented by writers like Frank McCourt, Irish playwright Brian Friel, Irish poet Seamus Heaney, and English novelist Nick Hornby (plus no loud music, no blaring TVs, and a no cell phone policy), it is easy to see why writers and normal everyday people are drawn to Old Town Bar.

This is one of the few remaining bars (another being My Brother's Bar in Denver) that is truly conducive for conversation between friends and strangers over drinks. It's a setting that unfortunately is quickly disappearing from today's pubs, where the ever constant cell phones, televisions, laptops, and iPods flood the atmosphere and douse any hope for quiet discussions.

The bar is a throwback to the way things were before all of the interruptions of digital gadgetry, to a time when people came to the bar to socialize with each other. And so today the bar is as it was, which makes it unique.

And speaking of unique, one of the most unique features of Old Town Bar is the ancient set of urinals found in the men's bathroom. Originally installed in 1910, the urinals have become almost as celebrated—and maybe even more so—than the bar itself. In fact, they are so celebrated that on November 1st, 2010, the bar celebrated the urinals' 100th birthday with champagne and a congratulatory letter from Mayor Bloomberg (which is still posted at the entrance to the restroom).

THE FOOD

The food is classic Irish/New York cuisine, including soups and sandwiches, pastas and salads. They are known for their hamburgers, so you'd do well to try one with a cold beer or nice red wine.

The seating area for the restaurant is located upstairs, as is the kitchen. If you order in the bar downstairs you'll have your food delivered by one of the last remaining, original dumbwaiters still used in the city.

THE DRINKS

Old Town Bar features a full service bar and a long list of beers on tap. You won't find much in the way of trendy drinks here, so plan on sticking to the classics, which they do well. A martini, a Manhattan or any other traditional cocktail should be the drink of choice when here.

NEARBY DISTRACTIONS

Theodore Roosevelt Birthplace—Website: www.nps.gov/thrb **Address:** 28 East 20th Street New York, NY, 10003, (Tuesday–Saturday 9am–5pm). Theodore Roosevelt is, to date, the only US President born in New York City, and this is your opportunity to visit the area of his childhood home. Located less than a quarter of a mile from Old Town Bar, Teddy spent the first 14 years of his life in this very location. He would later become an author, explorer, Governor of New York, Nobel Peace Prize recipient, Colonel of the Rough Riders and President of the United States. Though the house is a rebuilt replica (the original was demolished in 1916), it contains many of the original furnishings provided by Roosevelt's sisters and wife.

Broadway—Website: www.broadway.com (show times and theatre locations vary; visit website for schedule and tickets). A short distance—about 1.4 miles—from Old Town Bar is the start of the legendary Broadway Theatre District. With a long list of shows running year-round, numerous theatres to choose from, and some of the best live performances on earth, it has something for everyone. Check out their website and book early, as some of the more popular shows are sold out far in advance.

Times Square—Website: www.timessquarenyc.org, Times Square New York, NY. Few people think of New York or New Year's Eve without thinking of Times Square. Simply a major commercial intersection at the junction of Broadway and Seventh, Times Square has become one of the most visited tourist attractions in the world. A leisurely mile and a half from Old Town Bar, be sure to visit this electronically charged epicenter of New York City.

EAR INN, NEW YORK, NY

Address: 326 Spring Street, New York, NY, 10013, (212) 226-9060
Website: www.earinn.com **Video tour:** http://youtu.be/y4bqniYw-Qc
Food: Yes **Live Music:** Yes **Hours:** Monday–Sunday 11:30am–4am **Type of Bar:** Pub **What to Drink:** Shot of Jameson and a Guinness **Why You Should Go:** One of the oldest bars in the United States, serving continuously since 1833, brothel and grog shop for the waterfront

THE HISTORY

The history of the Ear Inn starts, as with so many other bars throughout the US, with some contested historical aspects.

The original building was built in 1817 for a man by the name of James Brown, a Revolutionary War veteran (which is not contested). Legend claims that Brown was an African-American soldier and an aide to none other than George Washington. In fact, some believe it's Brown featured at Washington's side in Emanuel Leutze's 1851 painting titled "Washington Crossing the Delaware".

Though some history of the bar and its original owner has been called into question, what's not disputed is that he opened a successful tobacco shop shortly after construction was completed. In 1833 the building was then sold to Thomas Cloake, who opened a bar on the ground floor. Cloake's bar was the start of one of the longest continually operating bars in American history.

After Thomas Cloake took ownership and installed the bar, the waterfront neighborhood quickly changed. At the time the Hudson River was a mere five feet from the Ear Inn, and the city and its commerce were booming. The bar was frequented by New York's immigrant gang members, river pirates, and visitors looking for female companionship (which could be found in the brothel located on the second floor).

At some point in the mid-19th century the bar became what some described as a "spiritual" establishment, where owner Thomas Cloake brewed beer and corn whiskey (a very rich, double-pot distilled bourbon), and continued to sell most of his products to thirsty sailors, pirates, and immigrant gang members. He also continued to use the top two floors as a brothel, a boarding house and a smuggler's den.

During Prohibition the bar passed itself off as a restaurant while continuing to operate as a speakeasy out of the bottom and second floors. After Prohibition ended the bar was nameless, though sailors and pirates called it "The Green Door," with the motto "Known from Coast to Coast." Up until 1977 the establishment had a pool table, gambling, and no music except singing by the patrons.

In 1977 the bar was purchased and renamed the Ear Inn so the owners wouldn't have to go through the Landmark Commission's lengthy review of new signs added to historical buildings. To achieve this, the owner simply painted the B on the neon Bar sign to look like an E and the Ear Inn of today was born.

TODAY

Today the Ear Inn is located on the fringes of Soho. If you were to spend the day there you would see the lunch crowd of nearby blue-collar workers give way to the trendy residents of the surrounding neighborhood as day turned into night.

They do feature a couple of TVs hanging above the bar, so it's a great place to sit and watch any number of games being televised.

As the day gets later the small building becomes more and more crowded, so get here before 5:00 pm to grab a seat at the bar.

Look around at the artifacts on the wall of the place, much of it spanning the bar's long history. You'll see many references to the second owner, Thomas Cloake. You'll also see many relics and artifacts relating to the sea, all found in the basement or elsewhere in the building. If you notice the many bottles above the bar, know that these were found in the basement as well, and date from as far back as the early 1800s.

THE FOOD

They describe the food as basic, but we must respectfully and heartily disagree. We tried the smoked salmon, chicken pie, steamed mussels, and shrimp salad. All were delicious, decent sized portions, and reasonably priced. If you find yourself at the Ear Inn we feel you can't go wrong with any one or all of these plates (we especially liked the mussels).

THE DRINKS

You won't find any sweet or fruity drinks at the Ear Inn. Their signature drinks, as described by long-serving bartender Gary, are either a pint of the Ear Inn Ale (which we can tell you from personal experience is delicious) or a pint of Guinness and a shot of Jameson. Stop in on the right night and Gary will probably partake in a shot and beer with you and may even give one of his signature toasts.

NEARBY DISTRACTIONS

Intrepid Sea, Air and Space Museum—Website: www.intrepid.org **Address:** Pier 86, 12th Ave. and 46th Street New York, NY, 10036, (877) 957-7447 (hours vary by season, with shorter hours in the winter. Visit their website for more info). Originally an Essex-class aircraft carrier built during World War 2, the Intrepid was in service until being decommissioned in 1974. Today she is a world-class museum featuring Sea, Air and Space exhibits including the submarine USS Growler, a Concorde, and the Space Shuttle Enterprise. A short three mile cab ride from the Ear Inn, it's a great opportunity to get close to some of the world's greatest crafts.

New York City Fire Museum—Website: www.nycfiremuseum.org **Address:** 278 Spring Street New York, NY, 10013, (212) 691-1303 (Monday–Sunday 10am–5pm, closed major holidays). Literally just steps from the Ear Inn, the New York City Fire Museum hosts one of the nation's greatest collections of firefighting memorabilia. Featuring art, artifacts and gear dating back as far as the 18th century, it gives visitors a glimpse into over 300 years of firefighting and the brave men and women who run into burning buildings while everyone else is running out.

Ghostbusters Headquarters—Website: 14 North Moore St. New York, NY, 10013, (always open. It's actually a real fire station). Only a half mile from the Ear Inn resides one of the most iconic locations in film history: the Ghostbusters headquarters. Today the building hosts Ladder 8, a company dating back to 1865, and the iconic Ghostbusters sign still hangs in the apparatus bay. For anyone who is familiar with this great New York-based movie, a trip to see this legendary building is well worth the short walk.

THE OLD '76 HOUSE, TAPPAN, NY

Address: 110 Main Street, Tappan, NY, 10983, (845) 359-5476
Website: www.76house.com **Video tour:** http://youtu.be/eyaYkLT0aEw
Food: Yes **Live Music:** Yes **Hours:** Monday–Thursday 11:30am–9pm, Friday 11:30am–9:30pm, Saturday 11:30am–10pm, Sunday 11am-9pm **Type of Bar:** Tavern **What to Drink:** Try a glass of wine from their extensive selection or an ale from the tap. **Why You Should Go:** Drink in the shadow of George Washington, sit in the room where the British first recognized the United States of America.

THE HISTORY

Originally built in 1668, the Old '76 House was initially a Public House in the Dutch colony located in current day Tappan, New York.

At the time of its construction a town would not be recognized as such unless it had a place a traveler could spend the evening, get something to eat and drink, provision himself and take care of his horse. Many towns built public houses to meet these needs as well as to be a place where townsfolk could relax, dine, drink, share news, receive and send mail and conduct business. In fact, almost everything related to business at the time was done in the local public house with the exception of legal matters, which were usually completed in the church (the original 1660s church is located across the street).

Old '76 House began life as one of these Public Houses and became a safe haven for Patriots to meet and plot during the years leading up to and during the Revolutionary War.

194

It is perhaps most well known for its role in the life of Major John Andre, the famous British spy who conspired with Patriot General Benedict Arnold to capture the fort at West Point. He was captured on his way back to British forces and found to be in possession of the blueprints to the fort and plans developed with Benedict Arnold. He was returned to Tappan by American forces and then locked up in the '76 House (known as Mabie's Inn at the time).

He stayed there through the length of his trial at the nearby church until he was convicted and then hanged just up the road on October 2nd, 1780. His last statement: "All I request, gentlemen, is that while I acknowledge the propriety of my sentence, you will bear me witness that I die like a brave man." His remains were later exhumed, and he was buried in Westminster Abbey in London where he is regarded as a Hero. Benedict Arnold escaped to England, where he lived out his life shunned by friends and foes alike.

Less well known but more importantly, the '76 House was also where, on or about May 3rd, 1783, England finally recognized the United States as an independent nation when General Carleton gave George Washington the plans for the British evacuation of the country. The meaning is pretty profound if you think about it. Our nation was finally recognized as such in a tavern!

In short, The Old '76 House drips with history.

TODAY

Today the Old '76 House is best described as a pristine, 300-year-old tavern. But it wasn't all that pristine until current owner Robert (Rob) Norden bought the place back in 1987.

Rob and a team of friends set about restoring the place to its former glory immediately after its purchase. Issues included a foundation that wasn't settling uniformly, an original floor and ceiling that were on the brink of collapsing, an inaccurate floor plan that had been established with smaller rooms and even a falsely marked "Andre's prison" that had been erected as a tourist attraction. There was, to put it mildly, a lot of work to do.

It took two years of remodeling to recreate the original public house. In that time 30 tons of foundation clay was removed by hand, and structural renovations were completed using authentic wood found throughout North America. Anything original that could be saved, was, and that includes the bar rail. It was at that very bar rail that none other than George Washington once drank and maybe even ate.

Rob is now happy to compare the '76 House to taverns that existed long ago. They play live music seven nights a week, serve great food and drinks, and take pride in creating an atmosphere that caters to the community. It's warm and comfortable and a great place to while away a Friday or Saturday night.

THE FOOD

The Old '76 House has teamed up with renowned chef Doug Mulholland to present its guests with a blend of traditional colonial foods like Yankee Pot Roast and modern-day dishes like Filet of Escobar.

Their food has won them acclaim in many local foodie magazines and journals, and they're consistently booked for weddings and receptions. Many of Mulholland's dishes feature local and seasonal ingredients and are his take on classic dishes. Try something from the period if you can.

THE DRINKS

Paired with their outstanding menu are their excellent and extensive wine list and a full-service bar. If you drink, do it at the bar standing up (as they would have done) with a hand resting on the large round rail.

Have an ale, glass of wine, or a glass of whiskey neat. Any of these would have been downed by Washington himself, who very well could have been right there where you're standing and at the very same bar rail (kind of humbling, actually).

NEARBY DISTRACTIONS

Major John Andre Monument—Address: 42 Andre Hill, Tappan, New York, NY, (always open but be mindful of the surrounding neighborhood, plus pretty creepy). Located just a half mile from the Old '76 House sits the monument to the British Spy Major John Andre. Major Andre was an assistant to British General Clinton, and at Clinton's order traveled to meet American traitor Benedict Arnold to discuss plans for the handing over of West Point. Andre was captured and subsequently tried and sentenced to death. His last request was that his captors bear him witness that he died like a brave man. Today the monument is a solemn reminder of the tragedies of war and the cost of freedom.

Defiant Brewing Co.—Website: www.defiantbrewing.com **Address:** 6 East Dexter Plaza Pearl River, NY, 10965, (845) 920-8602 (brewery and kitchen hours vary, visit website or call).

A short six mile drive from Old '76 House will get you to Defiant Brewing Company. Stop in for a tour and sample of their high-quality craft beer. They also recently opened a kitchen serving brisket, pulled pork and ribs served by the pound, so you decide on how big you want your portion.

Tallman Mountain State Park—Website: www.nysparks.com (hours vary by season). Just three miles away from the Old '76 House is Tallman Mountain State Park, offering an opportunity to view some of New York's wooded and marshlands while enjoying hiking trails, cross-country skiing and picnic areas. Spend a few hours exploring New York's "wilder" side, and then head to Old '76 House to try some outstanding food and drink at the bar rail at which George Washington once stood.

NEW YORK'S HISTORIC BARS

Pete's Tavern—Website: www.petestavern.com **Address:** 129 East 18th Street New York, NY, 10003, (212) 473-7676 (Monday–Tuesday, Sunday 11am–11:45pm, Wednesday–Saturday 11am–12:45am). Pete's claims to be the oldest continuously operating bar in New York City, a claim that's hard to pin down. It became a bar in 1864, making it younger than some of the others, but it is the only one that is documented as serving through Prohibition, which is how they get their claim—continuously operating. True or not, this is a haven for locals, students and tourists. This is where the famous short story, "The Gift of the Magi" was written by O. Henry, and it boasts a long line of celebrities and famous personalities through its doors.

White Horse Tavern—Website: www.whitehorsetavernny.com **Address:** 567 Hudson Street Manhattan, NY, 10014, (212) 989-3956 (Monday–Thursday and Sunday 11am–2am, Friday–Saturday 11am–4am). This was a quiet bar opened in 1880 to serve the longshoremen and seaside merchants and workers until writers and Bohemian artists began frequenting the place in the 1950s. The scene changed fairly quickly, especially when Dylan Thomas became so famous, and then the bar became a trendy spot for locals and tourists.

PJ Clarke's—Website: www.pjclarkes.com **Address:** 915 3rd Ave. New York, NY, 10022, (212) 317-1616 (Monday–Sunday 11:30am–4am). Opened in 1884 as a saloon for Irish locals, PJ Clarke's has become a favorite watering hole for New York residents and tourists alike. Its claim to fame is that the place simply didn't close. Anywhere else this wouldn't seem like quite an accomplishment, but considering the growth of skyscrapers in the surrounding area it's actually amazing to see this place still exists. They claim to have served through Prohibition (which they probably did), and then didn't allow women in until the 1960s. Much of the history hangs on the walls, though, and you'll find a picture gallery of the who's who of New York City.

Neir's Tavern—Website: www.neirstavern.com **Address:** 87-48 78th St, Woodhaven, NY, 11421, (718) 296-0600 (Monday–Thursday 11am–1am, Friday–Saturday 11am–2am, Sunday 12pm–1am). If you find yourself in Queens, you need to stop by one of the leading competitors for "oldest bar in New York." Neir's Tavern claims to have been founded in 1829, which certainly would make it the oldest. They also claim to have been continuously open since its founding (excepting prohibition, of course). What's interesting is that while McSorley's and Pete's often vie for the title of "oldest," Neir's seems satisfied to stay out of the fight. In fact, it bills itself as "the most famous bar you've never been to." This place is definitely notable, and a place you should try to have a drink at if you can. Order a classic cocktail and sit at the bar that Joe Pesci, Robert Dinero and Ray Liotta made famous in Goodfellas.

Stonewall Inn—Website: www.thestonewallinnnyc.com **Address:** 53 Christopher St, New York, NY, 10014, (212) 488-2705 (Monday-Sunday, 2pm-4am). In 1969 the bar at this address, called The Stonewall Inn, was raided by New York City Police Vice Squad Public Morals Division. The bar was a known gay bar, and apparently that was reason enough to raid the place and arrest those inside for acting "immoral." This happened pretty frequently and apparently the patrons had had enough: that night they fought back. The outcome was a riot, with fires, destruction of property, and the beginning of the gay right's movement. The bar that stood here in 1969 closed, but the space is remembered as important to the people who had been kept in the shadows for so long. In fact, the US Government made this a historic landmark. A tavern by the same name, also catering to the gay community, has since opened up and we highly recommend those that are into bar history swing by and have a drink.

Jimmy's Corner—Address: 140 W 44th St, New York, NY, 10036, (212) 221-9510 (Monday–Friday 11:30am–4am, Saturday 12pm–4am, Sunday 3pm–4am). This is the last true bar, and certainly the last dive bar, off of Time's Square. When you get tired of the Hard Rock Café and other corporate places, duck in here and have a beer. Founded by professional boxing trainer Jimmy Glenn, this place is popular for locals after work and on weekends. The place is often crowded (we've never been able to get a seat at the bar), but the service is fast and the people are pleasant.

7B Horseshoe Bar AKA Vazacs—Address: 108 Avenue B, New York, NY, 10009, (212) 677-6742 (Monday–Sunday 12pm–4am). This East Village relic has been here for decades, stretching back at least to the 1930s, but looks like it's been there significantly longer (and it may have, but we can't find any information on it). What we do know is that this dive is comfortable but loud, is regularly lined with grizzled regulars during weekdays (when we visited), and then with hipsters at night and the weekends. This place is a popular filming location, and you can see it prominently in The Godfather II, and Crocodile Dundee ("That's not a knife…"). Order a PBR, play some old school pinball, and get nostalgic for old New York in a gritty, last-of-the-dying-breed, dive bar.

PHILADELPHIA, PA

The City of Brotherly Love has a great past that anyone with any interest in history will appreciate. Not only that, but a couple of places have kept their personality despite the growth of the city into the monster metropolis it is now.

There's a certain sense of wonder you get when visiting this city that comes from knowing all of the events that took place here that shaped our country's future. But even more so, knowing how much the bar scene actually contributed to that shaping, drinking here is itself a rite for anyone that appreciates a good saloon.

Many don't know that the Declaration of Independence was written in a tavern in this city. Thomas Jefferson hunched over a small table in the Indian Queen Tavern for three days, drinking ale and Madeira wine while penning what was to become one of the most famous pieces of writing in history.

And just down the street from the Indian Queen you'll find the birthplace of the United State Marine Corps, or at least a marker denoting as much. The marker is actually for the Tun Tavern. That's right: the USMC was born in a tavern. The owner of the place was made chief recruiting officer for the newly formed USMC by the Continental Congress in 1775. And so he naturally set up a table in his own place and began getting his customers—drunk or sober—to sign up for the Corps.

Just about every important event that happened in Philadelphia had something to do with booze and bars. The politicking that went into our nation's founding? That didn't take place in Independence Hall; it took place in the taverns over ale and rum punches.

And in fact, one of the biggest parties in history was thrown in one of the bars you can visit today. On September 17th, 1787, after signing the US Constitution, the 55 delegates of the Continental Congress (plus General George Washington) met for dinner and a celebration at City Tavern. In the course of the evening the Founding Fathers put away 100 bottles of wine, 34 bottles of beer, 8 bottles of whiskey, 8 bottles of hard cider, and 7 bowls of rum punch. What makes this event even funnier is that the tavern-keeper added 2% to the bill for "damages" done. This place is, of course, a Bucket List Bar™; however, we don't suggest trying to reenact this historic event.

THE CITY TAVERN, PHILADELPHIA, PA

Address: 138 South 2nd Street, Philadelphia, PA, 19106, (215) 413-1443
Website: www.citytavern.com **Video tour:** http://youtu.be/Wf6mlZ__724
Food: Yes **Live Music:** Yes **Hours:** Hours vary by season, holiday, etc. Call or
check website for updates. **Type of Bar:** Tavern **What to Drink:** A Shrub, a
Tavern Cooler or Ales of the Revolution. **Why You Should Go:** This tavern
was the most important place in the city of Philadelphia during the founding
of our nation.

THE HISTORY

Originally built for the "convenience and credit of city" the City Tavern in
Philadelphia was established in 1773. Shortly after it opened its doors, John
Adams attended a meeting of the First Continental Congress there and it was
described as "the most genteel tavern in America."

Paul Revere rode to the Tavern on more than one occasion, reporting news
of the Boston Tea Party and later of the closing of Boston's port by the
British.

The Second Continental Congress began meeting in the Tavern in May of
1775, with members meeting every Saturday. Eight of them formed a "table"
and dined there daily.

Benjamin Franklin practically lived here, and John Adams and George
Washington met for the first time in the same room where you can now eat
and drink.

Things changed for the Tavern when British General Cornwallis marched
his troops directly to it on September 24th, 1777. British officers assigned
quarters in the Tavern had weekly balls. Two single officers advertised for "a

young woman to work in the capacity of a housekeeper, who can occasionally put her hand to anything. Extravagant wages will be given, and no character [references] required."

There are books devoted to the history of this amazing place. What's important for this book, though, was that this was the place to have food and drink in Philadelphia. In fact, on the night of September 17th, 1787 the members of the Continental Congress, chose the City Tavern as their spot in which to throw one of the most infamous parties ever recorded.

The 55 members of the Congress (plus George Washington) at that soirée went through 100 bottles of wine, 22 bottles of porter, 12 bottles of beer, eight bottles of whiskey, eight bottles of hard cider and seven bowls of spiked punch.

TODAY

The original City Tavern was demolished in 1854 but in 1948 the government designated parts of downtown Philadelphia as National Historic Parks. Part of the reconstruction included the rebuilding of the City Tavern, and construction was completed just in time for the nation's bicentennial. The tavern was rebuilt as an exact replica of the original, right down to the seating, the room layout and, of course, the bar (called the dispensary at the time).

Proprietor and Head Chef Walter Staib has converted the City Tavern into an award-winning restaurant with seven dining rooms, three wine cellars, and an award-winning menu inspired by 18th-century American cuisine. Himself a James Beard Foundation Nominee and Emmy Award-winner, Staib has poured himself into returning the City Tavern to its previous glory. From the Colonial food and drinks, to the decor and the furniture, sitting down for a meal or having a cocktail is like being transported back in time to the days of our Founding Fathers. No other place we have visited has been able to give us such an authentic feel.

The place to retire to is the dispensary. This small room hosts a collection of booths, a couple of benches and a few tables and chairs. It's from this little room that period drinks are mixed and served.

THE FOOD

The food at the City Tavern is some of the most unique (not to mention some of the best) we have ever tried. Chef Walter Staib has spent considerable time and effort researching true colonial food and period menus, and he presents his findings and recipes in his critically acclaimed television show, "A Taste of History."

The same enthusiasm evident in his show has been put into his menu at the City Tavern.

A great starter for any meal is his West Indies Pepperpot Soup. This was a colonial favorite (George Washington served it to his troops after crossing the Delaware) and consists of beef, taro roots, and greens.

Also try Chef Staib's Veal and Herb Sausage "Munchner Style." Consisting of handmade veal sausage, Pennsylvania Dutch-style sauerkraut, mashed potatoes and Dijon mustard, it is simply delicious (especially when paired with his beer).

THE DRINKS

Chef Staib also researched and reintroduced period beer and cocktails at the City Tavern to go with his period cuisine.

No visit to the Tavern is complete without trying the Ales of the Revolution sampler. The sampler is four different kinds of beers, each featuring original recipes from great brewers such as George Washington and Thomas Jefferson. Each is unique, all are great, and most are toned down slightly due to the high alcohol content in the original recipes.

After finishing off the beer, move on to the Rum Shrub. The Shrub dates back to the 1700s and was originally designed to hide flaws in rum as well as take advantage of fruit that started to turn before it was used. It's a mixture of fruit juice vinegar (called shrub), sugar (or other sweetener like simple syrup), water, and rum.

We can also recommend the City Tavern Cooler. Another period drink it's made with peach brandy, West Indies rum, whiskey, and then topped with apple cider and stirred with a cinnamon stick. The spirits mix amazingly well while the sweetness of the cider tones down the harshness of the liquor.

NEARBY DISTRACTIONS

Tun Tavern Memorial Marker—Address: Sansom Street & South Front Street Philadelphia, PA (always open). Located less than a quarter of a mile from City Tavern is the site of the legendary Tun Tavern. It was at this very location that on November 10th, 1775, the United States Marine Corps was born. The owner of the Tun was appointed Recruiting Officer by the Second Continental Congress, and so naturally he began signing up his patrons. Unfortunately, the tavern burned down in 1781, and today most of the location is covered by I-95. All that remains of this storied tavern is the historical marker, which makes a great photo opp.

Independence Hall—Website: www.nps.gov/inde **Address:** 520 Chestnut Street Philadelphia, PA, 19106, (215) 965-2305 (Monday–Sunday 9am–5pm except Christmas day). It is in this very building that on July 4th, 1776, the United States Declaration of Independence was approved by the Continental Congress. This is where America finally declared its independence from England, and this is where America was born. At only a half mile from the City Tavern, no visit to the area is complete without a visit to this historic building.

Liberty Bell Center—Website: www.nps.gov/inde/liberty-bell-center.htm, **Address:** 138 South 2nd Street Philadelphia, PA, 19106, (215) 965-2305 (Monday–Sunday 9am–5pm except Christmas day). Few iconic symbols stir as much within Americans as the Liberty Bell. A long-lasting symbol of

American independence, revolutionary progress and the American spirit, it's well worth the usually long wait in line for a glimpse of this American treasure.

MCGILLIN'S OLD ALE HOUSE, PHILADELPHIA, PA

Address: 1310 Drury Street, Philadelphia, PA, 19107, (215) 735-5562
Website: www.mcgillins.com **Video tour:** http://youtu.be/qNjMvs94kgU
Food: Yes **Live Music:** Yes **Hours:** Monday–Sunday 11am–2am **Type of Bar:** Pub **What to Drink:** McGillin's 1860 IPA **Why You Should Go:** A bar since 1860, a staple of Philadelphia, plus the century-old gallery of signs and advertising from Philadelphia-area businesses.

THE HISTORY

McGillin's opened its doors in 1860, making it over 150 years old, one of the oldest bars in America and Philadelphia's oldest continuously operating bar. Though it originally opened as The Bell In Hand, its patrons simply called it McGillin's after owner, William McGillin. Called "Pa" by his patrons, McGillin was an Irish immigrant who came to the United States because of the Irish Potato Famine in the mid-19th century. Pa used the upper levels of the building to house himself, his wife and his 13 children. As the bar quickly became popular William expanded, taking over the oyster house next door, the back alley/washroom and eventually even McGillin's own house upstairs.

Unfortunately, Pa McGillin passed away in 1901, leaving his wife, Catherine "Ma" McGillin, to take over the management of the bar and restaurant. A smart businesswoman, Catherine continued Pa's renovation and expansion plans, and continued to run the place until the mid-1930s.

Part of her tenure encompassed Prohibition, when she famously locked the front door and vowed that no one would enter through it until the Volstead Act was repealed (not realizing it would take 14 years). True to her vow she used the backdoor as the entrance to the restaurant (with speakeasy upstairs).

Ma passed away in 1937, at which time her daughter Mercedes took over operation until 1958 when she sold it to two brothers, Henry Spaniak and Joe Shepaniak (for some reason the brothers spelled their last names differently).

While always a popular neighborhood bar it was in the 1950s that it really started to come into its own thanks to a new crowd of patrons. Celebrities like Will Rogers, the Marx Brothers, Vincent Price, and Tennessee Williams would visit McGillin's for a drink, some food, and entertainment. As the number of celebrities increased so did the bar's popularity.

TODAY

Today the bar remains in the Spaniak/Shepaniak family and is run by Mary Ellen and her husband, Chris Mullins: Henry Spaniak's daughter and son-in-law. It's still frequented by celebrities, like Tony Danza, Will Ferrell and Bam Margera, local sports stars, politicians, and musicians in town for concerts.

Widely considered Philadelphia's best Irish bar, and on the top list of many magazines and culinary journals (like "Gourmet", among others), McGillin's looks like what you'd imagine a 19th-century Irish bar *should* look like. It'll seem almost familiar at first—the walls covered in bric-a-brac, the friendly crowd and the gleaming wood of the bar. It'll take a minute for you to realize that just about every chain, wannabe Irish pub and restaurant is copying this place in their bland formulas.

The real deal is worth it, though. The bric-a-brac on the walls isn't really random; it's been collected over 150 years—like the old assortment of liquor licenses behind the bar—and has a lot of significance to Philadelphia (especially the collection of advertising and signs belonging to once-landmark-stores like Wanamaker's).

THE FOOD

From Mile High Meatloaf to shepherd's pie, mussels, steaks and other Irish favorites, McGillin's features some excellent dishes. Most meals come with a bowl of soup from their self-serve station and they offer a different special every night of the week.

Most would describe the fare as comfort food, but they do spend an immense amount of time to make it even more comfortable. Many of the herbs are fresh from the owner's personal herb garden. They also take pains to get fresh fruit and vegetables, like tomatoes from nearby New Jersey, and fresh seafood.

We didn't sample any food ourselves, but owner Chris Mullins will gladly tell you what's in season and is best for that evening's meal.

THE DRINKS

McGillin's has a full-service bar that can mix up just about anything you could want, but their real specialties are their craft and custom-made beers. They're happy to point out that they were the first place in Philadelphia to embrace local craft beers, and so it's only fitting they commissioned a local brewery to produce some beers just for them.

McGillin's has three house beers: McGillin's Real Ale, McGillin's Genuine Lager and McGillin's 1860 IPA. The lager and the ale are both outstanding beers, but the real treat is their IPA. Originally created as part of the 150th anniversary celebration in 2010, the IPA is unfiltered, making it similar to the beers drunk in the 1800s. Unsurprisingly, the recipe is secret, but we do know that it contains multiple hop varieties, including Centennial and Amarillo.

McGillin's IPA is an outstanding beer available both on tap at the bar and at a select few distributors around Philadelphia and is the must-try drink when you visit.

NEARBY DISTRACTIONS

Masonic Library and Museum—Website: www.pagrandlodge.org **Address:** 1 North Broad Street Philadelphia, PA, 19107, (215) 988-1900 (tour times vary; refer to website for additional information). With origins dating back to the 16th century (and possibly even earlier) the Freemasons played a significant role in American History. Take the opportunity to visit this iconic Freemason lodge to get a new and unique look into the founding of our nation and the great men who molded it.

Simeone Automotive Museum—Website: www.simeonemuseum.org **Address:** 6825 Norwitch Drive Philadelphia, PA, 19153, (215) 365-7233 (Tuesday–Friday 10am–6pm, Saturday–Sunday 10am–4pm). A short five-mile drive from McGillin's will deliver you to the Simeone Automotive Museum. Featuring race cars dating back to the early 1900s, the museum is not only unique in its cars but also in the fact that many of the cars are still driven on Demonstration Days. Open to the public this is one of the few if not the only place you can still hear, see and smell these classic cars as they tear around the track.

The Rocky Statue—Address: Kelly Drive Philadelphia, PA, 19130, (always open). The statue of the fictional Rocky character is one of the city's most notable landmarks. An immortalization of the Rocky character, it was built to pay tribute to the underdog, much like the US was when it declared its independence from Britain. Only two miles away from McGillin's, it is a perfect stop for a free photo op and a run up the fabled stairs.

PHILADELPHIA'S HISTORIC BARS

Khyber Pass Pub—Website: www.khyberpasspub.com **Address:** 56 South 2nd Street Philadelphia, PA, 19106, (215) 238-5888 (Monday–Sunday 11am–2pm). This is typically called a "cozy dive bar," which really makes no sense. Maybe they mean small? Not threatening? We're not sure, but it is somewhat of a legend in this city. The selling point for historic bar lovers is that there has reportedly been a drinking establishment at this location since 1876, making it the third oldest location in Philadelphia (even if it did change names over the centuries).

Dock Street Brewery—**Website:** www.dockstreetbeer.com **Address:** 701 South 50th Street Philadelphia, PA, 19143, (215) 726-2337(Monday–Wednesday 3pm–10pm, Thursday 3pm–11pm, Friday 11:30am–12am, Saturday 12pm–12am). Founded in 1985 this is the first microbrewery in Philly and one of the first in the United States. It's a notable bar to visit simply because of this. The owners did something new and different, and now all of these new craft microbreweries opening up are a result of their legacy. Great place to go for some seriously good beer and even better history.

Dirty Frank's—**Website:** www.dirtyfranksbar.com **Address:** 347 S 13th St, Philadelphia, PA, 19107, (215) 732-5010 (Monday–Sunday 11am–2am). Founded in 1933, right after prohibition, this neighborhood bar has become more of a community center for the city. They are warm and caring, and serve a variety of locals. Serving cheap drinks throughout the day (and night), you can easily get your drink on for less than a $20. Speaking of which, be sure to bring actual cash, they don't accept credit card. They also don't serve food, so bring your own. When you get here, order a Dirty Frank's Special, which is a shot and a 7-ounce beer, all for less than $3.00.

McCusker's Tavern—**Address:** 2601 S 17th St, Philadelphia, PA, 19145, (215) 339-9238 (Monday–Sunday 11am–2am). This friendly, neighborhood tavern has been around since the middle of the last century and run by the same family for three generations. They have cheap beer and drinks, and instead of a stinky old dive, inside you find a clean, well-kept bar, the likes of which your grandad might have visited back in the day. They serve pub grub, like burgers and wings, and have an array of televisions with whatever games are being played at the time.

PORTLAND, OR

Portland was established in 1843 when two explorers, struck by the beauty of the area, beached their canoe and decided it would be a good place to start a settlement. As the settlement took shape, a name needed to be bestowed upon it, and, rumor has it, that the name was determined by a best-out-of-three coin toss. On the one side was a man who wanted to name it Portland, after Portland, Maine, and on the other was a man who wanted to name it Boston, after, well, Boston, Massachusetts. The Portland name won and the settlement stepped quickly into notoriety.

From 1859 to 1941, Portland was known as the "Unheavenly City," a name linked to rumors of the shanghaiing of innocent bystanders via an extensive tunnel system (the tunnel system is known today as, ironically, the Shanghai tunnels). The city went through multiple trials and tribulations as it grew into the city we know today. A fire almost destroyed the city in 1873, unsanitary sewers and gutters led to its being dubbed the "Northern States filthiest city" in the late 19th century, numerous unsavory union strikes and riots welcomed the 20th century, and organized crime ran rampant from the 1920s to the 1950s.

Today, Portland is the Pacific Northwest's second largest city, second only to Seattle, Washington, and, as far as we can tell, organized crime no longer runs rampant and the city has cleaned up its sewers and gutters. Now it's more known for its random and dreary weather, food trucks, urban gardening, bicycling, art, local brewers, and (as some would argue) quirky residents. The city is truly a unique metropolis. But through it all, and, most importantly for us, Portland has some great historic and classic bars.

KELLY'S OLYMPIAN BAR, PORTLAND, OR

Address: 426 SW Washington St., Portland, OR, 97204, (503) 228-3669
Website: www.kellysolympian.com **Video tour:**
https://youtu.be/FFuahSC8MZE
Food: Yes **Live Music:** Yes, 4 to 6 nights a week **Hours:** Monday–Sunday,
10am–2 am **Type of Bar:** Pub **What to Drink:** Olympia beer **Why You
Should Go:** Third oldest continually operating bar in Portland, one of the last
independently owned and operated bars in Portland, great live acts.

THE HISTORY

Kelly's Olympian was originally opened in 1902 as an Olympia-tied saloon.
In other words, Olympia helped the place get its start with monetary and
other forms of support (such as loans, equipment, furnishings etc.) and in
return, the bar agreed to only sell Olympia products. Known originally as
"The Olympian Saloon," the name Kelly was added years later after one of its
owners.

From its beginnings, Kelly's was a popular gathering spot with locals,
timbermen, sailors, shipyard workers, and other river-industry workers due to
its proximity to the river and shipyards. It's rumored, and some evidence has
been uncovered, that the bar originally had a urinal that ran the length of the
bar, which allowed clientele to relieve themselves without having to leave their
beer. The bar also had an exceptionally popular cardroom, which remains
today—though in a new digital form—and was one of the only ones in town,
helping to keep the bar packed around the clock.

The bar is believed to have been connected to the Portland Shanghai
tunnels, which date back to the early 19th century and of which evidence can

be found in the basement today. The Shanghai tunnels connected taverns and hotels to the waterfront and were originally intended to allow businesses to move goods without having to deal with street traffic. Legends and rumors would lead many to believe these tunnels were utilized to Shanghai individuals during Portland's darker days, by Chinese immigrants as a place to live, and, as prohibition took hold, to move illicit booze from the river to the many speakeasies around the city. The stories may or may not be true, but we do know the tunnels existed, and, it appears by the variations in the floor tiles and covered and patched openings, Kelly's was a part of that network.

As Portland grew and changed, Kelly's remained a cornerstone of the city and its community. It's seen few owners over the years, with the Power's family owning and operating it for 3 generations until just recently. Greg Powers, a 3rd generation owner, recently sold the place to a pair of local business partners who invested considerable time and money brining the bar back to its former glory and ensuring it'll remain both a living piece of Portland's history, and a favorite stop among locals and tourists alike.

TODAY

When you walk into Kelly's today, you feel like you were just swept back to the motorcycle hey-day of the 1960s and 70s. Vintage motorcycles and motorcycle memorabilia deck the walls and hang from the ceiling. We were told that the motorcycles are all road ready, you just need to drop them down, roll them out, start them up and ride off (a true dream for the motorcyclist at heart). Additionally, everything on the walls is vintage and original, from the old neon signs, to Evil Knievel's helmet and the motorcycles themselves. The collection belongs to one of the owners and, like the bar, are a nod to history.

The old card room remains but in a more modern form: the tables have been replaced with video poker machines (you can't go home again). You also won't find the old bar-length urinal at your feet (thank goodness), and they serve more than just Olympia products, though you can still get Olympia products or choose from more than 20 beers on tap. The kitchen is full-service and the food is made from scratch. If you arrive on one of the many nights featuring live music, you can slide over to the bar's expanded venue, located right next door, to catch the show. Or, simply post up on the expansive bar and enjoy the atmosphere.

In the end, Kelly's (like her vintage memorabilia) is a throwback to a different time. Not better or worse, just different. She has a great story to tell, a few secrets left to reveal, and a few stories waiting to be written. So, if you find yourself in downtown Portland, swing by and grab a bite to eat and a couple of drinks, and learn a bit more about this city's history.

THE FOOD

Kelly's has a full-service kitchen that makes everything from scratch. The Mac and Chees Balls are a pretty tasty appetizer as are the wings. The burgers are simple but delicious, and the breakfast choices filling (we really enjoyed

The Olympian). Cruise in on a Sunday and enjoy their all-day Mimosa and Bloody Mary specials.

THE DRINKS

Kelly's does have a full-service bar, but their real specialty is their more than 20 rotating tap system. We recommend exploring the tap selections or keeping it simple and ordering an Olympia beer.

NEARBY DISTRACTIONS

Powell's City of Books—Website: www.powells.com **Address:** 1005 W Burnside St, Portland, OR 97209, (800) 878-7323 (Open Monday–Sunday 9am–11pm). Claiming to be the world's largest independent new and used book store, this is a Portland institution not to be missed. Featuring multiple floors, nine color-coded rooms, and over 3,500 different sections, its continued success (while giants like Barnes and Noble flail) is a testament to the city's love of books. Grab a cup of coffee and a map (yes, they really have them available), and take in a literal, literary vault.

Portland Walking Tour's Underground Portland Tour—Website: www.portlandwalkingtours.com, (503) 774-4522 (Hours and tour times vary). Since you have visited a place that was a part of the Portland Underground, aka the Shanghai Tunnels, taking a tour of what remains of the tunnels will be exceptionally interesting. During the tour you'll not only learn about the notorious tunnels (including Portland's dark and sinister past), but also get to physically visit these locations in the subterranean levels of the Merchant Hotel.

HUBER'S CAFÉ, PORTLAND, OR

Address: 411 SW 3rd Ave., Portland, OR, 97204, (503) 228-5686
Website: www.hubers.com **Video Tour:** https://youtu.be/2DL6yIPkmaw
Food: Yes **Live Music:** No **Hours:** Monday–Thursday 11:30am–12am,
Friday 11:30am–1am, Saturday 11am–1am, Sunday 4pm–11pm **Type of
Bar:** Saloon **What to Drink:** Spanish Coffee **Why You Should Go:** Great
food and cocktails, old school bar, a testament to the American Dream.

THE HISTORY

Huber's is the story of the American Dream come true. Established in 1879
on the corner of 1st and Morrison, it was originally known as "The Bureau
Saloon" until Frank Huber purchased it and changed the name to Huber's.
Later, in 1891, Huber hired Jim Louie, a Chinese immigrant, as a cook. It
was a choice that would prove to be a fortuitous decision for both men.

In those days, if you purchased a drink at the bar you got a free turkey
sandwich and a side of slaw. The original location was small, with only a few
booths, and as such many patrons would simply walk around, drink in one
hand and a turkey sandwich in the other, mingling amongst themselves. This
is how the Turkey Tradition, still present today (though you no longer get a
free sandwich with a drink order), got its start.

Huber's was moved to its current location in 1910, and in 1912 Frank
Huber passed away. Jim Louie was promptly asked to manage the business for
the Huber family, which he immediately agreed to. When prohibition was
passed, Jim, encouraged by his loyal patrons, kept the place open as a
restaurant specializing in turkey-based meals. The place also served illicit
booze and the specialty was a Manhattan in a coffee or tea cup. Jim's nephew,

Andrew, joined him in the restaurant in 1941 and they were able to set up a 50-50 partnership with the Huber family. Jim tragically passed away, right after finishing up his normal day in the restaurant in 1946. His nephew Andrew took over as manager, and eventually purchased the restaurant outright in 1952. Andrews's son, James, came on board in the early 1970s and introduce Huber's signature drink, the Spanish Coffee.

From the start, Huber's was and still remains a family affair. As it passed from Frank Huber to his family, to Jim Louie, his nephew Andrew, and now Andrew's descendants, the tavern and restaurant are and remain a wonderful example of the American Dream realized.

TODAY

When you walk into Huber's today, you will immediately be struck by the class and elegance, which is refined but not pretentious. The turkey and Spanish Coffee traditions continue. In fact, they are famous the world over for their tasty Spanish Coffee, and they use more Kahlua than any other independent restaurant in the US.

When you arrive, one thing you will almost immediately notice is that Huber's has two entrances, the restaurant and the bar. The bar area is the original section, dating back to 1910, and should be your first stop. At one time it was considered the most elegant bar in all of Portland, and we would argue it still is, with many of the original fixture still present today. With the antique bar, stunning stain glass sky lights, and light fixtures, it is easy to imagine patrons from the roaring twenties walking around with cocktails and turkey sandwiches in hand, conversing about the idiocy of the 18th Amendment, and enjoying the atmosphere of Huber's.

After you enjoy the atmosphere of the antique bar, we recommend you move into the restaurant to enjoy an outstanding meal. Along the way check out some of the clippings and pictures displayed on the walls. These documents tell not only the restaurant's history, but also the story of its owners and employees through the years.

THE FOOD

Huber's has an expansive and enticing menu, but don't waste your time diving too deeply on your first trip. The place was founded on turkey, is known for its turkey, and many a customer's come back time after time simply for its turkey (Jim Louie was once heard saying he had carved over 50,000 of them in his lifetime). We recommend sticking to turkey and ordering their famous turkey dinner.

THE DRINKS

Huber's has a full-service bar featuring classic and craft cocktails, served by well-trained bartenders who can whip you up just about anything your heart desires. But, you would be remiss not to start off with their Spanish Coffee, which they have been serving since the 1970s. It's not just the drink itself, but the way they prepare it at the bar or your table that makes it so popular. With steps that include long, dramatic pours and melting sugar around the rim by setting rum alight, you'll find yourself hypnotized at first, then trying to drink it quickly so you can order another. We recommend starting with one of these before exploring the bars other offerings.

NEARBY DISTRACTIONS

Voodoo Doughnuts—Website: www.voodoodoughnut.com **Address:** 22 SW 3rd Ave, Portland, OR, 97204, (503) 241-4704 (Open 24 Hours). The brain child of Kenneth "Cat Daddy" Pogson and Tres Shannon (who spin quite the tale describing the businesses history), Voodoo doughnuts has become a Portland staple (though they also have shops in Austin, Denver, Hollywood and Orlando). The place is open 24 hours and makes some legendary and equally quirky doughnuts. A must during any visit to Portland (beware, they are cash only).

Pink Trolley Sightseeing—Website: www.graylineofportland.net, (503) 241-7373 (Hours vary). Pink Trolley Sightseeing's hop-on/hop-off trolleys are an easy and convenient way to check out the city while learning a little here and there. While narration is not as in depth as you will find on some of the specific tours, such as the walking tours, they do give you some general insight into the city and its history, and it's an easy way to see more the city, more quickly.

ALIBI TIKI LOUNGE, PORTLAND, OR

Address: 4024 N. Interstate Ave., Portland, OR, 97227, (503) 287-5335
Website: www.alibiportland.com **Video tour:**
https://youtu.be/221HCabpWYA

Food: Yes **Live Music:** Yes **Hours:** Daily, 11:30am–2:30am **Type of Bar:** Tiki **What to Drink:** Kumoniwanalaya (Come on, I wanna lay ya) or the Masturbating Monkey **Why You Should Go:** Founded in 1947, the Alibi Tiki Lounge is certainly not Portland's oldest bar, but it is one of best examples of old school Tiki bars left in the US.

THE HISTORY

The building that contains the Alibi has an extensive bar history dating back to the 1800s. It didn't become a Tiki Bar until Roy Ell, returning from World War 2 in 1947, purchased the bar, which was known as Max's Alibi at the time. Roy immediately set about converting the bar into a place that resembled tropical Polynesia and not the Pacific Northwest logging town that was Portland at the time. To outfit the bar, Roy was known to frequently travel to Hawaii to hand-select the décor. As the years progressed so did the bar, as it was filled with bamboo, Polynesian masks, and woven palms. A kitchen, serving Polynesian-inspired dishes, was added in 1950.

The 1970s and 80s were exceptionally hard on most Tiki bars in the US, and it was during this period many of them shut down. Fortunately for the Alibi, this wasn't the case, as it remained exceptionally popular among Portland locals. 1992 marked a passing of the torch for the Alibi as Roy sold the bar to Carla and Larry White, who had to promise not to change a thing in the bar. Larry, a huge Tiki fan himself, honored the agreement and expanded both the bar and kitchen menu plus introduced Karaoke, which was an immediate and continued hit.

The bar changed hands once again in 2017, when local historic bar managers Marcus Archambeault and Warren Boothby took over. Following some minor restoration and tweaks to the bar and food menu, the bar reopened to much fanfare.

TODAY

Today the Alibi remains one of Portland's most popular and beloved bars. When you walk in you are immediately swept away, no longer in Portland's (at times) rainy and dreary weather, but on an island oasis, complete with food and a full-service bar. The place is dimly lit, almost too dark (but still pleasant), expansive, and has red vinyl booths galore (the booths are comfortable enough to spend the whole day in by the way).

The afternoons tend to be laid back and relaxed, a time to stop by if you're looking to have quiet, Tiki-themed (and hangover curing) meal and strong, tropical cocktail, all while quietly getting lost in the ambiance that is the Alibi. But where the afternoons are relaxed, the evenings are a bit more energetic. As karaoke gets started so does the crowd as it increases in size, noise level, and alcohol-infused rowdiness.

The Alibi religiously hangs on to its Tiki past, not with desperation, but instead with noble confidence and style, sweeping you off to that imaginary island oasis with ease. If you're looking for a great Tiki bar while you're in the Portland area, this is your spot. Roll in, grab a tropical drink, a bite to eat, and then pelt out your favorite karaoke tune. There are few better ways to spend a night in Portlandia.

THE FOOD

The full-service kitchen was opened in the 1950s and has been serving Tiki-crazed patrons since. The recently introduced flaming PuPu platter has become a hit, and the Kahlua pulled pork is a longtime favorite.

THE DRINKS

This is a true Tiki bar, and the drinks are both strong and sweet. While they do many of the classics well—like the Scorpion Bowl or Mai Tai—the Kumoniwanalaya has become a popular choice as has the Masturbating Monkey.

NEARBY DISTRACTIONS

The Freakybuttrue Peculiarium and Museum—Website: www.peculiarium.com **Address:** 2234 NW Thurman St, Portland, OR, 97210, (503) 227-3164 (Monday–Sunday, 10am–8pm). Part sci-fi collectible exhibit, part urban-legend celebration, part oddity museum, the Freakybuttrue Peculiarium has been at the center of "weird" Portland for (according to them) over five decades. Find odd statues, creepy exhibits, and over-the-top kitsch. This place is a great find and a truly unique experience. Buy some stuff in the gift shop to pass out at the office when you get home, you'll be happy you did.

Washington Park—Website: www.explorewashingtonpark.org **Address:** 2760, 4033 Southwest Canyon Road, Portland, OR, 97221, (503) 319-0999 (Monday–Sunday, 5am–10pm). Get out of the hustle and bustle of the city and into some green space. Portland's Washington Park makes up one of the largest urban parks in the US, and gives you plenty of space to walk off the booze. The park hosts a zoo, amphitheater, trails, gardens, reservoirs and a railroad.

BrewCycle Portland–West—Website: www.brewgrouppdx.com **Address:** 1425 NW Flanders St, Portland, OR, 97209, (971) 400-5950 (Monday–Saturday, 10:30am–7pm, Sunday, 11am–7pm). What better way to explore the famous breweries of Portland than by a group-driven bicycle. Riders face each other over two bar tops while their guide steers them through the streets, taking them from brewery to brewery. The more you drink the easier the peddling gets (or so we hear).

PORTLAND'S HISTORIC BARS

Dan & Louis Oyster Bar—Website: www.danandlouis.com **Address:** 208 SW Ankeny St., Portland OR, 97204, (503) 227-5906 (Open Monday–Thursday 11am–9pm, Friday–Saturday 11am–10pm, Sunday 12pm–9pm). Dating back to 1907, this fourth-generation bar and restaurant is an ingrained part of Portland's history. The inside is full of nautical memorabilia lending to a feeling of being on a ship or in a restaurant on the beach, not in the middle of downtown Portland. Hit this place up on a sunny afternoon during happy hour, where you can post up in the alley and slurp on cheap oysters from the Washington and Oregon coasts. Top it off with a huge cherry-red Manhattan or local craft beer for a perfect happy hour experience.

Momo's—Address: 725 SW 10th Ave, Portland, OR, 97205, (503) 478-9600 (Open daily, 3pm–230am). Located in the center of downtown Portland is Momo's, probably one of the best worst kept secrets of the area. Featuring a normally cramped and dark atmosphere, complete with racy artwork and expansive and private leather covered booths, the real gem of this classic dive is one of downtown's few patios. A small menu, pinball machines, working stiffs, locals, hipsters and PSU students round out the experience. We recommend swinging by on a nice afternoon to enjoy the hidden patio and one of their popular grilled cheese sandwiches.

The Sandy Hut—Address: 1430 NE Sandy Blvd, Portland, OR, 97232, (503) 235-7972 (Open Monday–Friday 2pm–230am, Saturday–Sunday 11am–230am). Serving drinks since 1923, the Sandy Hut (sometimes affectionately referred to as the Handy Slut) is what we would refer to as an epic dive bar and restaurant combo. While pretty broken down and sometime downright dangerous in the 1980s and 90s, it was lovingly restored by the same pair that now own the Alibi. The entire bar was given a facelift and years of neglect were scraped from her walls to turn her back into the jewel that was the hotspot of Portland in the 1950s. Be sure to check out the original Al Hirschfeld mural on the wall, sister to the only other original found at the Frolic Room in Hollywood. If you find yourself bleary-eyed and hungry one Saturday or Sunday afternoon (or better yet, at about 1 am) and in need of a hefty, greasy meal and stiff drink, the Sandy Hut is your place. Opening at 10:30am on Saturday and Sunday and staying open until 2:30am every night, it is a perfect stop to grab a meal. The breakfast choices (such as the breakfast burrito or breakfast sandwich) are great choices, but the burgers are some of the best burgers you will find in Portland. They also feature great live music acts and yearly events, so check their schedule ahead of time to find out what's going.

SAN ANTONIO, TX

San Antonio is the city that many envision when they think of Texas history. And of course they think of it for good reasons. After all, this is the city in which Santa Anna laid siege to the Alamo and killed James Bowie, Davie Crockett and a small outnumbered force from the Texian Army.

This is also the heart of cattle country, and in the 1800s it saw many of the most successful cattle barons in the West walk her streets. The most famous and successful of these was Richard King, founder of the King Ranch, one of the largest ranches in the world.

It was also the host to Texas' first brewery (like Austin, San Antonio had a huge German immigrant population) and number of old West saloons. The brewery and all but one of the saloons are gone now, but their legacy lives on.

And like most cities, San Antonio has a darker side. In the 1960s they became home to the Mexican Mafia, a ruthless organized street gang that ran the underworld of the city, including one of our Bucket List Bars™.

Luckily much of that has changed. San Antonio has been cleaned up, and many of the bad elements have been escorted out of the city. It's still home to a huge military population, with Army, Marine and Air Force personnel stationed close by. The crowd you'll find will be a combination of business people, a stream of tourists, and military personnel looking to blow off some steam.

THE ESQUIRE TAVERN, SAN ANTONIO, TX

Address: 155 East Commerce Street, San Antonio, TX, 78205, (210) 222-2521
Website: www.esquiretavern-sa.com **Video tour:**
http://youtu.be/N7hRgIoDxVY
Food: Yes **Live Music:** No **Hours:** Monday–Wednesday & Sunday 11am–12am, Thursday–Saturday 11am–2am **Type of Bar:** Saloon **What to Drink:**
The Mas Chingoni **Why You Should Go:** Earliest post-Prohibition bar in San Antonio, gangland bar in the 1970s-1990s.

THE HISTORY

The Esquire was opened on December 6, 1933, by the Georges, a local family who intended to quench the city's thirst after the failed Great Experiment (that is, Prohibition). As you can imagine, it opened to much fanfare after 14 years of government imposed "dryness." In fact, opening day saw a line that stretched for over a block.

The Georges were immigrants from Greece and were pursuing the American Dream when they opened their bar. Originally they tried to open on Houston Street but were denied their request by the City. Instead they were given the rights to open a bar on Commerce Street, which is where the bar resides today. This turned out to be to their advantage because the location developed into a premier locale on San Antonio's famous River Walk.

From 1933 until the bar shut down in 2006, The Esquire's demographics ebbed and flowed with that of the city of San Antonio. From notorious gangsters of the 1930s (who used to purchase guns just down the road), middle class professionals, hipsters, and the notorious Mexican Mafia (who ran prostitution and drugs out of the bar), the Esquire has seen it all.

Speaking of the Mexican Mafia: located above the original bathrooms, which were originally placed in the back of the building, was a loft known as the VIP Room. The small room contained a bed, a sink, and for the right amount of money, a female companion. In short, the VIP room was The Esquire's "Champagne Room," or as is known in the masseuse realm, a place to obtain a "Happy Ending."

This was one of the products of the Mexican Mafia, a vicious gang of Latino street thugs that is rumored to have originated in San Antonio. From the late 1970s through early 2000s (when the bar finally closed), they used the Esquire to deal drugs and to run their prostitution ring. It was a rough place with a rough crowd. Nightly, The Esquire saw stabbings, shootings and fights. There were metal detectors at the door and they even sold t-shirts that read, "I Survived The Esquire Tavern."

In 2006 the bar shut down and took a five-year hiatus. It had garnered a bad reputation and was known as a place to expect trouble. But then in 2008 local businessman Chris Hill purchased the troubled saloon with the goal of restoring it. He told a local newspaper, "The more I looked at it, the more I realized I didn't want someone to open a barbecue joint there. I mean, I can remember going there and having a great time. I thought it was important to downtown that there's one old original space left on the river."

When Hill purchased the bar it was badly dilapidated and in desperate need of renovations. After over a year remodeling, he brought the bar back to life in 2011 with a custom but vintage look that welcomes patrons just like it did in 1933.

TODAY

Today The Esquire has been renovated and displays its heritage through custom, vintage-looking décor. The furnishings are still some of the original (though restored), and the bar is still the longest one in Texas (more than 100 feet long). It also features an upscale, full-service kitchen with great burgers and some of the best fried pickles in all of Texas. But what really sets The Esquire apart from other establishments on the River Walk (besides its age) is its traditional approach to cocktails.

THE FOOD

We had heard rave reviews about their food and were excited to try it as their executive chef is known to have blended regional cuisine and bar staples into a full menu of great choices.

For an appetizer we had the fried pickles, which were just remarkable washed down with a cold beer (for some reason fried pickles always seem to hide the fact that they're about a thousand degrees until you bite into them, so be careful). The Bison Burger is second to none - even the bartenders went on and on about them (they're bartenders, so we trust them) – and the lamb burger was a close second.

THE DRINKS

The bartenders at The Esquire have mastered the lost art of professional bartending. Drinks, both traditional and house specialties, are made to exact specifications, giving patrons a consistent and true taste to their cocktails. As a matter of fact, some of the regulars told us that they sometimes feel guilty drinking their cocktails after watching the level of work and pride the bartenders put into them.

During our visit we were lucky enough to spend our time with The Esquire's former master barman and cocktail aficionado, Jeret Pena, who just opened his own place, The Brooklynite. Besides being what some would consider a black belt in the art of barman-ship, Jeret is a libation artist who is responsible for the creation of one of The Esquire's most popular drinks, the Mas Chingoni, a spin-off of the traditional Negroni cocktail with a few key ingredient changes.

We recommend you grab a Mas Chingoni, head out onto the back deck and enjoy the view. Even better, make reservations well ahead of time and enjoy a table on the deck during the yearly "Taste of the River Walk."

NEARBY DISTRACTIONS

The San Antonio River Walk—Website: www.thesanantonioriverwalk.com, (always open, though restaurant, bar and shop hours vary by location). Probably the most famous of San Antonio's tourist attractions, the River Walk is a network of pedestrian walkways one story beneath the streets of downtown San Antonio. The paths follow the San Antonio River and are lined with just about every kind of bar/restaurant (including The Esquire) in the city ensuring something for everyone.

Ranger Creek Brewing & Distilling—Website: www.drinkrangercreek.com **Address:** 4834 Whirlwind Dr. San Antonio, TX, 78217, (210) 775-2099 (tour times and dates vary; call or check their website). Claiming the title of the only "brewstillery" in Texas, Ranger Creek both brews beer and makes Texas Bourbon Whiskey. Featuring once-a-month tours, for those interested in getting a look at how they make beer and whiskey, plus daily samplings, it is worth the short 13-mile drive from The Esquire.

Little Red Barn—Website: www.littleredbarnsteakhouse.com **Address:** 1902 South Hackberry San Antonio, TX, 78210, (210) 532-4235 (Monday–Thursday 11am–2pm, 4:30pm–9pm, Friday 11am–2pm, 4:30pm–10pm, Saturday 12am–10pm, Sunday 11:30am–8pm). In the mood for steak? Then head over to the Little Red Barn Steakhouse, which is only three miles from The Esquire. Established in 1963 and claiming to be the largest steakhouse in Texas the Little Red Barn has great steaks, fast service, picnic-style seating and an authentic Texas atmosphere, making for a unique and fun dining experience.

THE MENGER BAR, SAN ANTONIO, TX

Address: 204 Alamo Plaza, San Antonio, TX, 78205, (800) 345-9285
Website: www.mengerhotel.com **Video tour:** http://youtu.be/GroSRcM8eoc
Food: Yes **Live Music:** No **Hours:** Monday–Friday 11am–12am, Saturday–
Sunday 12pm–12am **Type of Bar:** Pub **What to Drink:** The house margarita
or a Lone Star **Why You Should Go:** More cattle deals struck here than
anywhere else in the United States, plus the legacy of Teddy Roosevelt, and
the Alamo is literally right next door.

THE HISTORY

Built on the site of Texas's first brewery (the Menger Brewery) and across
the street from the Alamo, the Menger Hotel was originally opened in
1859—just 13 years after Texas was admitted to the Union and a short 23
years after the battle of the Alamo. It was originally built as a 50-room hotel
and dubbed "the finest hotel west of the Mississippi," but its popularity grew
at such a dramatic rate that a three-story addition had to be built just after
opening. Just like any high-end establishment of the time it also contained a
spectacular and extravagant bar.

The bar itself was built in 1887 and is an exact replica of London's now-
demolished House of Lord's Pub. Dark cherry wood, beveled mirrors from
France, decorated glass cabinets, and brass spittoons created a bar of rare
sophistication. That isn't to say it didn't attract a wide range of clientele.
From Presidents, to generals, cattle barons, writers and poets, this bar has seen
them all… and more.

Teddy Roosevelt recruited some of the famous Rough Riders (the US
volunteer cavalry of the Spanish-American War) right here in the Menger

Hotel. During a particular set of drills Roosevelt was so impressed with these men he ordered an early end to the day and declared drinks on him at their favorite bar, which just so happened to be the Menger. Teddy was later reprimanded for his actions by his Colonel, who stated that an officer drinking with his men was not conducive to good discipline.

Teddy accepted the reprimand and left the tent. Within minutes he returned to the Colonel's tent, saluted, and then declared "Sir, I consider myself the damnedest ass within ten miles of this camp! Good night, sir!"

Along the walls of the bar and the hotel you'll find a huge assortment of photos showing some of the more prominent guests to have visited the Menger. Included are Presidents Theodore Roosevelt, Ulysses S. Grant, Woodrow Wilson, and Dwight D. Eisenhower.

Other guests have included Robert E. Lee, George Patton, Oscar Wilde, Jimmy Doolittle and even baseball great Babe Ruth (put simply, the list is distinguished). One could spend hours viewing the photos and memorabilia throughout the hotel.

TODAY

The Menger Bar is a favorite stop-off for tourists, who wander in from the heat after perusing the nearby Alamo. At times the small bar can feel a bit crowded as a tour bus drops people off right outside the door, but they generally fade away to view the rest of the hotel. The bar is also a favorite of local or visiting celebrities, so be on the lookout.

An unusual feature is the upstairs, loft-like seating area. We'd prefer to sit at the bar, but you should walk up and take in the different perspective it affords of the entire room. It's also nice to think about all of the deals that were struck here between ranchers long ago.

In addition to prominent guests from its past, some guests and employees decided to never leave. The Menger, like so many of the establishments we've visited, is rumored to have its fair share of ghosts. We were told it has a ghost from every era, including the ghost of Richard King, The King Ranch founder and time-to-time Menger guest, Sallie White, a previous house keeper, and even a Confederate soldier. Experiences range from smelling cigar smoke in rooms, the feeling of being tucked into bed, hearing the expression "pardon me" when no one is near you, and the occasional call for room service from empty rooms.

THE FOOD

The Hotel has an upscale restaurant—the Colonial Room Restaurant—that you can order from while sitting in the bar. It features many of the entrees you'd expect to find in a San Antonio eatery—steak, fish, chicken and some pastas.

THE DRINKS

When you walk into the Menger Bar you would expect the drink menu to reflect the sophistication. But in this case looks can be deceiving. If you have a more refined palate and are looking for a martini or Old Fashioned you will be well served here, but if you are a fan of the everyday bottle of cold beer or a nice margarita, then you've definitely come to the right place.

There are really two drinks you need to try here. The first is a bottle of Lone Star and the second is their house margarita.

Lone Star is a Texas favorite, founded and brewed in the expansive state, is served ice cold and is perfect on a hot and humid summer day in San Antonio. The house margarita is made in the traditional manner, with fresh ingredients, and is one of the best, if not the best in all the state.

NEARBY DISTRACTIONS

The Alamo—Website: www.thealamo.org **Address:** 300 Alamo Plaza San Antonio, TX, 78205, (866) 769-8419 (Monday–Saturday 9am–5:30pm, Sunday 10am–5:30pm, except Christmas). Directly across the street from the Menger sits the world-renowned Alamo. Home of the Battle of the Alamo, where all but two defenders were killed, it was on these hallowed grounds that while ultimately defeated, Texans found a common rallying point and beat Santa Anna's army.

Ripley's Believe It Or Not—Website: www.ripleys.com/sanantonio **Address:** 301 Alamo Plaza San Antonio, TX, 78205, (210) 224-9299 (Sunday–Thursday 10am–7pm, Friday–Saturday 10am–10pm). Sitting across the street from the Menger as well as from the Alamo is San Antonio's Ripley's Believe It Or Not. Featuring artifacts, stories and images that will blow you away, it is sure to be fun for anyone.

Chunky's Burgers—Address: 4602 Callaghan Rd. San Antonio, TX, 78228, (210) 433-9960 (Tuesday–Thursday 11am–9pm, Friday 11am–10pm, Saturday 11:30am–10pm, Sunday 12pm–6pm). Up for a challenge? Then head over to Chunky's Burgers & More, about 11 miles away, to tackle the Four Horsemen Challenge! To win all you have to do is consume a half a pound of beef with the Ghost Chile in under 25 minutes. Good

SAN ANTONIO'S HISTORIC BARS

VFW Post 76—Website: www.vfwpost76ontheriverwalk.org **Address:** 10 10th St San Antonio, TX, 78215, (210) 223-4581 (Monday–Thursday 9am–10pm, Friday–Saturday 9am–12am). That's right: we're suggesting a VFW post. Why? Because it's the oldest post in Texas, of course. But more than that, this place actually has some great history attached to the Menger Bar and San Antonio in general. The post was founded in 1904 by veterans of the Spanish-American war. The hundred-year-old house was donated to them in 1946 and is a museum of the military history of the area. If you want a history lesson while knocking back Lone Star beers, this is a great place to get it.

Buckhorn Saloon—Website: www.buckhornmuseum.com **Address:** 318 East Houston Street San Antonio, TX, 78205, (210) 247-4000 (Monday–Sunday 11am–varied, call for closing times). The saloon was founded in 1881 and is a good slice of San Antonio's history. Be advised that the "museum" portion really is little more than a tourist trap, with $20 prices to see some stuffed animals (you can see a better collection at the Buckhorn Exchange in Denver for the price of a drink). The saloon, though, is the real deal, and there's no charge for admittance. It's rumored that Pancho Villa planned his revolution here, and that Teddy Roosevelt stopped in for a drink.

SAN DIEGO, CA

San Diego was the first place on the West Coast to be touched by Europeans, who sailed into the bay in 1542 and immediately claimed the place for Spain (despite the fact that there were already people living there). Since then, it's been popular for its mild weather and natural beauty. A lot goes on in this city with its long history, so there's plenty to see and do. But more importantly, for the purposes of this book, it's one of the best drinking towns in the country!

Much of the drinking climate here is owed to San Diego's many breweries. This is the place where Stone, Ballast Point, and Green Flash Brewery all chose to call home. At last count, there were about 125 craft breweries in the area (the largest concentration in the US). So, it's pretty obvious the people here enjoy a tipple or two. With the huge concentration of US Navy sailors and Marine Corps personnel, the bars in San Diego are also really busy.

But, despite the influx of all these new, shiny breweries, the city also has a great variety of old and historic bars.

Imagine the stories these places can tell! After all, Wyatt Earp had four saloons and gambling halls here in what was called the Stingaree District. In this place was found all manner of sin, just as vile as any derelict district you'd find on earth. Here the police wouldn't patrol at night because it was too dangerous! With people coming by ship to San Diego from all over the world, you'd hear dozens of languages spoken and witness despicable acts you couldn't even imagine.

What a fun place!

During prohibition, San Diego, was flooded with illegal booze. Ships would anchor off the coast, three miles out to sea in international waters, and sell rum and whiskey brought from Canada to bootleggers in small, fast moving boats that would in turn sell to the hotels and speakeasies found throughout the city. Law enforcement couldn't do a thing to stop it.

And if they did shut down your favorite speakeasy it was only a matter of driving south to get as much booze as you could want legally in Mexico. During prohibition, dozens of new bars popped up throughout Tiujana to sell beer and tequila to the thirsty Americans. They were also too happy to export the stuff as well—during prohibition alcohol exports from Mexico grew 8 times, and you can bet a lot of that was passing through San Diego.

The bars here span the decades and represent a cross-section of the city's history. From a place that would have hosted Wyatt Earp himself to a dive that was popular with the region's immigrant population, you won't be disappointed to drink here!

THE WATERFRONT, SAN DIEGO, CA

Address: 2044 Kettner Blvd, San Diego, CA, 92101, (619) 232-9656
Website: www.waterfrontbarandgrill.com **Video Tour:**
https://youtu.be/S2WlkJVb_fQ
Food: Yes **Live Music:** No **Hours:** Monday–Sunday 6am–2am **Type of
Bar:** Dive **What to Drink:** Craft beer or a Purple Hooter **Why You Should
Go:** Open since 1933 this place has the city's oldest liquor license and a great,
historic pedigree.

THE HISTORY

Sitting for over 80 years in San Diego's seaside village of Little Italy, the
Waterfront has a past that is closely knit with the surrounding community,
and is beloved by the people who frequent her. It was founded in 1933 by
friends Clair Blakley and Chaffee Ulysses Grant, grandson of President
Ulysses S. Grant. If you look closely at their liquor license, dated 1933, you'll
notice it's the oldest one in the city, a fact they're very proud of.

Fishing nets and model ships recall the past of the area and the bar. Though
now it's lined with shops and trendy restaurants, Little Italy was no more than
a fishing village when The Waterfront opened (the marinas and Seaport
Village are only about two blocks to the west). Sicilian fishermen would mend
their nets outside the front door on Kettner, and then retire to the bar for
drinks and cigars after their day's work (or sometimes before). But much of
that is gone now. If you peruse the many photographs on the wall, you'll see a
lot of this history reflected in them. Pictures of fishermen, their grizzled faces

stretched in smiles of pride, watch over the people lined at the bar and help tell the story of this place.

The community was tight-knit, and the owners of The Waterfront were part of it. So much so in fact that we were told that if the staff hadn't shown up by opening time (bright and early at 6 am), a few of the locals had keys and would open up the place themselves. Mornings, afternoons and nights might find a group enjoying drinks and playing Scopa, an Italian card game that's taken pretty seriously by the people who play it (and we understand the games could get rowdy). But in any case, the locals treated the place like home, and respected the owners and the bar. For them, it was somewhere to gather throughout the week to share gossip, to play cards, and to tell tall tales of the fish they didn't catch. It was the unofficial community center for their part of town.

Originally, the bar was much smaller than the space it now occupies. It started out quite humble in fact, but over the years it slowly grew. The clientele began changing slowly as well. Fishermen and their families were joined by members of the military stationed at the nearby Naval and Marine bases. The Waterfront proudly served these men and women through a world war, a Korean conflict and a Vietnam policing action (not to mention the many scuffles in between). The neighborhood started attracting young professionals and it too slowly changed.

In 1973, after 40 years of original ownership, The Waterfront was sold to the current owner's parents. They ran it along with a partner for yet another decade before their daughter, Nancy Nichols bought out the partner and took sole ownership. Nancy has since stood at the helm of The Waterfront ever since, driving it through good and bad times and turning it into the iconic San Diego destination we have today.

TODAY

The fishermen are now all gone (except for the one on the roof), mostly replaced by young professionals. No more nets are mended on Kettner, and the surrounding buildings have gone vertical—expanded and remodeled into hip condos and apartments. New restaurants featuring Italian-fusion cuisine can be found occupying every few spaces along the sidewalk. And the neighborhood, Little Italy, is now thick with tourists. In short, everything surrounding The Waterfront today has little in common with what used to surround it in 1933.

But as the neighborhood and population changed, The Waterfront never really did. Sure, the place may be bigger, perhaps two or three times the footprint of the original, but honestly that might be about it. They still keep the same hours they always did, 6am–2am, and they still serve a lot of the food that was introduced long ago. The people who work there and the people who go there are warm and welcoming, and there's still a sense of community. In fact, many of the regulars are locals—either living in the condos that surround the place or stationed nearby in the military.

They have a huge craft beer selection (which isn't all that surprising considering the immense crowd of craft breweries in the area) and a full bar, so they can also make any drink you can order. If you're hungry they have a full kitchen and serve food from 6am until 1:30am, making it the place to start and/or end a night out. If you're looking to catch the game they have plenty of TVs above the bar, unless you're a Raider's fan, in which case they have an old black and white TV in the back you can watch.

They are absolutely dedicated to the local military as well. To help locally, they throw a yearly party (their biggest party of the year) on December 5th (Repeal Day). It's the only day of the year they charge a cover, but it makes them a ton of money. But that money—all that cash from the door and from various auctions and sales throughout the day—doesn't go to them. Instead, 100% of it goes to the Marine Family Fund, which provides Christmas dinners for local veterans and their families. It's a lot of work, but it's for a great cause.

When you go, the place will be crowded – it's always crowded. When we visited early in the day, the patio seating was already gone and there was little room at the bar. If you walk around you'll find a dining room in back with a few scattered tables and televisions tuned to sports shows. But the fun place to sit is up front, where everybody walks in and you can scan the crowd, the shoppers, and the tourists walking up and down Kettner. Wait for a seat here and jump in when you can. You'll find the people surrounding you to be pretty diverse, with business people, locals from the neighborhood, tourists, college kids, and drunks like us. You might even spot local politicians, sports stars and celebrities.

THE FOOD

The breakfast includes classics like omelets or chicken fried steak and eggs. They also have a lot of the basic pub grub they serve from lunch on, like hamburgers, sliders and such.

One thing they pointed out was their Italian style fish and chips, which uses Italian spices in the breading and has been a hit for them for decades. It's also a little nod to their history. We had the chili and hamburgers and can attest to both of them, but we're pretty sure you'll be happy with just about anything you order.

THE DRINKS

You are in craft beer country here, so pick one and enjoy a pint. They have a couple dozen on tap, so you won't run out of options. They also have a full bar so can make you just about any cocktail you can think of, and even some you can't. We asked about a signature drink and the owner, Nancy, told us to try a Purple Hooter, a drink with vodka, Chambord and soda. It's not bad, and yes, it's very purple.

NEARBY DISTRACTIONS

Little Italy—Website: www.littleitalysd.com, running for about 10 blocks north and south between I-5 and North Harbor Dr. and Laurel St. and W. Ash St., Little Italy is where immigrants from Sicily and other parts of Italy made their homes in San Diego in the early 20th century. This was the fishing village that hosted The Waterfront for so many years. Now this area is full of chic, trendy shops and restaurants. After a few drinks at The Waterfront, work off the booze by checking out the local stores.

Maritime Museum of San Diego—Website: www.sdmaritime.org **Address:** 1492 N. Harbor Dr., San Diego, CA, 92101, (619) 234-9153 (Monday–Sunday 9am–8pm). What better way to celebrate the history of The Waterfront bar than by checking out the history of sea going in San Diego only two blocks away? The museum features a number of restored, vintage vessels, including sailing ships, steam ships and a submarine. They also feature permanent and rotating exhibits that really help visitors understand the maritime legacy of San Diego.

USS Midway Museum—Website: www.midway.org **Address:** 910 N. Harbor Dr., San Diego, CA, 92101, (619) 544-9600 (Monday–Sunday 10am–5pm). Just up the road from the Maritime Museum is the USS Midway, a decommissioned aircraft carrier that served the United States from 1945 until 1992. At one time she was the largest ship in the world, and she helped keep the peace through the Cold War. Now, visitors can tour this beautiful ship and see what it took to defend freedom after World War 2. Rotating exhibits are found throughout, as well as demonstrations and guided tours.

AERO CLUB BAR, SAN DIEGO, CA

Address: 3365 India St, San Diego, CA, 92103, (619) 297-7211
Website: www.aeroclubbar.com **Video tour:** https://youtu.be/AzWIgMg03Yk
Food: No **Live Music:** No **Hours:** Monday–Sunday 2pm–2am **Type of
Bar:** Dive **What to Drink:** Whiskey **Why You Should Go:** Opened by a
female pilot in 1947 this place has become one of the best whiskey
destinations on the West Coast.

THE HISTORY

In the mid-1940s a pilot named Maryanne Prophet wanted a place to hang
out with her friends, also pilots, and so decided to go into the bar business. By
1947 she and her husband had built a small place on India Street, directly east
of the airport, and named it the Aero Club Bar. Think of all the significant,
forward-thinking elements of this simple story. For starters, the pilot in
question who wanted a bar to hang out with other pilots was female. In 1947,
there weren't a lot of female pilots, so this itself was pretty progressive. Also,
just the fact that Maryann—not her husband, not her son—opened the bar is
also interesting, because, again, this wasn't something women did at that
time. We give a lot of credit to Maryann for her courage and foresight.

When the Aero Club Bar was built, there was little else around it. I-5 had
not yet been constructed, and so there was a clear view of the airport. It's easy
to imagine pilots coming into town, getting through with flights for the day,
and then taking a short cab ride over to the Aero Club to knock a few down

and swap tales about their time up in the air. That's what Maryanne wanted anyway, and that's exactly what she got.

Unfortunately, though, she didn't enjoy it all that much. Maryanne Prophet sold the bar within just a few months, starting a trend of short-term ownership. In fact, over its 70 year history the place has seen about 15 different owners. The array of owners is also pretty impressive. At one time it was the hangout for police officers in this part of town. When the owner was ready to go home, he'd leave the keys with the cops and they'd lock up for him. Then in the 1980s a group of Greyhound bus drivers pooled their money together and bought the place. Finally, it was bought by Bill Lutzius in 2004, making him one of the longest tenured owners of the bunch.

The place has seen its share of changing clientele to. In the 1960s the bar was informally known as the San Diego Gun & Knife Club, a statement about how rough it was and how equally rough the patrons were. Then in the 1970s it was a gay and leather bar. Finally, by the time the 2000s rolled around, the place was simply a dive, with cheap beer and troublemaking customers. Throughout it all, however, the place did keep much of the character that Maryanne built into it. The small, cozy place where friends can hang out and chat might have looked differently through the years, but the feel never left it.

TODAY

Bill admits that when he bought the place it was a little worse for wear (or "rough around the edges" as he put it). It was a dive, but a dive in the worse sense of the term, with low-rent patrons that were ready to start something with the slightest provocation and enough alcohol. So how do you change the crowd to one a bit better? According to Bill you simply stop serving what the "assholes" are drinking. And that's exactly what he did.

He also brought the bar back to its previous luster, restoring the interior and exterior, and putting up pictures and paintings that evoke the Aero Club Bar's past. Throughout the place, you see scenes of aviation from the 40s, 50s and 60s. The murals, photographs and assortment of bric-a-brac inside look like they were put up by Maryanne herself, and you get the sense that this is probably what it looked like in the late 1940s. Even the iconic, neon sign is the shape of a Delta Dart, a US Air force jet from the 1960s that really reflects the era.

But perhaps what strikes people the most when they walk into the Aero Club Bar, is the wall of whiskey to the left behind the bar. Lovingly named, La Mer, this wall stretches from floor to ceiling and is at least 20 feet long if not more. And it contains over 1000 different bottles of whiskey. There are different kinds, like Irish whiskey and Scotch, bourbon and rye whiskey, as well as different brands—many of them rare and hard to find.

Much of the credit for this huge display of tasty libations goes to the general manager and bartender, Chad Berkey. Chad, author of a book on whiskey and owner of an innovative new barware company called Tin Play, has been finding new bottles for the place since he started slinging drinks here. He also creates new and interesting, seasonal cocktails that feature whiskey as the primary spirit. But, he and his coworkers can mix up just about anything you like. They can also suggest new whiskies for you to try if you're unsure which one you might want.

While once composed of blue collar workers and the occasional vagrants like us, the crowd is now made up of professionals from around the region. Doctors and lawyers, accountants and business people now fill the booths and seats at the bar, and spend their time laughing with friends over cocktails. It gets crowded—very crowded—starting at about 4 in the afternoon. As the business day comes to an end it's hard to find a seat in here, so go early if you can. This is a great place to start or end an evening, but they don't serve food so get a meal before you stop in.

THE DRINKS

Where to start? The most obvious place is the whiskey. This is the time to try something you haven't tried before. It can be intimidating trying to choose, but take your time and ask the bartenders questions—they'd be happy to answer them. If you don't know exactly what kind you want, let the bartender suggest something based on what you typically like.

Also, be sure to ask what their seasonal cocktails are. Chad creates these based on local and seasonal ingredients, so they're sure to taste fresh and flavorful.

NEARBY DISTRACTIONS

Ocean Beach Pier—Website: www.oceanbeachsandiego.com **Address:** Niagara Ave, San Diego, CA, 92107, (619) 226-3474. Located in the Ocean Beach neighborhood, this is the longest pier on the West Coast, extending over 1900 feet into the Pacific Ocean. First build in 1966 to help fishing enthusiasts, the pier is one of the most iconic features found in San Diego. Surrounding the pier is Ocean Beach, filled with shops and restaurants. This is a great place to spend a day in the sun and to sweat out some of the whiskey you'll be drinking at the Aero Club Bar.

Stone Brewing World Bistro & Gardens-Liberty Station—Website: www.stonebrewing.com **Address:** 2816 Historic Decatur Rd #116, San Diego, CA, 92106, (619) 269-2100 (Monday–Sunday 11:30am–9pm). Sure, the Aero Club Bar serves beer, but they're known for whiskey. So, if you want beer, why don't you go to the place that makes some of the best. Stone Brewing World features all of your favorites from Stone, as well as a number of their specialties and seasonals, plus beer from other surrounding breweries. The location was once a US Navy mess hall, but now features a beautiful outside restaurant space with gourmet dining, bocce ball and outside theatre.

Old Town San Diego State Historic Park—Website: www.oldtownsandiego.org **Address:** 4002 Wallace St, San Diego, CA, 92110, (619) 220-5422. Established in 1769, this is the location of the first settlement in California. Here you can see what the area was like in the early

1800s. You can also wander through historic shops or stroll through gardens and find some interesting history. There are even great restaurants to grab a bite at while exploring living historical exhibits, like a blacksmith or woodworker's shop, where experts reenact scenes from the early 19th century.

TIVOLI BAR, SAN DIEGO, CA

Address: 505 Sixth Ave, San Diego, CA, 92101, (619) 232-6754
Video Tour: https://youtu.be/xIabGgz9Fqs
Food: Yes **Live Music:** No **Hours:** Monday–Sunday 11am–2am **Type of Bar:** Saloon **What to Drink:** Margarita **Why You Should Go:** This place became a saloon in 1885 when this was San Diego's red light district. It's seen gambling, prostitution, and a whole cast of seedy characters come through in its history.

THE HISTORY

San Diego's Gaslamp Quarter was at one time the city's red light district. Built in 1867 in what is now downtown San Diego, the place was known as Stingaree from the 1880s to about 1916. Here was found brothels, saloons and gambling halls. These were typically filled at just about any hour of the day by thousands of sailors who would arrive on ships from all over the world. And to many of them, those who had been at sea for months at a time, this place was Valhalla.

Just about every building in this area housed some den of inequity—there were hundreds of them. Even the famous Wyatt Earp ran four saloon and gambling halls in this area. Many of the saloons had "hotels" above them that

233

were available by the hour. Brothels were found all over the place. And all of this is also true of Tivoli Bar.

The building that houses Tivoli Bar was built in either 1864 or 1872, depending who you talk to (the owner says 1865, so we'll take that). In either case, though, it's one of the earliest built structures in the Gaslamp quarter. In 1885 the place became a general store and bar in the front half of the building (the saloon portion). In the back of the building was a blacksmith shop.

At the turn of the century the saloon was bought by an Italian family who renamed the place Tivoli Bar after a small town outside of Rome, Italy. The place drew a crowd, serving the degenerates of the city until San Diego started cracking down on crime in 1916. Then, prohibition went into effect, and the place turned into a diner and café…at least that's what they told the cops. Downstairs in the basement it turned out they were making wine and whiskey, so the place was a speakeasy until 1933 when it reopened as a saloon.

Like other saloons, the place had nine rooms upstairs. These were used for ladies of the night even through World War 2. In fact, the owners found a button located under the stairway that, when pressed, would turn on lights in the rooms to alert the Johns when the place was being raided. Pretty useful if you ask us.

In 1970, Tivoli Bar was sold to the Romero family who still own it today, and who have spent an immense amount of time restoring the old saloon to bring it back to its former glory.

TODAY

The Gaslamp Quarter was pretty run down through the late half of the 20th century, and it continued to live up to the hard-won notoriety from the first half of the 20th century. It was still known for prostitutes and drug-addicts all the way through the 1980s. The area was full of warehouses and produce dealers, so not the most lucrative crowd for an old saloon. Then, in the 1990s, developers moved in and things started changing. By the time Petco Park was opened just a stone's throw away in 2004, Tivoli Bar was surrounded by condos and apartment buildings. Trendy restaurants, bars and shops can now be found throughout the area, which has become a destination for tourists and locals alike.

The Romero family spent much of the late 1990s restoring the Tivoli Bar, and today it's a favorite hangout of local business people and visitors touring the area. The bar and bar back on your left as you enter is all original from the 1800s, and it's easy to imagine thirsty cowboys and sailors hunched over it, swapping stories and sipping whiskey. Notice the bric-a-brac and décor hanging on the walls. One is of Wyatt Earp, who was rumored to be a patron of the bar back in the day. Also notice the period painting of the reclining nude woman above the middle of the bar—nudes were pretty common back then, but today not so much. The nudes were painted by a San Diego artist named Larry Vincent Garrison, who simply went by the name of Vincent. He had a studio close by and would frequent Tivoli Bar. Much of his work was made for the Las Vegas casinos that had a western-type theme, and his paintings are now quite valuable.

Also, be sure to peruse the many photos they have scattered throughout the place. These tell the story of the bar: where it came from and the type of people that went there. They help put the saloon into perspective and help visitors understand its place in the community and the city.

The crowd here is pretty diverse. When we visited, there were a few regulars and a handful of tourists. We're told that they get a lot of the people from surrounding businesses during the day for lunch and then after work for drinks. Later at night the crowd is young, ranging from military to college students. It also gets really crowded when there's a baseball game or other event at Petco Park. In fact, during a game it's pretty tough to find parking in the Gaslamp Quarter so be prepared for that (as well as the crowds in the bar itself).

They have a full-service bar and serve just about anything you can think of. With 15 taps they do sell a lot of regional beer, so you'll be able to find a craft brew you like as well. One thing to point out is that their prices are much more reasonable than any other bar in the area by a longshot. Plus, they also have specials during baseball games and other events (such as Mardi Gras or Saint Patrick's Day). All in all, this is a great piece of history that you'll be happy you went to.

THE FOOD

Tivoli Bar does serve food, but they don't make it themselves. Instead the lease the space towards the back of the building (where the blacksmith shop was). When we were there, the space was occupied by a barbecue restaurant and we were told it's really good. They serve the standard bar food—hamburgers, fries, and such—but they also serve barbecue. Nevertheless, regardless of what's being served when you visit, just know that you can get a meal to soak up all the booze you'll be putting down.

THE DRINKS

Beer and whiskey are the staples here, and they pride themselves on being the cheapest in the Gaslamp Quarter. We can vouch for that, as we went to a nearby place and paid about double for a beer. The beer selection at Tivoli Bar is also pretty good, with the standard domestics but also a good array of locally brewed craft beers. Their whiskey selection also has most of the familiar brands, so if you're looking for something on the rocks or a shot, you'll be satisfied here. However, when we asked the owners what people should order, they told us to suggest the margarita. So, have a margarita.

NEARBY DISTRACTIONS

Gaslamp Quarter—Website: www.gaslamp.org, You're already here so why not explore? Surrounding Tivoli Bar are hundreds of other historic buildings that make up downtown San Diego. You can go to the Balboa Theatre, built in 1924, and catch a live performance. Or, you can go to any of the numerous nightclubs that often feature live concerts or DJ's. Aside from these there are trendy shops, restaurants and classic hotels. Spend a day wandering the streets then slip into Tivoli Bar for your drinks.

Petco Park—Website: www.padres.com **Address:** 100 Park Blvd, San Diego, CA, 92101, (619) 795-5555 (seasonal baseball and live events). This is one of the main reasons people come downtown, to visit Petco Park. Built in 2004 this very modern and beautiful baseball stadium is home to the San Diego Padres, so it sees activity from spring through fall. It also hosts a number of concerts and events after baseball has ended. During a home game, downtown becomes pretty festive, and Tivoli Bar hosts a pre-game tailgate and post-game party.

Haunted Hotel—Website: www.hauntedhotel.com **Address:** 424 Market St, San Diego, CA, 92101, (619) 231-0131 (Seasonal September–November opens 6pm). This is one of the longest running haunted houses in the country, stretching back over 25 years. The themes change yearly, but every fall it's considered one of the most exciting, thrilling and scary attractions in the city. Be sure to get your tickets online in advance, otherwise there's a good chance it'll be sold out.

SAN DIEGO'S HISTORIC BARS

Tower Bar—Website: www.thetowerbar.com **Address:** 4757 University Ave, San Diego, CA, 92105, (Monday 5pm–2am, Tuesday–Sunday 4pm–2am). The place was originally opened in 1932 as an ice cream parlor but eventually turned to booze as we all do when we get older. It's known for a huge absinthe selection that they serve in the traditional manner with a water fountain. The drinks here are cheap and the customers eccentric, with lots of live music to listen to and people to watch.

Pacific Shores—Address: 4927 Newport Ave, San Diego, CA, 92107, (Monday–Friday 12pm–2am, Saturday–Sunday 10am–2am). Known (sadly so) as the bar that opened the day before Pearl Harbor, this place has been serving sailors and locals since 1941. It has an underwater theme that's now pretty kitschy, but that just makes it really cool in our book. They have a great jukebox with lots of variety and cheapo drinks.

Red Fox Steakhouse and Piano Bar—Website: www.redfoxsd.com **Address:** 2223 El Cajon Blvd, San Diego, CA, 92104, (Monday–Friday 11am–2am, Saturday 4pm–2am, Sunday 4pm–12am). This place has an awfully strange history. It started out in life as an inn in Surrey, England that dated back to the 16th century. Then, actress Marion Davies thought it would look better at her Malibu beach house and so in 1926 it was dismantled, sent to the US and reassembled there. Finally, the place sold in the 50s and again this part was dismantled and put into storage before it was finally bought and reassembled here as a lounge and steakhouse attached to the Lafayette Hotel. The place is known for great cocktails and an intimate, classy, throw-back vibe. Stop by before it's whisked off someplace else.

SAN FRANCISCO, CA

The history of San Francisco is one of wickedness and debauchery. It didn't start out that way of course. In fact, San Francisco was little more than a Spanish mission and fort until 1849. After gold was discovered, the population boomed and smart entrepreneurs from around the world rushed to the Bay Area to make their fortunes—whether it be from mining or something else.

Because of the sheer amount of wealth—in the form of gold—that travelled through San Francisco, anything could be had. In one account of a standard mercantile store was a list of 110 different alcoholic beverages for sale, including Scotch ale, English porter, port, champagne, burgundy, claret, rum, gin and whiskey. There was, in short, no shortage of booze.

And places to consume booze were even more bountiful. The Barbary Coast, a three-block-long area of the most depraved booze joints in the country, drew thousands of gamblers, sailors, prostitutes and bandits every week. Here any kind of drink, drug or vice could be had for little, and human lives were worth even less.

In 1906 much of the area was leveled in the great earthquake and then subsequent fire. Most every bar—heck most every structure—was destroyed. Some remained standing, but most were rebuilt. The outcome is that any historic saloon in this area is a survivor and has a great story waiting to be discovered.

ELIXIR SALOON, SAN FRANCISCO, CA

Address: 3200 16th Street, San Francisco, CA, 94103, (415) 552-1633
Website: www.elixirsf.com **Video tour:** http://youtu.be/ANwtfxrgsI8
Food: No **Live Music:** No **Hours:** Monday–Friday, 3pm–2am, Saturday–
Sunday 12pm–2am **Type of Bar:** Saloon **What to Drink:** The Bloody Elixir
Why You Should Go: An original from the days of the Barbary Coast where
human life was less important than the next drink.

THE HISTORY

Located on the corner of 16th and Guerrero and smack dab in the middle
of the area once known as the Barbary Coast, an area known for its bars and
prostitutes, sits the Elixir Saloon. Originally opened in 1858, it is one of the
oldest continually operating establishments on the West Coast and the second
oldest in San Francisco still open today. To give you an idea of what the city
was like when the saloon was open, simply consider that in 1851 San
Francisco had 537 places serving alcohol and only 8 churches. Or, for every
church there were 67 bars.

The first recorded owner was Hugh Mooney, who owned the bar from
1873 until 1893. In 1893, Mooney sold the bar to Patrick J. McGinnis
Esquire, a prominent city lawyer. McGinnis owned it through the infamous
earthquake of 1906—the cause of widespread fires that swept through the city
and claimed thousands of structures including the Elixir. McGinnis
immediately rebuilt his beloved bar in 1906/1907 (his original floor plan is
still displayed proudly by the front door) making it the only bar in San
Francisco to be rebuilt in the same location and by the same owner after the
1906 earthquake.

Also of note, during McGinnis' ownership was the period of Prohibition during which the Saloon was listed as a "Soft Drink Parlor." During this period there is no concrete evidence of it being turned into a speakeasy or of any illegal activity occurring at the site. But the current owner believes, and we agree, that a place like the Elixir didn't simply shut down or suspend all activity in regards to alcohol; few places ever truly did at the time. Instead McGinnis, as a well-informed lawyer, probably continued to operate the bar using his legal smarts to avoid any issues with the law.

As time progressed the bar changed owners, layouts, and even its name a few times. It was known as The Hunt-In Club from 1940-1965, which was the first known name change. From 1965-1985 it was Swede's, named after the owner and discussed in the book "The Great and Notorious Saloons of San Francisco." 1985-1990 saw the place transformed into a club known by two names, Club Corona and La Bandita, and was a popular gay and transvestite Latino bar. In 1990, it was Jack's Elixir Bar. And finally in 2003, "H"—the current owner—bought it, restored it and gave it the name it continues to be known by today.

Over the years the bar has changed, the clientele has changed and the neighborhood surrounding it has reinvented itself a time or two. But one thing that has never changed is the fact that the place has always been a bar (or a "Soft Drink Parlor"). Through the earthquakes, fires, worldwide tragedies and the push and pull of mainstream culture, the Elixir has remained a saloon. It is a true neighborhood bar that is ingrained into the neighborhood, gives back part of what is given and is a place where anyone and everyone is welcome.

TODAY

Today the bar is owned by H. Joseph Ehrmann ("H") who, wanting to preserve the bar and its history, jumped at the chance to begin restoring it immediately after signing the papers. He told us the bar itself was hidden behind peeling paint and bumper stickers, the floor was more of a trampoline than a floor, the bathrooms were something we probably didn't want to know about and the ceiling was barely staying up. To put it simply, it was neglected and run down. H spent the next several months working on the bar, calling in favors from his friends and acquaintances, stripping the place down to its core and then returning it to its past luster.

In addition to the physical and visual improvements, H made some improvements to the Elixir's cocktail list. In addition to the traditional cocktail menu, he added both seasonal and regional selections. From great local craft beers (some brewed specifically for the Elixir), cocktails that change with the season, and right down to H's specialty (The Bloody Elixir,) the place has a drink for everyone.

THE DRINKS

Often we list a drink that is a must-try, and we plan to do so here, but never have we listed one that has been more recognized than the Bloody Elixir—H's take on the Bloody Mary.

This drink made it to number four on GQ magazine's "20 Best Cocktails in America" for 2008, as well as local Audience Choice awards for 2005 and 2006, and the 2008 Editor's Choice Best of Citysearch, San Francisco: Best Bloody Mary. Needless to say, if you find yourself in the Elixir it is at the top of the list of must-tries.

Every Saturday and Sunday morning, the Elixir also offers a Make Your Own Bloody Mary bar. Adding a piece or two of bacon makes for a unique and great tasting twist to the traditional drink.

NEARBY DISTRACTIONS

Fisherman's Wharf—Website: www.fishermanswharf.org, Less than four miles from the Elixir is San Francisco's most popular tourist destination: Fisherman's Wharf. The Wharf features a long list of restaurants (some featuring breathtaking views of the bay and the Golden Gate Bridge), seafood stands (featuring outstanding clam chowder and Dungeness crab), hotels, street vendors, street performers, gift shops, an aquarium and even a few bars. Though it is almost always crowded with tourists, it's a must-visit location when in the area.

Trattoria Pinocchio—Website: www.trattoriapinocchio.com **Address:** 401 Columbus Avenue, San Francisco, CA, 94133, (415) 392-1472 (open for lunch and dinner 7 days a week). Trattoria Pinocchio is less than three miles from the Elixir and worth every mile walked or driven. Owned by Sicily native and renowned Chef Giovanni Zocca, it has the best Italian food we've ever tasted. Featuring homemade pastas, pizzas, seafood and steaks, it is a truly Italian dining experience and one not to be forgotten. So if you find yourself in the mood for Italian, look no further than Pinocchio's as you will not be disappointed.

HEINOLD'S FIRST AND LAST CHANCE, OAKLAND, CA

Address: 48 Webster Street in Jack London Square, Oakland CA, 94607, 510-839-6761
Website: www.firstandlastchance.com **Video tour:** http://youtu.be/mSxoE2bM1tE
Food: No **Live Music:** No **Hours:** Monday 3pm–11pm, Tuesday–Thursday, Friday–Saturday 12pm–1am, Sunday 11am–11pm **Type of Bar:** Saloon
What to Drink: Local craft beer or glass of local wine **Why You Should Go:** Connection to Jack London, last surviving example of Gold Rush-era saloon.

THE HISTORY

Originally built on a dock in Oakland's East Bay in 1880, Heinold's Saloon was constructed from the timbers of an old whaling ship and used as a bunkhouse for men working at the nearby oyster beds. Johnny Heinold bought the place in 1883 for $100 and, with the help of a ship's carpenter, transformed the place into a saloon specifically built for the seafaring men roaming the waterfront.

After operating successfully for over 30 years, the bar was renamed Heinold's First and Last Chance Saloon for two notable reasons. First, during the 1920s the city of Alameda was dry and Heinold's just happened to be right next to the dock for the ferry running between Oakland and Alameda. It was literally the commuters' first and last chance for a drink on their way to and from Alameda.

Second, the bar also served as the first and last chance for a drink for servicemen deploying and returning home from the Port of Oakland. To have a drink here is a fairly powerful tradition as is evidenced by the memorabilia strewn throughout the bar today.

Over the years, the saloon has played host to millions of patrons from all walks of life. It was a huge part of legendary writer Jack London's life beginning when he was only 10 years old.

The bar served as the source of ideas for many of his books as he listened to the tales of visitors from all over the world. It was in this saloon that Jack met Alexander McLean who was the inspiration for the powerful and morally questionable Captain Wolf Larsen in the novel, "The Sea Wolf". McLean was known to shanghai drunks in the saloon and force them into service on his ship nicknamed, "The Hell Ship" because of his rumored cruelty at sea (he was probably more in line with the fictitious captain of the Sea-Wolf than anyone ever imagined).

On Wednesday, April 18th, 1906 an estimated 7.9 magnitude earthquake struck Northern California's Bay Area causing wide-spread devastation. The resulting fire destroyed a large percentage of what wasn't destroyed by the earthquake and the total death toll in San Francisco is estimated to have been at least 3,000 people. Ironically, The First and Last Chance was one of the few structures in the entire Bay Area left standing, though it had some additional dimensions added.

The earthquake caused the pilings under the saloon to settle into the mud, some more than others, giving the saloon a noticeable slope from the front to the back of the bar.

Unsuccessful efforts were made to shore up and level the floor and as such, the slope continues even today. When you step in, you also step down and immediately notice that everything in the bar is sloped, even the bar itself. The sloping isn't quite enough to make your drinks slide down the bar, though you do tend to keep a firm grasp on them just in case. The bartenders are accustomed to putting just the right amount in your glasses to avoid accidental spillage. We did a little experimenting and found that after a few drinks, things tend to level out.

TODAY

This place is more akin to a museum than a bar, and most of the items inside should probably actually be in a museum. You can literally walk in, order a drink and sit down at the same table where Jack London used to study, write, and listen to tales from the ever-present adventurers and sailors.

The artifacts on the wall are all historic and protected by a simple layer of chicken wire. Take a close look at the clock on the wall, it doesn't move, and hasn't since the earthquake of 1906 (there was nothing wrong with it, Heinold simply never restarted it). From the stained ceiling, caused by the gas lamps (still in operation), to the antiques throughout, and right down to the very floor, this place really tells the history of San Francisco and Oakland.

A few modern touches have changed its exterior just a bit. For example, the place is no longer sitting on the dock (the city extended the landmass to encompass the bar and other surroundings), there is now a patio, and a 1/2 size replica of Jack London's cabin built from the very timbers of his original Alaskan cabin (there's also an identical cabin made from the remaining timbers located in Alaska as well). But, with the exception of the surrounding landmass, a modern bathroom and a few other updates to make the place safe, it is as close to original as you could possibly hope for.

Speaking of the bathroom. If you happen to find yourself at the First and Last Chance and are with a first timer or someone not as educated as you've become from reading this book, then you have the perfect victim for a great joke.

When someone from your party heads to the bathroom ask the bartender to say hello to them via the hidden speaker. Throw the bartender a couple of bucks, give them the individual's name, and watch as they really make the visit memorable.

THE DRINKS

There's a full-service bar at the First and Last Chance Saloon, so order up whatever you might like. Of particular interest are the local craft beers on tap and the local wines (we had a great conversation with their wine distributor and he assured us this was local stuff).

But it somehow seems more fitting to simply sip something on the rocks. That's what Alexander McLean probably would've had as he sat in the corner eyeing the drunks and trying to figure out which one to kidnap. A whiskey over ice is a drink worthy of drinking at Heinold's.

NEARBY DISTRACTIONS

Jack London Square—Website: www.jacklondonsquare.com **Address:** 466 Water St. Oakland, CA, 94607, (510) 645-9292 (open year round but business times vary). Heinold's First and Last Chance Saloon sits right in the middle of Oakland's renowned Jack London Square. Named after the very man whose life was forever changed by the storied First and Last Chance Saloon, Jack London Square is steeped in maritime lore. Lining the natural estuary leading to the San Francisco Bay, the square contains a long list of restaurants, shops, businesses, walking paths and, of course, marinas. Events like live music, fundraisers and farmers market are common so be sure to check the events schedule posted on their website before heading out.

USS Hornet Museum—Website: www.uss-hornet.org **Address:** 707 West Hornet Avenue Alameda, CA, 94501, (510) 521-8448 (Monday–Sunday 1pm–5pm). Keeping in the maritime tradition and in the spirit of Heinold's First and Last Chance Saloon, a visit to the USS Hornet is a fitting destination. Less than four miles from Heinold's, the USS Hornet is a decorated World War 2-era aircraft carrier that participated in the Doolittle Raid, saw action in Vietnam and participated in some of the first moon missions.

SAN FRANCISCO'S HISTORIC BARS

The Saloon—Address: 1232 Grant Avenue San Francisco, CA, 94133, (415) 989-7666 (Monday–Friday 12pm–2am). This North Beach watering hole was founded in 1861, so it's a true remnant of the city's wilder days. The structure survived the 1906 earthquake and fire (it's said the fire brigades kept the fire away to protect the hookers upstairs) so when you drink here you're drinking in the real deal. It is maybe one of the scariest places you'll ever set foot into. The bouncers look like rejects from a biker gang and the décor is full of dive bar clichés, but it really is a great place. They have live music and some of the best blues bands in the Bay play here.

Little Shamrock—Address: 807 Lincoln Way San Francisco CA, 94122, (415) 661-0060 (Monday–Thursday 3pm–2am, Friday 2pm–2am, Saturday–Sunday 1pm–2am). Opened sometime in the early 1890s (the claim is 1893 but there are several problems with that claim), the Little Shamrock rocks its status as second oldest bar in San Francisco differently than the oldest (the Saloon). Chiefly, it doesn't stink as badly. After a century, it can't help but have a bit of a stench, but the bathrooms are clean and the service is friendly. It's become a favorite locals' bar and has earned a good reputation over the years.

The Buena Vista—Address: 2765 Hyde St. San Francisco, CA, 94109, (415) 474-5044 (Monday–Friday 9am–2am, Saturday–Sunday 8am–2am). If you find yourself in need of a warming cup of coffee while visiting the area, why not make it Irish and head on over to the Buena Vista? Featuring a legendary cup of Irish Coffee developed back in 1952 when owner Jack Koeppler challenged Stanton Delaplane, to help re-create the legendary Irish Coffee served at Shannon Airport in Ireland. After much research (that is, repetitive mixing and drinking) and a trip back to Ireland, they were able to create the delicious recipe still served today. Located next to the Powell-Hyde Cable Car's last stop and close to Fisherman's Wharf, it is a favorite among tourists and locals alike.

SEATTLE, WA

The Pacific Northwest was a wild place back in the day. And by "back in the day" we mean only about 70 years ago. Seattle was the stomping grounds for two different, very rough and tumble populations. First, there were the gold miners who set sail from Seattle to Alaska. Eventually, these men would come back either dead broke, or flush with gold. If broke they'd go on their way, but if they'd gotten lucky and had a bag full of gold, they were happy to spend it in the saloons and brothels that the city was positively crowded with

The other group was just as fun. Loggers or lumberjacks who spent their days in the forests surrounding Seattle converged on the city each payday. Like the gold miners, these were a thirsty, rowdy crowd, that was happy to spend every last cent they had on skid row. In fact, even that term, "skid row," was coined here. Back in the late 19th century and early 20th century, all the timber that was cut down had to be transported, and the easiest way to do that was by simply rolling (or skidding) them down a hill. In Seattle, at the bottom of Yesler Way, was Henry Yesler's sawmill. So, to make life easier for themselves, lumberjacks skidded the logs down the road to the mill. Eventually it came to mean an area that was run down or derelict, which is a bit ironic considering the property values along Yesler Way nowadays.

The crowds now are a lot less exciting than they used to be, however, the bars are much better. This place is flush with great dives and saloons to visit, so we're just scratching the surface here. At the same time, it's important to remember that each of these bars might be gone tomorrow. One of the places we visited when we came here happened to be the oldest gay bar in the country (opened in 1933). It was a great dive with great stories and friendly people. Sadly, it quietly closed only four months after our visit, and now all those stories are gone. Hopefully that doesn't happen to any of the joints in this chapter, but just to be sure, get here as quick as you can and visit as many as your liver will take!

CENTRAL SALOON, SEATTLE, WA

Address: 207 1st Ave S, Seattle, WA, 98104, (206) 622-0209
Website: https://www.centralsaloon.com **Video Tour:** https://youtu.be/-1b52eXV2NI
Food: Yes **Live Music:** Yes **Hours:** Monday–Sunday, 11am–2am **Type of Bar:** Dive **What to Drink:** Whiskey on the rocks **Why You Should Go:** One of two oldest bars in Seattle, a staple of the historic Pioneer Square, and the birthplace of Seattle's music scene.

THE HISTORY

In 1892, following the Great Seattle Fire of 1889, Thomas Watson built and opened this three-story brick building, naming it the Watson Bros Famous Restaurant. From that moment until today, the place has been serving the citizens and visitors of Seattle food and drinks, though under many different names and owners. In 1919, the saloon was renamed the Central Café, and has kept some form of that name ever since.

Pioneer Square, the oldest section of the city, saw the area's most fun-loving crowds. Loggers, railroader, sailor and miners all wandered through this part of the city back in the early 20th century, and they found just about every kind of delight you can imagine in this small section of Seattle. At some point in its life, the Central has been a saloon, restaurant, post office, card room, and a brothel. It has, therefore, a great legacy backing it up.

And this notoriety didn't change with the closing of the sawmill, which subsequently led to a decrease in the number of loggers. Nor did the disappearance of the miners as the gold boom of Alaska finally ebb detour the legacy of the Central. In fact, activity actually increased during World War 2 when it was servicemen that prowled the bars and "hotels" of downtown Seattle. Eventually, though, the downtown district—Pioneer Square more specifically—became pretty run down, and so was the haven for bums and winos, but also artists and musicians. The area has since been preserved and the buildings saved, and has even been declared a historic district, further helping in restoration efforts.

Music was another prominent attraction at the Central Saloon, and apparently musicians loved playing here. Perhaps the most famous performer at the saloon, up until the 1990s, was none other than Seattle native, Jimi Hendrix, who played here in the late 1950s. But then the late 80s approached, and Seattle music was going in a different direction from the rest of the country. Nirvana, Alice in Chains, and Soundgarden all played their very first shows at the Central, and it was the epicenter of the Seattle grunge music scene in the 1990s.

TODAY

Music is still a big part of the Central Saloon, and the saloon itself is still a big part of Seattle's night scene—an amazing feat considering the many newer and flashier bars opened (and closed) over the last 20 years. They feature a live event every night, and while these are typically bands and shows, they might feature other events as well (check their website for shows, times and prices).

They're also really well known for their food. This seems to be another bit of legacy (aside from the music), because the saloon was noted for its great food in the late 1800s as well. Though, to be honest, how much competition could there have been? In any case, today they feature a number of different burgers, sandwiches, wraps and salads. If you want starters and pub grub they have that too, so you're sure to find something to fill you up.

And speaking of filling up, they've got over a dozen beers on tap with some good variety, so you'll be able to get some locally made craft brews as well as national brands. They also have a full bottle selection and full bar, so you'll be able to get most any mixed drink you might need. As with most other bars in this book, this isn't a craft cocktail lounge, so don't expect something too unreasonable.

When you come in you'll notice the many pics of famous rockers that have passed through the doors. What's striking is the shrine to those who have died over the years—it's a long list.

The beautiful oak bar takes up the entire left of the room, with a few scattered tables and chairs towards the back and to the right of the bar. Be sure to take a moment to linger at the raised stage at the back. This is where rock and roll history was made almost three decades ago. If you were a product of the 90s, this is a pretty special place.

Try to make it when there's a live show. Alternatively, since this is the closest bar to the stadiums, try it out on a game night. The place will be packed but will also be a party that goes well into the morning hours. But, whenever you get here, you'll be happy you did.

THE FOOD

We've heard great things about the pulled barbecue pork sandwich, which is made in-house and served with their own slaw. They also have home-made tater tots, which we didn't know existed until we came here. If you're looking for a couple of quick picks we definitely recommend these.

THE DRINKS

Beer and alcohol flow pretty freely here—though they also have locally-made wines. What's great about the bar is that the prices of the drinks are still very low despite their ability to get a premium for them. In fact, they were about the cheapest we found in the area, which is saying something for a place with this kind of history. The drinks were also really strong, with honest pours in everything we tried. Our advice would be to order a straight whiskey (your call). As far as we're concerned, this simple drink is historically what they served when the doors opened in 1892, so why change?

NEARBY DISTRACTIONS

Seattle Great Wheel—Website: www.seattlegreatwheel.com **Address:** 1301 Alaskan Way, Seattle, WA, 98101, (206) 623-8607 (Monday–Thursday 11am–10pm, Friday 11am–12am, Saturday 10am–12am, Sunday 10am–10pm). Opened in 2012 and standing at 175 feet, the Seattle Great Wheel gives you amazing views of the city and the coast. It has 42, climate-controlled gondolas that each seat 8 people (with a limited number of pricier, VIP gondolas with more extras and fewer seats).

Gum Wall—1428 Post Alley, Seattle, WA, 98101. In Post Alley under the Pike Place Market, and adjacent to the box office of the Market Theatre, is the second germiest attraction found on earth (second only to the Blarney Stone). Back in 1993 patrons of the theatre began sticking gum to the wall. Workers scraped it off at first, but then gave up when more gum showed up. By 1999, the wall, actually both walls, were completely covered in gum and people came from all over to stick their gum on the wall. It's pretty disgusting to be honest, but maybe that's what makes it worth seeing.

Seattle Pinball Museum—Website: www.seattlepinballmuseum.com **Address:** 508 Maynard Ave S, Seattle, WA, 98104, (206) 623-0759 (Sunday–Monday, Wednesday–Thursday 12pm–6pm, Friday–Saturday 12pm–8pm). Opened in 2010, the Seattle Pinball Museum bills itself as an interactive display of kinetic art. They feature a collection of over 50 vintage and new machines, all of them restored to their perfect, new conditions. Some of their games date back as far as 1934, while others have only recently been manufactured. This is a great way to have some fun, preserve some art, and explore a bit of the past.

MERCHANTS CAFÉ, SEATTLE, WA

Address: 109 Yesler Way, Seattle, WA, 98104, (206) 467-5070
Website: www.merchantscafeandsaloon.com **Video tour:**
https://youtu.be/cp0jEgEEhyQ
Food: Yes **Live Music:** No **Hours:** Sunday–Thursday 11am–11pm, Friday–
Saturday 11am–2am **Type of Bar:** Dive **What to Drink:** Whiskey on the
rocks **Why You Should Go:** Amazing history and story here, with a brothel
above the saloon (not there anymore, calm down), and a speakeasy
downstairs.

THE HISTORY

The property at 109 Yesler Way, in the Pioneer Square section of Seattle,
has legitimately been slinging drinks longer than any other saloon in this
town. Originally, there was a two-story wooden building sitting here built by
John Hall Sanderson, an early Seattle businessman and land developer. The
building had businesses on the ground floor, and a photographer's studio
upstairs. Then, the Great Seattle Fire of 1889 swept through downtown, and,
like most of the other wooden buildings surrounding it at the time, it was
completely destroyed.

Sanderson wanted to make sure that didn't happen again, so he
commissioned the building be rebuilt out of terra cotta brick and had a new,
three story building built here in 1890. When he had it built, he designed it
specifically to hold a liquor store and café on the bottom and a hotel on the
top two floors. This started a legacy of dispensing alcohol from this address,
and it hasn't stopped since.

The building was sold in 1892 and the name of the bar was changed to Merchant's Exchange Saloon. It was during this time that the upstairs apartments began to accept hourly rentals (if you know what we mean). Osner, the new owner, recognized how lucrative prostitution was in a town full of burly—and lonely—lumberjacks and gold miners, and so imported women (discreetly called, "seamstresses") into Seattle and housed them upstairs.

At the back of the saloon were a number of framed paintings of women. It's reported that this was, in essence, the menu for the happenings upstairs. The gentleman (to use the term very loosely) pointed to the one he wanted to have hem his trousers (so to speak), and then paid the proprietor before making his way up to have his inseam taken in.

The building was sold again in 1898 to a gold-rich businessman named Franz Xavier Schreiner. Schreiner, or "FX" as he was known, set up a bank downstairs and exchanged cash for gold dust. He would reportedly cash out as much as $100,000 worth of gold over a weekend. As it did to all things fun, prohibition tried to put the kibosh on the good times in 1916 (early dry laws in Seattle), but instead of giving up the bar, FX simply paid off the police and moved the alcohol sales (as well as a gambling room) downstairs.

Seattle stayed pretty rowdy all the way up through World War 2, and though we have no records to prove it, there's no reason to think that the prostitution stopped in 1933, despite the fact that the saloon went legit with alcohol sales. There's a good chance this place has only been on the straight and narrow for the past 50 or so years.

TODAY

We think FX would be happy with his saloon. Okay, there isn't still a brothel upstairs (we asked), however it is a boutique hotel, so the rooms ARE for rent (Netflix and Chill?). There's no longer the need for the speakeasy downstairs, and they've done away with the card room, but they do still have a bar down there which is a great place to lounge and drink.

Inside the main bar upstairs you find the intricately-carved bar that was shipped around the Cape Horn in the late 1800s. You find the wooden floors, the pressed tin ceilings, and a décor reminiscent of 1898—no beer signs or anything tacky (though they do have a few televisions for local sports).

You also find a great bar program. The manager, Luke, told us that either the Old Fashioned or the Margarita would be a great drink to order. Yes, they are worlds apart, but so are people's tastes. Each, though, is made traditionally with fresh ingredients. We tried the Old Fashioned and were really happy with it. Especially the fourth one, which went down even better than the first.

At the back of the bar you still find the picture gallery that the burly lumberjacks and miners pointed to with trembling fingers as they chose their companion for the evening. And one of those paintings, the "Oriental Girl" is said to be haunted. Also, they've had many reports of haunting upstairs in the women's bathroom and downstairs in the underground bar. It's in the underground bar, in fact, where two small children died in a fire in 1938. They apparently still roam the place and like to play tricks on guests.

Merchant's Café is in the middle of the excitement in downtown Seattle, so there's a good chance you'll be in the area anyway. It's only around the corner from the Central Saloon, so it'll be easy to hit both spots in a short time. We definitely recommend seeing this place before you leave the city. If you visit, take the time to explore the place, look at the paintings, and try to imagine this place filled with loggers, miners and sailors.

THE FOOD

Merchant's Café has a full kitchen with tasty, local pub grub as well as more upscale features. We had the fried cheese curds (of course), made with locally sourced Beecher's Handmade Cheese, and would definitely recommend this as a starter. We also tried their burgers, which were also delicious. If you don't feel like eating with your hands you can sit down to meatloaf, salmon or a selection of salads or soups.

THE DRINKS

They have a full bar program here and made a pretty wide variety of cocktails. There is a little more freedom to order more obscure cocktails if you like, but the manager himself told us to try the Old Fashioned (we did) and the Margarita (we'll take his word). They also have a wide selection of locally brewed craft beers as well.

NEARBY DISTRACTIONS

Bill Speidel's Underground Tour—Website: www.undergroundtour.com **Address:** 614 1st Ave, Seattle, WA, 98104, (206) 682-4646 (Sunday–Wednesday 8:30am–7pm, Thursday–Saturday 8:30am–9pm). If you haven't heard of the Seattle Underground, you should look it up. After the fire of 1889, the city rebuilt on top of itself, entombing storefronts and tunnels underneath the streets and shops you see now. These tunnels were often used to smuggle humans or other goods from one house of ill-repute to another. This tour takes visitors through those passages and teaches the dark history of this city and what it's hiding underneath your feet. Make reservations in advance through their website.

Chinatown-International District—Address: Fifth Ave. S. and S. King St. (Chinatown Gate). Designated as Seattle's Chinatown in the 1800s and then put on the National Register for Historic Places in 1986, the Chinatown-International District spans 23 acres just to the east of Pioneer Square. Not a touristy place, necessarily, this is a space for a mishmash of all Asian cultures that dwell in Seattle. Here you find grocery stores selling a variety of Asian products, with everything from Korean to Japanese, as well as more specialty stores, where shoppers can find herbs and traditional medicines. Of course, there is also a wealth of great restaurants with authentic cuisine. Expect to gain a few pounds here.

Klondike Gold Rush-Seattle Unit—Website: www.nps.gov/klse **Address:** 319 2nd Ave S, Seattle, WA, 98104, (206) 220-4240 (Monday–Sunday 10am–5pm). We're not big on museums (in fact, this whole book was written to get you out of the museums and into the bars of American cities instead), but every now and then we have to make an exception. The story of the bars of Seattle, especially the few surviving pre-prohibition bars, is intertwined with the gold rush that happened in Alaska. That event gave Seattle much of its identity and it brought many a traveler through this city, and some of them ended up staying. Going to this museum gives you a better perspective about the people that used to frequent places like Merchant's Café or the Central Saloon.

SEATTLE'S HISTORIC BARS

Jules Maes Saloon—Address: 5919 Airport Way S., Seattle, WA, 98108, (206) 957-7766 (Monday–Sunday 11am–11pm). When you read their literature, they'll date themselves to 1888, however, extensive research has shown that the building wasn't built until 1889, and that the first bar in here was 1907. Jules Maes himself only worked in here for a year before he died (though he was a bar owner with different bars throughout the area before and after prohibition). That doesn't really matter though, as this is a pre-prohibition era bar with a beautiful interior that will transport you to 1910 and firmly keep you there until you stagger out. Be sure to peruse the walls and look at all the mementos that have been collected and then hung up over the years. The food is heavy, diner-type grub, that will fill you up and help soak up the booze you're sure to be pouring down your throat. Like most dives, the drinks are cheap and strong, and you'll find a good selection of local and regional beer and booze.

The J&M Café—Website: www.jandmcafe.cafe **Address:** 201 1st Ave S, Seattle, WA, 98104, (206) 402-6654 (Monday-Sunday, 11am–2am). The J&M Café started life where the Central Saloon now stands. Business partners Jamieson and McFarland opened up the J&M Café at that location in 1892, and then moved to the current location some years later. In terms of Pioneer Square saloons, this place is legit, and was serving in the area when it was nothing more than loggers, miners, sailors and other riff-raff. There's no word on whether the hotel above the saloon was used as a brothel, but it wouldn't surprise us. When you go, be sure to check out the beautiful mahogany bar and bar back, constructed and shipped around the cape in the 1890s (as most of the old bars in this city were). They serve a selection of delicious, and different appetizers, like fried oysters and Baba Ghanoush. They also serve other pub grub, like burgers and sandwiches, but also pizza, which is always a great find. They have a wide variety of drinks, from a decent beer selection to a full bar, and have TVs to watch sports. One of Seattle's haunted tours starts at the J&M due to a suspected ghost in the basement, ask one of the bartenders about this when you go by.

Blue Moon Tavern—Website: www.bluemoonseattle.wordpress.com, **Address:** 712 NE 45h St. Seattle, WA, 98105, (206) 675-9116 (Monday–Friday 2pm–2am, Saturday 12pm–2am, Sunday 1pm–2am). This historic dive, popular with the university crowd, was opened in 1934. Known for great happy hour specials and an extensive list of locally made beers, you'll find a crowd of students at any given time of the day. At one time, the bar was popular with the counterculture literary crowd, including novelists and poets. It was also a place that harbored the more progressive professors of the University of Washington as they were being hunted by anti-communists in the 1950s. In the 1980s and 90s the place was under serious pressure to either close down or get completely remodeled. Luckily, in all instances, the community has banded together to stop these efforts and save what many say is the last, blue-collar hangout in the area. In truth, places like this are getting harder and harder to find, and we definitely recommend having a beer or three here when you travel to Seattle.

The 5 Point Café—Website: www.the5pointcafe.com **Address:** 415 Cedar St., Seattle, WA, 98121, (206) 448-9991 (Monday–Sunday 24 hours). Opened in 1929 by C. Preston Smith and his wife, Francis, the 5 Point Café started life as a typical greasy-spoon, serving the downtown business population before, during and after their work hours. After prohibition in 1933, the 5 Point got its liquor license and converted half of the building into a bar, separating it from the diner by a wall. Now as you walk in you see a half dive-bar and half diner, both of which have been helping the Seattle community either get drunk or sober for over 80 years—not a bad run. Parked under the landmark Seattle Space Needle, the 5 Point is a dedicated part of the community and spends an enormous amount of time helping out its neighbors. For example, during the spring and summer they sometimes hire bikini-clad girls on roller skates to "plug" expired parking meters for cars along the surrounding streets, and if that isn't community minded, we don't know what is.

Mecca Café—Website: www.mecca-cafe.com **Address:** 526 Queen Ann Ave. N., Seattle, WA, 98109, (206) 285-9728 (Monday–Friday, 7am–2am, Saturday–Sunday, 7am–3am). Opened in 1929, this is the sibling to the 5 Point Café, and will look quite familiar to you if you've already stopped by the 5 Point. It, too, is split up into a diner on one side (the right as you enter) and a cramped dive bar on the other (the left). The café serves breakfast all day, so think something greasy and sweet after a night of boozing. The bar itself is cramped and stuffed with knick-knacks and bric-a-brac from its decades of serving drunks like us. The drinks are oh, so cheap, and the pours are big and strong. The crowd ranges—during the day you're surrounded by regulars, and at night by revelers trying to sober up. It gets crowded when the third shift gets off, early in the morning, and also late at night when people are meeting up for a pre-party. You'll notice the neighborhood is a selection of new condos, pharmacies and chain restaurants. This tells us the Meccas is probably under pressure to sell and move, so get here while you can.

Tucson, Arizona and its surrounding area are chock full of some of the best and wildest history in the United States. It was in this desert that Wyatt Earp tracked down the rival "Cowboys" gang and took revenge for his brother's murder. It was also in this desert that people lost their lives for little more than an insult.

Tucson, and nearby Tombstone, were dynamic places and are pretty emblematic of what many think of when they think of the Old West. And for good reason…much of what people think is probably true.

Tucson grew up though, even while Tombstone threatened to fade away. Luckily, they both kept the history and the uniqueness that makes them so special.

Tucson features a great entertainment scene with an abundance of distractions to keep you busy. Aside from the Bucket List Bars™ in this book, 4th Avenue, next to the University of Arizona, is teeming with nightlife. Weekend nights there can be crowded and a lot of fun.

Just down the road from Tucson is Tombstone, a town that epitomized the wild west of lore. People lost their lives on a daily basis in this small town for as little as a sideways glance. At the same time, every sin and vice to be had in the late 1800s could be had on her streets and in her saloons.

Unlike Tucson, Tombstone didn't grow. Instead it almost passed into obscurity. Had it not been for the tourist industry the town "too tough to die" would have, in fact, died. But luckily much of what was there in the late 1800s is still there today. This goes for both the bars and the spirit. If you can muscle past the tourist-trap feel of this place, there's a great bunch of locals to get to know.

THE BUFFET BAR & CROCKPOT, TUCSON, AZ

Address: 538 E. 9th St., Tucson, AZ, 85705, (520) 623-6811
Website: www.thebuffetbar.com **Video tour:**
http://youtu.be/mDJwxsGkVpE
Food: Yes **Live Music:** No **Hours:** Monday 10am–2am, Tuesday–Sunday
6am–2am **Type of Bar:** Dive **What to Drink:** Maker's Mark or Stoli on ice,
Coors Banquet Beer **Why You Should Go:** Oldest post-Prohibition dive in
Tucson, friendly hospitality, drink specials.

THE HISTORY

Located in the Ironhorse District of Old Town, Tucson, the Buffet Bar and
Crock Pot is Tucson's oldest watering hole. The building was built in 1929
and it actually began serving alcohol in 1934 under the name The Lantern
Bar.

The area is known as the Ironhorse District because it's geographically
within one mile of the original Tucson train depot. During the early 20th
century, railroad workers had to live within a mile of the train depot in order
to hear the whistles of arriving trains (and trains in that period were, of
course, known as *iron-horses*), hence the name Ironhorse District. It's
composed mainly of single-room bungalows that originally housed the rail
road workers and their families.

The Buffet has been continually serving the Tucson community for over 77
years and is not only the premier dive bar of Tucson, but arguably one of the
premier dive bars of the whole United States.

TODAY

Today the Buffet is one of the most welcoming bars we've been to and has taken the term dive bar to new (ahem) heights. It was recently featured in Esquire Magazine's "Best Bars in America" section, which said the hot dogs "should never be consumed sober." Not only did we try them, and survive, we really liked them.

Likewise, the Tucson Weekly asked, "…where else but the Buffet can you order a beer and study the weird mix of college kids, drunks, and the potentially mentally ill? Ah, paradise!" To many the Buffet is just that…paradise.

The décor could be considered eccentric—if graffiti was décor. You'll notice the darkness (standard for a good dive) and the walls covered in magic marker and paint. It's a combination of names, philosophical references, quotes and pictures—and it all kind of runs together in some kind of perfect, Berlin Wall-esque pattern. We were told it's painted over about once a year to be filled up again.

You'll also notice the great decoupage of artifacts from the years scattered about. Most are pretty meaningful so feel free to ask. They also have cheap pool and even cheaper shuffleboard.

The Buffet opens at 6 am daily (except on Mondays when they sleep in until 10 am) and doesn't close until 2 am. While it seems a bit superfluous to open at 6 am, the bar actually caters to those working night shifts, who are just getting off work when the place opens. We're told in the mornings the bar is crowded with delivery people, healthcare workers from the local hospitals and others who work the graveyard shift.

The Buffet has regularly low prices, so they don't offer a happy hour. They do, however, offer a happy minute (two to be exact, one at 6pm and one at 11pm). During the 6pm happy minute you get a two-for-one drink deal, you call it. The 11pm happy minute gets you a fresh drink of whatever you have in front of you for one dollar more. Regardless of what it is you're drinking, it's only a buck.

THE FOOD

They're also known for their bar food, specifically hot dogs, quarter pound polish sausages and pickled eggs. The hot dogs and polish sausages are steamed in beer and served with a huge tray of fixings. The pickled eggs (died red in beet juice) are made with the original owner's recipe. Esquire says you shouldn't eat this stuff sober. We can't say we agree, but if you drink here like you should, then you probably won't be sober when you do try them anyway.

THE DRINKS

They're primarily known for three drinks. First, they have sold more Coors Banquet Beer on tap than any other bar in Arizona. So much of it, in fact, they were presented a plaque in 1996 from Coors thanking them for selling over 500,000 gallons. Today a 16 ounce glass of draft Coors will run you $2 (yes, you read that right).

Their second and third signature drinks are shots of Makers Mark (they sell more than any other bar in Arizona) and Stoli vodka. For $3.50 you get a 1 ½ ounce shot over ice. It's that easy.

NEARBY DISTRACTIONS

Frog & Firkin—Website: www.frogandfirkin.com **Address:** 874 East University Blvd., Tucson, AZ, 85719, (520) 623-7507 (Sunday–Thursday 11am–1am, Friday–Saturday 11am–2am). Not in the mood for pickled eggs or brats? Then head on over to Frog & Firken, which is less than a mile away from The Buffet. Featuring some of the best Chicago deep dish style pizzas in Tucson and some outstanding domestic, micro and imported draughts and bottles. It's sure to help you soak up some Stoli and Maker's Mark. Check their website for upcoming events and nifty coupons.

Kino Veteran Memorial Stadium/MLB Spring Training—Website: www.kinosportscomplex.com **Address:** 2500 E. Ajo Way, Tucson, AZ, 85713, (520) 434-1343 (Game/Event time vary). Tucson plays host to a multitude of Major League Baseball teams for their yearly spring training. Most games occur at the Kino Veteran Memorial Stadium, less than 5 miles from The Buffet and offers attendees a chance to watch some of their favorite teams and players get ready for the upcoming season. Not spring training during your trip? That's ok, the stadium also plays host to the Tucson Padres minor league team.

KON TIKI, TUCSON, AZ

Address: 4625 E. Broadway Blvd., Tucson, AZ, 85711, (520) 323-7193
Website: www.kontikitucson.com **Video tour:** http://youtu.be/OprpvwfS-n8

Food: Yes **Live Music:** Yes **Hours:** Monday–Thursday 11am–1am, Friday–Saturday 11am-2am, Sunday 11am–1am **Type of Bar:** Tiki bar **What to Drink:** Scorpion Bowl **Why You Should Go:** Classic 1960s Tiki bar in the middle of the desert, great classic drinks, original hand-carved Tikis.

THE HISTORY

Kon Tiki was started at the height of the Tiki bar phenomenon in 1963 by a couple of Tucson's leading restaurateurs: Dean Short and Tom Chandler.

Many of the Tiki bars around the country at that time were part of a chain called Kon Tiki and therefore very similar in appearance, food and drinks. But the owners of *this* Kon Tiki wanted something unique and so they brought in designers from all over the country to make their place stand out from the rest. Everything inside the bar, from the fountains to the Tikis, is custom and one-of-a-kind made specifically for Kon Tiki.

As a matter of fact, the Tikis themselves were made by renowned Tiki carver Milan Guanko who hand-carved each, making them unique in both their style and representation. Kon Tiki has over 20 of the Guanko Tikis, more than any other location in the entire United States.

As Tiki bars declined in popularity in the 70s and 80s so did Kon Tiki. The bar changed ownership multiple times throughout the years and fell into disrepair and neglect and was finally forced to close its doors in 1993. Then current owner Paul Christopher—originally a dishwasher at Kon Tiki at 14 years old—bought the bar, cleaned it up and reopened it in 1994.

TODAY

With the reopening of the bar by Christopher in 1994, Kon Tiki became a fixture in Tucson and in the worldwide Tiki Bar community. Upon arriving, you will be greeted by Kon Tiki's mantra, "Welcome to Paradise," right above the front door. And as you step into the bar be prepared to be transported to a new world. Though it may be a blazing 105 degrees and bright outside, the first two things you will notice when stepping in is that it is cool (thankfully) and that it's dark. Not dark in the sense that you can't see anything, dark in the sense that you have no idea what time of day it is, what season it is or if the apocalypse is going on outside. The glow of the lights, the sound of the fountains, the Tikis and the Polynesian décor all combine to disconnect you from the real world when you step in.

This feeling of being swept away to somewhere new and different is the perfect example of how a Tiki bar is supposed to make you feel—like a Vegas casino: that's what they're designed for. And to be honest, Kon Tiki is one of the best at it.

People travel from all over the world to visit Kon Tiki and they regularly get visitors from Australia, England, China, Japan, Brazil, Argentina and Canada to name a few.

THE FOOD

Kon Tiki has a full-service kitchen with Polynesian-fusion cuisine. Much of it is in the form of tapas or finger foods, like their Monkey on a Stick: skewers of marinated beef (the marinade, called volcano sauce, is like the Scorpion Bowl mix in that it is a closely guarded secret), and is served on a bed of rice. They have two kinds: spicy and regular (go with the spicy).

THE DRINKS

Without a doubt you must try Kon Tiki's signature, Scorpion Bowl. Like most Tiki bars, they keep their recipe secret so we don't know exactly what's in the mix, but we can tell you there's no hint of alcohol at all. Because of the large amount of alcohol contained in just one Scorpion Bowl, it can't be served to just a single person (you need a partner in crime to enjoy the whole thing….perfect for a date). Don't despair if you are flying solo though, you can still try the Mini Scorpion, a single serving of the Scorpion Bowl with the same great taste, just a smaller quantity of alcohol.

Related to the drinks are the mugs that Kon Tiki occasionally has made for them by renowned Tiki artists, Tiki Farm. Each series is limited and one of a kind, no two series are the same, and each is based on one of the Tikis actually at the bar.

NEARBY DISTRACTIONS

Pima Air & Space Museum—Website: www.pimaair.org **Address:** 6000 East Valencia Rd. Tucson, AZ, 85756, (520) 574-0462 (520) 574-9238 (Daily 9am–5pm closed Thanksgiving and Christmas). Though it is a bit of a drive (10 miles from Kon Tiki) the Pima Air and Space Museum is worth the trip. Featuring over 300 different aircraft from the US and all over the globe. It is one of the largest Air and Space museums in the world (and the largest not funded by the government). Taking up over 80 acres, it is easy to spend an afternoon marveling at some of mankind's greatest aircraft.

Trail Dust Town—Website: www.traildusttown.com **Address:** 6541 East Tanque Verde Road #22 Tucson, AZ, 85715, (520) 296-4551 (times vary by attraction, call or visit their website). Less than 5 miles from Kon Tiki sits Trail Dust Town. This Old West themed attraction features the Pinnacle Peak Steakhouse, one of the most popular steakhouses in Tucson, a Wild West themed stunt show, rides, shooting gallery, shops and the Museum of the Horse Soldier. Most attractions are open until 8 pm or later so you may want to plan your visit after the hottest hours of the day during the summer.

THE TAP ROOM, TUCSON, AZ

Address: 311 E. Congress St., Tucson, AZ, 85701, (520) 622-8848
Website: www.hotelcongress.com/club/the-tap-room **Video tour:**
http://youtu.be/AwzK8j93fAM
Food: Yes **Live Music:** Yes **Hours:** Monday–Sunday, 11am–2am **Type of
Bar:** Pub **What to Drink:** Martini or Bloody Mary **Why You Should Go:**
John Dillinger captured here, the jukebox, original Pete Martinez artwork.

THE HISTORY

The Tap Room bar is located in probably one of the most notorious hotels
in Tucson's history, the Hotel Congress. The hotel was opened in 1919 and
sits directly across from the Tucson railroad station where thousands of
travelers passed through on their journey to the Southwest from all over the
world. Two of the most notorious area visitors were John Dillinger and Wyatt
Earp.

Wyatt shot and killed Frank C. Stilwell in the Tucson rail yard during a
shootout that is believed to have been committed in revenge for the killing of
Wyatt's younger brother Morgan. The shootout occurred before the hotel and
bar had initially opened but it was the start of a series of events that put not
only the towns of Tucson and Tombstone on the map, but also the Hotel
Congress and the bar it houses.

The bar and hotel were built to serve the area's growing agricultural
industry and the railroad passengers arriving in or passing through Tucson. Its
location was a perfect stop for travelers since it was a short walk from the
station and had all the required services any weary traveler needed: a bed, a

restaurant and a bar. Though the train station achieved notoriety for Earp's killing of Stillwell, the hotel and bar existed quietly until January 22, 1934.

On that fateful day, a fire started in the basement under mysterious circumstances and quickly spread to the third floor via the elevator shaft. Staying at the hotel at the time was the gang of bank robber John Dillinger. The group escaped unharmed via exterior fire escapes but left their suitcases behind. Once safely out of the hotel, they bribed a couple of firemen to go back into the hotel and retrieve the gang's luggage containing guns and more than $20,000 in stolen cash.

One of the firemen later recognized the gang members and notified authorities. In the course of hours the small Tucson police force was able to round up the entire Dillinger gang, including John himself, without firing a single shot. When captured, John Dillinger is quoted as simply saying "Well, I'll be damned!"

TODAY

Today the Hotel Congress still stands proudly in downtown Tucson, though one story shorter because of the 1934 fire. Inside, the Tap Room looks like little has changed since its opening in 1933. Visitors find themselves surrounded by period neon, a glimmering waist-high wooden bar, art deco mirrors, old movie poster, priceless works of art and a 1940s Wurlitzer jukebox still belting out jams like the day it was installed.

Much of the art work was created by world-famous painter, rodeo clown and Tap Room regular Pete Martinez. Though they regularly get offers from art collectors and galleries from around the world for the classic paintings, they refuse to sell them, saying Pete's art work belongs in the place he felt most at home.

If you're here towards the end of January, try to catch Dillinger Days, a celebration to honor Tucson's police force, and to remember the capture of John Dillinger. Events include a 1930s-themed gala featuring a street festival, re-enactments from the time period (including the capture of Dillinger), classic cars, music, tours, lectures and much more.

Regardless of when you're here, keep your eye out for the celebrities who frequent the Tap Room. While visiting we ran into Joey Burns, front man for the alt-country band Calexico. And we're told that ZZ Top's Billy Gibbons calls this place his favorite bar.

And, like many old places, the Hotel Congress may be haunted. According to whispered rumors there is a ghost in a grey suit by the name of T.S., who many have seen peering out of windows on the second floor. Another rumored ghost is that of a woman dressed in a Victorian dress who has been seen smelling the roses in the stairwell and lobby.

But creepiest of all is the rumored goings' on in rooms around the hotel, none more feared or active than the ghost that inhabits room 242, considered the most haunted room in the hotel. A stay here, after a having a few drinks down at the bar, could prove to be exceptionally interesting.

THE FOOD

Hotel Congress features a café (the Cup Café) with offerings throughout the day. They claim an eclectic menu and feature regional fare like huevos rancheros as well as more ethnic cuisine, like Asian-fusion dishes.

THE DRINKS

The Tap Room itself is a full bar. They are renowned for the Bloody Mary and the martini. In fact, local papers have often claimed this to be the best place in the area for sipping a dry martini. No doubt the atmosphere really helps—you can sit at a gleaming Formica countertop listening to Frank Sinatra sing his lungs out on the Wurlitzer behind you while pondering how many olives it really takes to make the drink perfect. Not a bad way to spend an evening.

NEARBY DISTRACTIONS

Southern Arizona Transportation Museum—Website: www.tucsonhistoricdepot.org **Address:** 414 N. Toole Ave. Tucson, AZ, 85701, (520) 623-2223 (Tuesday–Thursday 11am–3pm, Friday–Saturday 10am–4pm, Sunday 11am–3pm). Located directly across the street from The Tap Room, the Southern Arizona Transportation Museum focuses on the history of Arizona's railroads. But one of its most interesting ties to history is in the form of Wyatt Earp, Doc Holliday and the Cochise County War. It was at this very station that the Earp family, escorted by Wyatt, Doc and others, was preparing to leave from the area when Wyatt spotted and eventually shot Frank Stillwell for his alleged involvement in Morgan Earp's murder. Today the event has been immortalized both in movies and with a statue of Wyatt Earp and Doc Holliday.

The Rialto Theatre—Website: www.rialtotheatre.com **Address:** 318 E. Congress St. Tucson, AZ, 85701, (520) 740-1000 (operating hours vary by show). Literally right across the street from The Tap Room/Hotel Congress sits the Rialto Theatre. Opened in 1920 and featuring mainly vaudeville—dance, singing, bands, comedy—performances, the Rialto Theatre has withstood the test of time. Today it features a wide range of acts, from music and comedy, to lectures and plays. It is a popular destination for locals and tourists alike.

THE CRYSTAL PALACE, TOMBSTONE, AZ

Address: 436 E. Allen St., Tombstone, AZ, 85638, (520) 457-3611
Website: www.crystalpalacesaloon.com **Video tour:**
http://youtu.be/pCCAjlH-bws
Food: Yes **Live Music:** Yes **Hours:** Monday–Sunday 11am–1am – or so **Type of Bar:** Saloon **What to Drink:** Old Overholt Rye Whiskey **Why You Should Go:** Classic American saloon from the Old West, restored almost to original, waiters and waitresses in period dress, gunfight reenactments.

HISTORY

The bar began life as the Golden Eagle Brewery on the corner of Fifth Street and Allen Street, which was to become known as one of the bloodiest street corners in the Wild West. Close to midnight on December 28th, 1881, Virgil Earp was walking to the bar when multiple shotgun blasts struck him. Virgil survived but lost the use of his left arm.

Earlier that year, on June 22, a huge fire broke out in Tombstone which wiped out almost the entire town. One of the few surviving buildings was the brewery and bar due to the dedicated work of a bucket brigade (an example of the priorities of the time). Less than a year later, on May 26th of 1882, another fire broke out and an even more valiant effort by the bucket brigade couldn't save the doomed building. Swift action by the town's people saw to it that the establishment was rebuilt quickly, at which time it took on the new name, Crystal Palace, and a whole new personification.

After being rebuilt, the Crystal Palace became THE destination for fine dining and entertainment by stage coach passengers making the journey to San Francisco. It was said to feature oysters and other delicacies (though we're still trying to figure out how they got oysters out in the middle of the desert during the 1880s), and a fountain that the Tombstone Epitaph said "spouts forth streams of pure water." The saloon also featured gambling, including faro and wheel of fortune, and some of the finest wines and hard liquor available anywhere in the US at the time. Upstairs it housed the offices of Virgil Earp (Wyatt's older brother) and Dr. Goodfellow (portrayed in the movie, "Tombstone" as the doctor pulling bullets out of Wyatt's younger brother Morgan when he died).

TODAY

Over the years the bar has opened and closed numerous times, has served multiple roles including a movie theater and a greyhound bus station, gone through a rash of owners, and even sold all of its gambling tables and the original bar to a bar in Naco, Mexico during Prohibition (unfortunately the original bar perished in a fire). Though the Crystal Palace has had a rough life, it was eventually bought and restored by owner, Kimmie, and today is a cornerstone in both the town and the experience of Tombstone.

The miners, cowboys, outlaws, gunfighters and prostitutes, of yesterday have long since left the building (so to speak) only to be replaced by fake bullets, tourists and a hand full of locals. That's not to say the bar has lost any of its appeal though. The current owner, along with her son, R.J., have done their best to make the Crystal Palace feel much like it did in the 19th century, both in the physical makeup (there are still original bullet holes in the ceiling, a fake second story and many of the original fixtures) and the authentic costumes of the waitresses and bartenders. Adding to the authenticity are actors dressed as gun-slinging cowboys who regularly act out historic gunfights both in and outside of the bar.

THE FOOD

Gone are the oysters (and we must reiterate our dubiousness at their claim of freshness in the middle of the Arizona desert in 1886) as well as the other attempts to woo the crowds on their way to San Francisco. Here you find simple bar-menu fixings, like their burgers, fries and sandwiches. However, they're known for their smoked barbeque ribs. We'll suggest this at the passed-on suggestion from the cook, R.J., who swears by them (but then, of course, he's the one that makes them…).

THE DRINKS

At the Crystal Palace you really must try the Old Overholt rye whiskey. Old Overholt was originally distilled in Broad Ford, Pennsylvania and claims to have been founded in 1810. Today it is a subsidiary of Jim Beam and is distilled in Clermont, Kentucky. Regardless of the change of venue or ownership, it's the oldest whiskey brand in the United States. What makes the drink even more special is that it was Doc Holliday's drink of choice. In the 1880s, he would regularly sit at the Crystal Palace sipping a bit of Old Overholt while playing cards. We can't think of a more fitting drink in a place like this.

NEARBY DISTRACTIONS

The Bird Cage Theatre—Website: www.tombstonebirdcage.com **Address:** 535 East Allen St. Tombstone, AZ, 85638, (520) 457-3421 (Monday–Sunday 8am–6pm). A mere 341 feet from the Crystal Palace, The Bird Cage Theatre is a must see for any visitor to the area. Once known as the wildest and wickedest night spot on the western frontier, it featured varying kinds of shows, prostitutes and gambling. Believed to have been the scene of at least 26 murders and containing over 100 bullet holes, it's a rare and unique look into life as it was during one of America's most storied chapters. Be forewarned though, guests and employees alike claim to see ghosts on a regular basis.

Boothill Graveyard—Address: 408 N. Hwy 80 Tombstone, AZ, 85638, (520) 457-3300 (Monday-Sunday 730am-Dusk). Probably one of the most notorious graveyards in the entire US, it features some of the most well-known and even humorous gravestone inscriptions. Does "Here lies Lester Moore, four slugs from a 44, no Les, no More" sound familiar? You'll find this as well as gravestones evidencing the infamous Earp and Cowboys war throughout the graveyard. Best of all, it is one of the few free attractions still available today.

The "Good Enough Mine" Underground Tour—Website: www.tombstonechamber.com **Address:** 5th & Toughnut St. Tombstone, AZ, 85638, (520) 255-5553 (open daily, call for hours). Discovered by Tombstone founder Ed Schieffelin, the "Good Enough Mine" was one of the initial mines responsible for causing the silver rush that helped to turn Tombstone into a boom town. Informative and fun, the tour features a glimpse into mining in the 1800s including a trip underground to view a small portion of the historic and vast mine.

TUCSON'S HISTORIC BARS

The Shanty—Address: 401 East 9th Street Tucson, AZ, 85705, (520) 623-2664 (Monday-Sunday 12pm-1am). Not far from Buffet Bar, The Shanty is Tucson's oldest continuously serving bar, opening right after the repeal of Prohibition. This is definitely a locals' joint, with a healthy mix of college students and young professionals. It's also the only bar in the immediate area with pool tables, so those partying in some of the local clubs like to duck in here to relax for a bit. They serve strong drinks and cold beer, and their bar snack of choice—popcorn—never goes out of style.

Chicago Bar—Website: www.chicagobartucson.com **Address:** 5954 East Speedway Boulevard Tucson, AZ, 85712, (520) 748-8169 (Monday–Sunday 10am–2am). This live music bar is a favorite of Tucson natives and students alike. They feature live music and cover bands most every night of the week, including some very good local blues bands. A bit divey, but the drinks are cheap and the music is loud.

Big Nose Kate's—Website: www.bignosekates.info **Address:** 417 East Allen Street Tombstone, AZ, 85638, (520) 457-3107 (Monday–Sunday 10am–12am). A short walk down the wooden sidewalk from the Crystal Palace is the other famous saloon in Tombstone, Big Nose Kate's. Named after Doc Holliday's prostitute girlfriend, it was originally the site of Tombstone's Grand Hotel, a richly appointed hotel where visitors traveling to or from one of the coasts could rest in elegance. The place isn't as authentic as the Crystal Palace (which actually was the Crystal Palace), and it's the quintessential tourist trap, but it's still a fun place to spend a couple of hours drinking.

WASHINGTON, D.C.

If there was ever a city that needed to drink, it'd have to be Washington, D.C. Nowhere else on earth is there more political energy than in this place. Politics, as you probably well know (or perhaps should), was always one of the topics that was off-limits in a decent bar (the other being religion), so it can be complicated to find a place that offers some peace and quiet. Luckily, though, we did the work for you and were able to discover a few dives (and a couple of nice places) where you can relax and get away for a bit.

As a city, the area has a long bar history. And, as bars go, these places are important to the running of America. Bars, after all, are where many of the most important events in our nation's history actually occurred. The Boston Tea Party was planned in a tavern. Ben Franklin, John Adams and George Washington all met for the first time in a bar. And when the British had to deliver their plans to finally leave this country, they did so in a pub. It makes sense. Bars are where we can talk privately, out of earshot of anyone trying to eavesdrop. If you wanted to discuss the affairs of the government without anyone listening in, where else would you go?

Bars were some of the first buildings in this city. In fact, John Adams lived above a tavern after he became president because construction on the White House wasn't completed yet. And even the term "lobbyist" came about because of a bar. President Grant enjoyed his evenings at the bar in the Willard Hotel, where he'd drink brandy and smoke cigars after a long day in the Oval Office. When leaving the bar, he was often hounded by political advocates who were waiting for him in the lobby of the hotel. It became so common, they began labeling them "lobbyists."

All in all, bars have always been an important part of America's Capital. Unfortunately, that Capital has grown substantially, and in all directions. Very little remains of the old Washington, D.C. that Adams or Grant would recognize, and that's especially true for the taverns and bars. Most all of the historic saloons in the city have been torn down and replaced with offices, stores or apartments buildings. As progress always does, it bulldozed taverns that most likely played some type of historic role in our country. Now all that history is gone. There are a couple, though, that still have that past and those memories. You'll find them in this section.

One thing to note before you begin, though. As you explore the bars in this section keep an eye out for people you might recognize. Many of these places are still popular with the folks we elect to Congress, or at least to the folks who work for them. You might also spy pundits and talking heads that you recognize from various cable news shows. In any case, you can expect to hear a lot about the things we see on the nightly news. It's unfortunately unavoidable in this city.

OLD EBBIT GRILL, WASHINGTON, D.C.

Address: 675 15th St NW, Washington, DC, 20005, (202) 347-4800
Website: www.ebbitt.com **Video Tour:** https://youtu.be/Hogt3F8Bg7E
Food: Yes **Live Music:** No **Hours:** Monday–Thursday 7:30am–2am, Friday
7:30am–3am, Saturday 8:30am–3am, Sunday 8:30am–2am **Type of
Bar:** Tavern **What to Drink:** Cocktail or straight whiskey **Why You Should
Go:** Oldest bar left in Washington D.C. with a who's who of political visitors.

THE HISTORY

In 1872 the Ebbitt House Hotel was built by Henry A. Willard on the
southeast corner of F Street NW, and 14th Street NW, in the young city of
Washington, D.C. It wasn't the first structure there, though, as there was a
series of houses built on this property as far back as 1800. In 1856 the two
structures on this lot were bought by William E. Ebbitt, who turned them
into a boarding house that he renamed after himself (the Ebbitt House).
When Willard got hold of them in 1872, he leveled the buildings and built a
new, 6-story hotel in the same spot, naming it after the previous proprietor.

One of the hotel's most prominent features was an elegant dining room and
bar at the rear of the building (where a brothel was actually located years
before…somehow fitting). The places—both the hotel and the dining
room/bar—became the trendiest places in the city, and a gaggle of some of
history's most celebrated politicians of the day passed through the doors.
People like Army Generals William Tecumsuh Sherman and Ulysses S. Grant
dined alongside President Andrew Johnson and abolitionist Henry Ward

Beecher to name just a (very) few. Imagine, then, all of the things that were talked about or settled or agreed upon at this place over drinks and dinner! It staggers the mind to think that our nation's course may have been changed over brandies and cigars here.

After a long, slow decline in the early 20th century (and after it passed through numerous owners), the hotel was razed in 1926. All of its furnishings, including all of the furnishings in the dining room and bar (right down to the paneling), were auctioned off. The furnishings of the dining room and bar were bought by local restaurateur Anders R. Lofstrand, Sr. Lofstrand relocated the restaurant and bar to 1427 F Street NW, and named it the "Old Ebbit Grill." He ran it for only two years before selling it to a friend in 1928. The story from there gets a bit tedious. Yet more owners bought it and sold it over the next fifty years before finally landing in the hands of the Clyde Restaurant Group, which still runs it today. It also moved in 1983 to its current location at 675 15th Street NW, where it has remained ever since.

The place, throughout all the moves and owners, remained pretty much the same. The interior contains all the original furnishings, artwork and taxidermy that the original contained (with additions made throughout the years). It has been known throughout the area for its food and drinks, and its elegance and service, elements that also refused to change. And even the clientele and stories still include a who's who list of Washington D.C. insiders, politicians, and celebrities. Perhaps most notable was that the Old Ebbitt Grill made headlines in the 1970s when it was discovered it was being used by a Russian spy ring. Throughout the 1980s, all the way up to today, the grill has remained an important gathering place for politicians, locals, and tourists.

TODAY

If Grant, Sherman, or even Johnson were to walk into the Old Ebbitt Grill today, they'd see a lot that was familiar to them. Though it's expanded substantially and now includes multiple dining rooms and bars, all of the décor that had been there since day one (that could be salvaged through the years, anyway) is still there. Much has been added through the years of course. Of the newer additions, our favorite has to be the taxidermy. We aren't necessarily endorsing the wanton slaughter of beautiful, exotic creatures, but the fact that there's the head of walrus and whole stuffed alligator hanging on the walls is pretty unusual. Factor in the fact that these animals, indeed all of the stuffed fauna, were bagged by none other than Teddy Roosevelt himself, and you begin to understand the place of the Old Ebbitt Grill in our nation's capital.

As you enter, you see the main bar to the right. This is the original bar and is the most popular and the loudest. It's tough to find a seat here anytime beyond 3:30 in the afternoon. Locals getting off work swarm this section, as do tourists and visitors, making it hard to find room. If you can find a seat, you'll also find yourself having to shout over the noise from the crowd. All the work you put into finding a seat and trying to have a conversation is worth it, though, considering all the history at this bar. Above you will be the aforementioned taxidermy, with many a stuffed, horned animal. Also, readily seen are the numerous paintings, photographs and prints found here and throughout. Many of them are closely connected with the region or the city itself, and provide a small bit of insight into the part that the Old Ebbitt Grill has played in D.C.'s history.

There are numerous dining areas, including a sprawling dining area to the left, and also one beyond the main room. Actually, if you're looking for peace and quiet, that's easily found beyond the main room in Grant's Bar, named for the general and president who used to like to tie one on at the Old Ebbitt Grill when it was located in one of its previous spots. At this bar, the noise from the crowd becomes a dull murmur, there are fewer prying eyes, and the lighting is a bit lower. It makes for a much more intimate spot.

Another thing that really hasn't changed is the opportunity for people watching. As before, the place is still very popular with the Washington, D.C. insider crowd, so you never know who might show up. In fact, you'll notice that at around 5:15 pm, the crowd is rotten with groomed, well-dressed, young men and women. Most all of these people are working in some capacity for lawmakers or in government agencies. You need only to quietly sip a drink to get a new insight into the inner workings of our government. Then find a quiet spot to cry.

THE FOOD

Old Ebbitt Grill features an extensive, full menu with fine dining options. They're known for their Italian dishes and steaks, so be sure to try either. For us, the starters were really something we enjoyed. We tried their crab cakes featuring freshly caught crab, and Oysters Rockefeller made with local oysters—both were amazing and paired well with the locally-made craft beer we were drinking. They also have standard pub grub (though a bit more expensive), including hamburgers and chicken wings. Lastly, if you like oysters, they have a number of fresh, local oysters at their oyster bar.

THE DRINKS

This is a great place to duck into for a drink. They make a really good cocktail here. We tried an Old Fashioned and Manhattan and were delighted with both. They also have an extensive whiskey (and whisky) collection, so if you're looking for something new to try on the rocks, you won't be disappointed. The same can be said if you're looking for a great wine (they have selections in various ranges). And lastly, their beer selection is also really good and features local craft brews.

NEARBY DISTRACTIONS

Ford's Theatre and the Peterson House (house where Lincoln died)— **Website:** www.nps.gov/foth/the-petersen-house.htm **Address:** 516 10th St NW, Washington, DC, 20004 (202) 426-6924 (Monday–Sunday 8:30am– 5pm). Just a few blocks from the Old Ebbitt Grill is the theatre where one of our greatest presidents was shot. Ford's Theatre, still an active theatre with occasional shows, offers tours and a museum free of charge. Once done, stroll across the street to the Peterson House, where Abraham Lincoln was carried and eventually passed. The house is restored and furnished to circa 1865, and the two of these places provide a unique perspective about the death of our 16th president.

International Spy Museum—Website: www.spymuseum.org **Address:** 800 F St NW, Washington, DC, 20004 (202) 393-7798 (Monday–Sunday 9am–7pm). This private museum, which does charge entry, is probably one of the most interesting and offbeat museums you'll find. Dedicated to the tradecraft of espionage, the museum offers exhibits that trace the history of spying from well before the Revolutionary War until today. Included are a wealth of artifacts, like hidden microphones and cameras, and even a James Bond car. There are many interactive exhibits as well.

National Portrait Gallery—Website: http://npg.si.edu **Address:** 8th St NW & F St NW, Washington, DC, 20001 (202) 633-8300 (Monday–Sunday, 11:30am–7pm). You know all of those portraits of presidents you see on TV and elsewhere? Well they all end up here, at the National Portrait Gallery. We include this place, the only Smithsonian museum in Washington, D.C. we do include, because it's so far off the beaten path and most people miss it. But once in, you'll be glad you stopped. Stroll the portraits of not only our various presidents, including famous portraits of George Washington and others, but also other historical figures that have played a significant role in our nation's history.

GADSBY'S TAVERN, ALEXANDRIA, VA

Address: 138 N Royal St, Alexandria, VA, 22314, (703) 548-1288
Website: www.gadsbystavernrestaurant.com **Video Tour:**
https://youtu.be/4JXEKdtU0bw
Food: Yes **Live Music:** No **Hours:** Monday–Sunday 11:30am–3pm, 5pm–
10pm **Type of Bar:** Tavern **What to Drink:** Rum Punch **Why You Should
Go:** George Washington, among other dignitaries, dined here, and he even
had his birthday party here.

THE HISTORY

There has been a tavern on this corner in Alexandria, Virginia, a stone's
throw from the Nation's Capital (which is why it's included in this chapter),
since 1749, according to historical records. These taverns were torn down and
rebuilt over the years until finally in 1785 the Georgian-style, brick building
now located here was built (another tavern was built right next to it in 1792).
These were owned by local businessman John Wise, and then leased to
Englishman John Gadsby (described as the Donald Trump of his day—but
we think they mean the Donald Trump before people hated him).

John was certainly a bon vivant for his time. He invited dignitaries and
politicians on a regular basis to dine, attend elegant balls he threw (we would
call them parties, today), and to regularly stop by. This had the effect of
turning his tavern into the destination for the socially elite of the time: if you
wanted to be seen, you would be seen at Gadsby's. John Adams, Thomas
Jefferson and even the Marquis de La Fayette tipped a glass here. And the
interior of the tavern reflected the draw for the affluent regulars. While other
taverns may have been rustic or pedestrian, Gadsby richly appointed his place

with beautiful wood paneling (especially the ball room on the second floor), expensive furniture, and elegant crystal and flatware.

All of his hard work had its desired effect, because one of Gadsby's regulars was George Washington himself, perhaps the most famous man there was at the time. He even attended two birthday celebrations (birthnight balls they called them) thrown in his honor. And remember, Washington enjoyed drinking and could also put it away, so his presence here was a ringing endorsement.

Unfortunately, as often happens, the place started a decline after John Gadsby moved away in 1808 and John Wise died in 1815. By the mid-19th century, while still partially a tavern, it was also a set of offices. By the early 20th century the place was in complete disrepair and was threatened with demolition. Luckily, the American Legion and other patriotic groups bought it and spent an enormous amount of money and time in restoring it. It finally reopened in 1976 with the main building leased to a restaurant serving period drinks and food, and a museum next door.

TODAY

Today the restaurant and museum continue to be popular places to visit. Any given time of day will find locals dining and having a drink alongside visitors and tourists. Next door at the museum, the City of Alexandria continues to educate the public and restore the old tavern. In fact, the second floor has been completely renovated to look identical to the ballroom in which Washington and his entourage would have partied. And the first-floor restaurant, too, looks much like it would have looked when Jefferson or Madison dined here.

They don't have a bar as we know it. Instead they have what's called a dispensery, like the City Tavern in Philadelphia has. This is essentially a small, square room that's stocked with spirits and other items with which to create cocktails and period drinks. People didn't belly up to the bar in those days, rather they just requested a drink at the dispensary, where it would be made and then "dispensed" to them.

What makes this place really unique are the events, which all give a nod to the tavern's history. For the purposes of this book, the two most important events are George Washington's Birthnight Banquet and Ball, and the Great Rum Punch Challenge. For the Birthnight Ball, visitors are treated to a reenactment of what Washington's celebrations might have been like. Actors in period dress recreate the dancing and festivities of the evening, and visitors get to join in, partaking in a meal and dancing (and drinks, of course). At the Great Rum Punch Challenge, visitors get to sample rum punches (a period drink) made by different, local distilleries, and then vote on their favorite. The best will be crowned at the end of the evening.

THE FOOD

This is a fine dining restaurant with amazing food served throughout the day. Unlike the City Tavern in Philadelphia, they aren't restricted to only period cuisine. Here they serve burgers and salads for lunch and dinner. But, they also serve crab cakes from locally farmed lump crab, steaks, meatloaf and other great options. One thing we'd recommend is "Washington's Favorite," which consists of grilled duck breast, scalloped potatoes and corn pudding.

THE DRINKS

Though the drinks come from a dispensery and not a bar, that doesn't mean the selection is limited. They have an extensive wine list, but they also serve most all spirits you could want. They do have some period drinks, but our recommendation is a rum punch. This is a drink that does go all the way back to the Founding Fathers (before them, in fact), and this is a great place to try one.

NEARBY DISTRACTIONS

Saint Paul's Cemetery—**Website:** www.stpaulsalexandria.com **Address:** 228 S Pitt St, Alexandria, VA, 22314, (703) 549-3312. About three blocks to the south of Gadsby's is this historic cemetery that you might want to check out. There are a lot of old cemeteries in the older sections of Arlington, and many are older than this one (which was founded in 1809). But this one has a special connection to Gadsby's. In 1818 a 23-year-old woman fell ill on the ship she was travelling on with her husband. She died in room 8 of Gadsby's, but only after swearing everyone in the room to tell no one of her identity. They kept their word and in the cemetery is a large, notable gravesite marked only, "The Mysterious Stranger." Legend says she now haunts Gadsby's.

Escape Room Live—**Website:** www.escaperoomlive.com **Address:** 814 King St, 2nd Floor, Alexandria, VA, 22314, (800) 616-4880 (Monday–Thursday 5pm–10pm, Friday 5pm–11pm, Saturday 10am–11pm, Sunday 12pm–8pm). If you haven't been to an escape room yet, this is definitely one to try. In short, escape rooms are attractions that lock you (and your friends) into a room, and then you have to find clues to help you escape in a certain amount of time. This attraction features four different rooms with different themes that will have you using the ol' noodle. You probably shouldn't be drinking before you visit. Book online in advance.

Mount Vernon Distillery—**Website:** www.mountvernon.org/the-estate-gardens/distillery **Address:** 5514 Mount Vernon Memorial Hwy, Alexandria, VA, 22309, (703) 780-3383 (Seasonal, April–October Monday–Sunday 9am–5pm). Did you know that when he died, George Washington was the biggest whiskey producer in the United States? His distillery, complete with water-powered mill, has been faithfully reproduced and allows you to see how our first president made rye whiskey over two centuries ago. They also occasionally have some whiskey for sale, so maybe you'll get lucky. Either way, though, this is a must-see when you're in the area!

WASHINGTON D.C.'S HISTORIC BARS

The Tune Inn—Address: 331 Pennsylvania Ave SE, Washington, DC, 20003, (202) 543-2725 (Monday–Sunday 8am–2am). Founded in 1947, this Capital Hill dive has been helmed by the same family for three generations. Inside you find memorabilia, signs, knick-knacks and even taxidermy collected over the decades. Though a fire closed the place down in 2011, and forced them to remodel a bit, resulting in much of the grime collected since its opening to be polished off, it still has that great dive feel. The drinks are still cheap, the crowd is still questionable (that includes the people in suits), and the atmosphere is still a bit mysterious. They have a full kitchen that cranks out some great pub grub, much of it with their own twist. Like Tony's Beer Battered Burger, which starts as a plain old cheeseburger, and then gets battered and deep-fried. Despite the fact that this is one of Guy Fieri's favorites, it really is pretty delicious. Another one is the Fireman's burger topped with that Pennsylvanian favorite: scrapple (we're still unsure what it actually is). This is one of the last true dives in the city, and definitely deserves a tour when you're visiting the other monuments.

Off the Record—Website: www.hayadams.com/dining **Address:** 800 16th St NW, Washington, DC, 20006, (202) 638-6600 (Sunday–Thursday 11:30am–12am, Friday–Saturday 11:30am–12:30am). At the basement of the Hay-Adams Hotel, cattycorner to the White House and opened in 1928, is this historic bar that's served the political elite for decades. Off the Record features richly appointed, red velvet booths and cushions, with beautiful mahogany covering everyplace else. They serve elegant and pricy, traditional cocktails here, but they'll be some of the best-made cocktails in the city. Try ordering a martini, Old Fashioned, or Sazerac, and you'll be happy. At one time, this was the meeting place for US Senators, Congressmen and even US Presidents. Each wanted a quiet place to sip a drink and talk politics without the formality that the rest of the city demands. Here they could find it, and even today the bartenders won't tell you any of the people they've served across the bar. After all, here, it's truly off the record.

The Tabard Inn—Website: www.tabardinn.com **Address:** 1739 N St NW, Washington, DC, 20036, (202) 785-1277 (Monday–Sunday 4pm–10pm). Another great bar found in one of Washington DC's oldest hotels. Built in 1922, the Tabard Inn (named after the inn that Chaucer's travelers depart from in the Canterbury Tales) has been serving locals and travelers from its elegant lounge and bar for almost a century. Here you have three choices of places to position yourself: along the bar on leather-topped bar stools, in the ivy-covered patio, or in the lounge with its warming fireplace. The decision often comes down to the weather outside. If it's warm, go for the patio for sure. All seating is first come, first serve, so arrive early or at least expect to wait to sit at your desired place. The drinks are often traditional, but they also have a lot of signature drinks that are seasonally made.

Martin's Tavern—Website: www.martinstavern.com **Address:** 1264 Wisconsin Ave NW, Washington, DC, 20007, (202) 333-7370 (Monday–Thursday 11am–1:30am, Friday 11am–2am, Saturday 9am–2:30am, Sunday 8am–1:30am). How could anyone not include this place in any list of one of the top bars in the city of Washington DC (or Georgetown, more precisely)? Martin's was opened by Irish immigrant, William S. Martin and his son in 1933. The family has owned it ever since. In fact, this is the oldest family run place in the District, and now run by the fourth generation. And while the outside suggests it's just another faux Irish bar in the city, the reality is much different. After all, this is the bar where every president since Harry S Truman has stopped in to have a drink. And, it's also the bar where JFK popped the question to one Jacqueline Bouvier (in booth 3). All in all, this place has a lot of stories to tell about the city, and drinking here helps to make you feel like you're part of it.

INDEX

284

CONNECT WITH US!

Questions or comments about the bars in here? Are we completely, arrogantly wrong about the details? Do YOU have a Bucket List Bar we just have to include in the next book? Let us know!

Mail
Bucket List Bars
c/o AO Media LLC
2015 Cotton Ave.
Las Cruces, NM 88001

Email
info@bucketlistbars.com

Find Us on the Web
http://www.bucketlistbars.com

Follow Us on Twitter
@BucketListBars
@DrunkenHistory

Connect on Facebook
Facebook.com/drunkenhistory

ABOUT THE AUTHORS

Photo by Fizelwink Photography

Clint Lanier

Fascinated by the hidden history of bars, Clint Lanier has traveled the world to find out-of-the-way watering holes with great stories to tell. From the juke joints of the Mississippi Delta, to the cantinas of Mexico, he's always on the lookout for the next saloon, tavern, or dive that brings a neighborhood or a whole city together. When not on the road, he is writes about booze and teaches at New Mexico State University in Las Cruces, New Mexico.

Derek Hembree

As a military brat, Derek Hembree began traveling and exploring the world at a very young age. A bartender during his college years and an adventurer at heart, he is intrigued by historic bars, their stories, the art of mixology, and sharing it all with the world. Along with traveling and bars, Derek is passionate about finding the perfect wave, the freshest powder, and exploring the world on two wheels.

CPSIA information can be obtained
at www.ICGtesting.com
Printed in the USA
LVHW011125311018
595216LV00017B/490/P

9 780692 182741